TAMING THE PITS

A Technical Approach to Commodity Trading

TAMING THE PITS

A Technical Approach to Commodity Trading

ROBERT M. BARNES
Shearson Hayden Stone, Inc.

A RONALD PRESS PUBLICATION

JOHN WILEY & SONS
New York   Chichester   Brisbane   Toronto

Library of Congress Cataloging in Publication Data:

Barnes, Robert M
    A management science approach to commodity
trading.

  "A Ronald Press publication."
  Bibliography: p.
  Includes index.
  1. Commodity exchange. I. Title.

HG6046.B34   332.6′44   79-12107
ISBN 0-471-05795-9

Printed in the United States of America

10 9 8 7 6 5 4 3 2 1

Dedicated to
Serious Investors

Preface

On a cold January night in 1966 I started reading a soft-cover book on commodity trading. The high leverage, fast pace, and pyramiding profits stirred dreams of the fast buck, but I was even more interested in the intriguing challenge of developing methods for unlocking the treasure chest to see how and why prices moved. That is still my principal interest—the study of investment methods.

In those early days many traders, including myself, investigated relatively simple techniques, such as charting and moving averages. The first sophisticated method I examined was linear regressions, a form of forecasting. At that point I used daily data only, and for analysis I usually considered just closing prices. But as time went on, price models became more sophisticated (due to influence from academic articles—mostly on random price behavior) and timing techniques more complex. I also started using more advanced methods, from forecasting to testing, from mathematical statistics.

The concept of systems evolved from applications in other industries. I had applied diverse ones (computer simulations, sampling, game theory) to oil research, military war gaining, and airline income problems. The idea of treating commodities trading as a *total system,* with disparate but interlocking and dependent parts such as timing, risk capital, capital allocation, selection of investments, and even the trader himself, slowly began to gel. After all, much of life today depends on things that are highly coordinated. A car will not work unless each part works, in conjunction with all other parts. Success of commodity trading also depends on each part doing well and interlocking with the others.

The intent of this book is to look at a systematic way of commodity trading and to examine all parts of trading as a related matter. I do not intend to discuss the basic mechanics of commodities, such as how to open an account, how to place orders, or what wheat contracts are. This, hopefully, will constitute an inclusive study on proper trading for profits.

Various texts and articles on commodity trading (see the Bibliography) are currently available to the investor. Some are broadly oriented toward the basic mechanics of trading, explanations of terms, information available, and methods of trading. Others are more intensive and present specific models and mathematical concepts for timing trades. The former are aimed at the general investing public with no background in commodities or mathematics, whereas the latter limelight one or two aspects of trading and require sometimes little quantitative experience and other times a great deal.

I have tried in this book to explore, sometimes in depth and other times in a survey manner, various topics that make up the elements of a total commodity system—risk, selection, timing, capital management, and discipline. In some cases the topic does not require advanced training in mathematics. The sections on risk, selection, and discipline, and the introductory chapters that explore and tie everything together, do not demand extensive quantitative background. Likewise some chapters on timing methods (for example, charting) are elementary and well described in prior texts.

Some approaches in other sections to the timing of trades and capital management, however, do require at least one year of college mathematics to fully understand and use the results. Specifically, one should be familiar with basic concepts of calculus and probability to follow all the material in these particular chapters. I have endeavored, however, to briefly explain in nonmathematical terms in those chapters the rationale, general principles, and results of more rigorous mathematics. In most cases simple usable calculation procedures have been arrived at, even though the development of some might require more background than the reader possesses.

The depth of treatment varies from chapter to chapter, reflecting both the state of the art and my attempts to elaborate and expound on new and relatively new concepts. For instance, charting is well known and extensively described in the literature; hence I considered it superfluous to expound on and on about it and be redundant in addition. This and other well-tread subjects can be read in more depth by choosing from the Bibliography. In other areas, such as new timing methods (statistical testing methods, Chapter 16) and account growth simulation (Chapter 22) have not been explored at all and require extensive treatment. Even in these areas the work is new, there is a lot of unexplored material, and entire texts could be built around them (for example, velocity and acceleration methods).

The objective of this text is manyfold. For many it can serve as an introduction to the elements of the total trading concept (exclusive of mechanics, treated extensively in other texts). It may be a springboard to other, more intensive studies covered elsewhere. Others may use the book as a reference text on many timing systems, for example. The Bibliography may spur some on to other studies. Individual chapters on timing methods, risk attitudes, or capital management may give enough detailed information to the commodity trader to apply to trading without additional work.

Most chapters do not require any preparatory reading or courses. Even many of the timing chapters are self-contained and do not require prerequisite or supplementary outside reading. Some, like the chapter on wave theories, are survey in nature and are so broad that extensive, reasonable coverage would encompass a text on each. Here it is advisable to consult the Bibliography (for example, books on Eliot wave theory and Dow theory) to have complete understanding and be able to apply the concepts in actual trading.

Some chapters, however, require careful attention and a good mathematical bent on the part of the reader. Specifically Chapters 16–22 require, in varying amounts, calculus and probability background. If the reader does not have it, he can still understand the results and final formulas applications and accept the critique of the method. Barring taking a year of calculus and probability, he may wish to borrow the services of an engineer or scientist friend. However, he can still, in most cases, use the final formulas, without too much difficulty. For instance, he could use the little probability formula in Chapter 21 and some data on his account's growth to project future account decays to let him know how bad the account could falter and to see whether its growth was still on target.

Greenwich, Connecticut   ROBERT M. BARNES
April 1979

Contents

TAMING THE PITS

A Technical Approach to Commodity Trading

Introduction

Perhaps the space age did it, maybe industrial engineering made it happen, or possibly even transcendental meditations revealed it. In any case, people are talking systems. A transportation system, federal budgeting system, or stereophonic sound systems—all involve sophisticated parts interdependent on each other for a complete effect.

And so it is with commodity trading. First, the complete effect (profitable results) depends on having enough *risk moneys* to start trading and to withstand periods of losses. Second, it means an investor in this arcane endeavor must *select* the right commodities for trading to ensure the most efficient use of the investment dollars. Third, *timing* of trades is ultraimportant to make sure trades are basically profitable. Fourth, the investment dollar must be *well-managed*, too, to bring about optimum growth at minimum risk. Managing an account means also knowing what to expect in trading performance. Fifth, the trader must be a guru, self-disciplined and able to run the trading system like an automaton. I try to cover all aspects of a systematic approach to trading in this book.

Section 1 is devoted to general discussions of a trading system. Chapter 1 compares different areas of investments (stocks, bonds, real estate, commodities, etc.) for risk and return and different ways commodity traders now have for attaining success in trading. Chapter 2 is an essay about how to define, model, and solve trading problems and how to construct and use a general systematic method for trading profitably. The latter part of this chapter serves as a broad introduction to the whys and wherefores of the rest of the book.

Section 2 (Chapter 3) concerns risk: who, why, how much, and under what circumstances. A survey and psychological examination of risk attitudes toward investments and commodities in particular is also reviewed.

Section 3 (Chapter 4) is devoted to selecting proper commodities for trading. Judged against many criteria, some commodities are shown to be unsuited for systematic trading opportunities and others ideally so. Each commodity is discussed, graphed, and examined in detail.

Section 4, timing, contains fifteen chapters, each devoted to a major or innovative trade timing (when to buy, when to sell) method. There are essentially four schools of timing: forecasting prices, detecting trends, no trend (trading market), and pattern recognition. The fifteen timing methods pretty much span the gamut of new or used interesting approaches: fundamental, charting, moving averages, contrary opinion, oscillator, congestion phase, breakout, wave theories, secondary reaction, marrying methods (trend and contrary here), statistical testing, velocity and acceleration, equilibrium, and adaptive forecasting.

Section 5, capital management, concerns the optimum initial and reinvestment strategies (Chapter 20); evaluating how well or poorly an account is doing compared to preset guidelines (Chapter 21); and simulations of several account growths—one a coin-toss, and two examples of actual account statistics fed in (Chapter 22).

Section 6 discusses personal trait characteristics needed to assure good investment discipline to follow a trading system faithfully. Nearly twenty traits are considered.

Section 7 concludes with an extensive bibliography on writings bearing on investment methods.

THE TRADING SYSTEM

1 The Sweet Smell of Success

Success is a funny thing. Like beauty, it is in the eye of the beholder. Most people desire it. But unlike beauty, it has a more tangible meaning to individuals. Most often success is measured by the possession of material objects (e.g., house, office, boat). Climbing the corporate ladder also has the obvious material reward of high salary with the added ego gratification of increased recognition and power.

Others, especially since the onslaught of the beatnik and hippie eras in United States history, have different concepts of success. The definition has widened and stretched. Success can encompass a wider variety of areas—from acrobatics to Zen Buddhism. Success to some, then, depends on very personal achievement—virtuosity in craftmaking, home (commune) building, growing vegetables, and so on.

But success in intangibles also becomes important. The attainment of inner calm, control, and sharpening of all the senses are considered just as or more desirable than monetary or other tangible achievements. Recently, transcendental meditation, extrasensory perception (ESP) and Eastern religious rituals have greatly influenced United States and Western goals and mores, too. Physical training (participatory sports such as tennis,

3

hiking, jogging) has become both an aid and an end in itself in attaining success.

In fact, it is not uncommon to see an individual wake up early, meditate in an awkward position with a funny smell lingering about; jog and sweat for a few miles, play a set or two of tennis, shower and sauna, and then drive to a client's office and close a $3 million deal.

SUCCESS IN INVESTMENTS

Perhaps second only to the recent deluge of books on attaining inner (self) success is the proliferation of writings on investment success (see bibliography). They range from rather esoteric self-discipline treaties to hard-nosed mathematical concepts of trading formulas. Included are a number of important books and essays on stock-market techniques, and details and critiques of a few that would pertain to the commodity futures markets. But the main body of references and discussion in this book concerns the area of commodity futures.

THE SPECTRUM OF INVESTMENTS

Generally, the first decision a person seeking success in investing must make, after deciding he does indeed have enough moneys for investments, is to determine which area or areas in which to concentrate his capital commitments. Of course, this decision is dependent on funds available for real risk and how much riskbearing he can afford. This clinker can be serious; if an individual has an adequate income to meet current and projected needs but only has $4000 of idle capital, he probably would want to consider only investments that have little risk and great liquidity to meet sudden or unanticipated living needs. Assuming this individual has real investment money (not needed for any foreseeable living needs), he is faced with a kaleidoscope of possibilities for investing. Figure 1 presents a representative (but not complete) spectrum of investment alternatives, a speedometer of investments. The stepping order is approximate, and in particular times and instances some places should be interchanged.

On the low edge of the risk rainbow lie government obligations: mortgage notes, treasury bills, savings bonds, and so on, which are backed by the United States government. Obviously, if the federal government can-

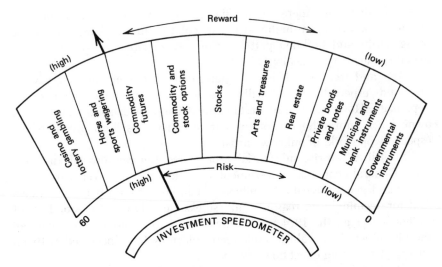

Figure 1. The spectrum of investments.

not meet its obligations, the entire economy is really in jeopardy and it doesn't matter whether your particular investment is safe. *Nothing* would be safe at this point; anarchy may occur.

Next, with a higher degree of risk, are municipal bonds and various bank instruments. Cities will generally be around and solvent for a long time and banks are backed, to a large extent (though limited to $40,000 for each savings account), by the federal government. But even here there are occasional pitfalls. Banks (recently even large ones) have gone bankrupt, and more and more frequently, towns and cities and even New York City have or are faced with possible defaults on interest and principal payments. Further on up, private (corporate) bonds and interest-bearing notes are paid to holders before profits to stockholders but are still vulnerable to corporate failure.

Real estate represents solid footing in the investment arena, as values generally increase year to year (reflecting general inflationary tendencies in the economy and the fact that it is a limited, nonproducible good). But individual circumstances vary. Lake and ocean-front recreational property values have been rising steadily and fast for the past several decades, reflecting an acute shortage of space, increasing prosperity of individuals and their rising aspirations for recreational space; likewise for suburban property, especially around large cities. Here the situation is accentuated because of growing population and racial overtones. In the other direction, however, there are many borderline properties, especially in big-city urban areas, which are highly risky, speculative undertakings. Changing living habits and building patterns can and do affect real-estate values over the years very radically.

Arts and treasures, like real estate, can hold their value very well. Diamonds especially do and will move up easily with inflation but rarely depreciate. However, like real estate, great bargains or solid values (e.g., owning a Rembrandt) can occur, but so can values drop precipitously, especially on works of unknown artists.

Securities can rise substantially, of course, but can also fall dramatically. General economic, governmental, worldwide, and even narrow industry and geographical area influences can be felt on a particular stock. And for seemingly no reason at all, stocks can plunge. Investor lack of confidence (e.g., the 1974 market crash) due to economic recession can sharply affect stock values. Prolonged doldrums have persisted with an adverse, frustrating effect on stock owners.

Stock and commodity options probably rank next highest in risk. For a certain period of time the holder of an option has the right to purchase (or sell) a given amount of the stock or commodity at a previously set price. For this right he pays a fixed amount of money (the premium). If the stock's price prior to the expiration date is considerably better than the set price and results in a profit large enough for him, he will exercise the option. However, there is often less profit or even none before the period is up, resulting in partial or total loss of the investment (the premium).

Commodity futures can be even more speculative than options. Because the investor is putting up only a small portion of the value of what he is trading (e.g., typically 30¢ on a $3.00 bushel of wheat), a change in price of 10% or more could not only wipe out his original investment but make him owe the broker more (if the price of wheat dropped, say 40¢ from the price at which he had bought and he had only put up 30¢). This type of risk can be reduced substantially (but not eliminated) by the use of loss-mitigating and -limiting methods, such as stop losses, diversification into many commodities, and adequate reserves.

Finally, two areas of quick return—quick loss are, from a probability basis, the most risky of investments. Horse and other sports betting results in either gain or total loss (of the committed money). Usually within minutes (horses) or hours (sports) you'll know whether you've won or lost. With casino games (blackjack, roulette, one-armed bandits, or craps) and state lotteries, the elation or disappointment will register on your face within seconds. Here, too, loss of the investment is total.

Curiously, there is a relationship between the extent of risk and the speed with which the outcome occurs. The faster the outcome, the larger the potential loss. In a craps throw it takes seconds to find out if you've won or lost, whereas a government bond won't mature in perhaps twenty or thirty years.

Likewise, there is a strong correlation between risk and reward (return) of the investment. Gambling returns can pay as low as two or three times the original stake up to hundreds of times. Lotteries are cherished by afficionados for the instant millionaire potential of a dollar bet or less. Of course, the risk of total loss is very high, balancing off the high potential reward.

Going down the spectrum, horse bets pay off from 20% return to 20 : 1 gains and sports bets generally less of a range.

Commodity futures, with less risk from a practical standpoint (few lose their whole stake or more right off the bat), can produce winnings in the same range as horse bets. There is also more information handy and less luck involved than with horses.

Commodity and stock options generally have less reward to investment ratios than with commodity futures because the premiums for options are generally larger than the margins or deposits required to trade the same commodity futures or stocks.

Stocks have the great potential for doubling, tripling, or even ten- and twentyfold increases, but the time involved to accomplish that is long compared to commodity futures and occurs less often.

Real estate values can also skyrocket—three and fourfold increases over five years is not completely rare. Occasionally you hear about Las Vegas real estate increasing from $100 an acre before World War II to several hundred thousand dollars now, but such cases (including Florida booms) are fairly rare, over and done with, or touched by scandal. Normally, real estate will keep pace with a combined growth rate of inflation and population.

Corporate bonds and notes usually pay better than do bank interest but are held to 7–20% per year payouts. Convertible corporate bonds add a little tickler to this category and act a little like a stock or stock option, with a mixture of (low) fixed return plus good-sized growth potential, depending on its cousin's, the stock's, price-movement inclinations.

Bank savings pay nearly the lowest reward of any of the investments, although they are quite safe. Inflation, however, makes this investment worth less in buying power in the future almost certain; hence this is an almost certain *losing* investment, with virtually no hope of reward if any sizable inflation is present.

Finally, federal-government instruments pay low also and are in the same reward–risk bracket as bank savings, except for greater safety.

WHY COMMODITY FUTURES?

Throughout time individuals have wrestled with the problem of how best to invest surplus moneys. Wars, famines, inflation, and the ever-increasing complexity of modern industrial societies have made the choices more difficult and uncertainty greater. Traditional forms of investing no longer yield high returns or safety.

Real-estate values no longer climb steadily upward and may be hard to realize (liquidate). Stock-market prices plummet with more regularity and for longer periods (the long-term outcome is uncertain—a slow growth economy like Britain's?). Even bonds fluctuate widely and are dependent on inflation, and sometimes defaults in payments are made. Worst of all, money is slowly but certainly eroded in savings institutions, leaving an individual with roughly half the purchasing power he had ten years ago.

Many have invested in commodities to escape inflation or to realize greater gains than in most any other investment media. Knowledge and expertise can be concentrated on just the small but diverse number of commodities traded, costs of trading are relatively small, and large profit opportunities abound frequently. Super trends result from extreme weather conditions (e.g., drought) or political events (Russian wheat or soybean deals), and virtually all traders have equal access to the information about each commodity; there are no real insiders who have special, secret knowledge of either price direction or unreleased information, as happens in the stock market.

The commodity markets are big and liquid. Last year over $1,400 billion in commodity value was transacted, compared to less than a fourth of that in the stock markets. Trades are entered and completed instantaneously, credits and debits are made, and checks sent at the end of the trading day.

Securities tend to move together in the same direction, whereas commodities such as potatoes, cocoa, and wheat often go their own separate ways.

The philosophy of this book is that one can protect and enlarge his capital best by aggressively seeking the most leveraged investment media and applying the best skills and knowledge to it.

Specifically, management science tools—the application of mathematics, modeling, statistics, and computers to economic and social environments—are the best tools to use on the most consistent area of profit potential, *commodities*.

SUCCESS IN COMMODITY TRADING

Contrary to this subheading, very few commodity traders *are* successful. In fact, those who are successful are a rare breed. According to the U.S. Department of Agriculture (USDA), one survey of 8782 speculators in the grain futures markets showed that only 25% made net profits after commissions (see *Commodities* magazine articles). Professor Hieronymous at the University of Illinois estimates the losing percentage as closer to 90%. Interestingly, if you eliminate those who are neophytes or who stop trading after losing $500–$1,000, the loss drops to around 60%, similar to stock-market rates.

A number of academic sources (see bibliography) point out that both the stock and commodity markets are random sequences of price changes and are not predictable, given past price information alone. If this is true, it certainly explains why very few people, on balance, make money in commodities. Most traders use technical methods (based only on price, volume, open interest, etc.) for investing. If, on balance, their price approaches yield no predictability, then cumulative profits must be zero. Thus they lose only commissions, on balance, on each trade. This explains why after only twenty-five trades they have lost all their money, assuming 4% commissions on each trade round turn, and investing all the money each time (twenty-five trades times 4% net loss due to commissions, equals 100% losses). Keeping some funds in reserve would slow the rate of loss, but the end result would be the same.

The question of whether technical trading methods can produce net cumulative profits after costs on a somewhat consistent basis has not really been answered, however. On the one hand are brokers, advisors, and some individual traders who claim fantastic profits and who are incensed at the thought that their trading results were due just to luck. The academics, however, claim that the traders' successes were due to a string of luck, not skill on the individual's part.

There are some who do seem to make somewhat consistent profits (so we hear, anyway). The truth is probably in the middle of the opposing viewpoints. The large loss rate certainly suggests the public at large has no better skill than flipping coins in commodity markets, with losses after commissions surely eroding capital.

Yet there are people that seem to have a steady knack of picking price drifts and making net profits. Second, current academic studies have not scratched the surface in terms of adequately modeling and testing price behavior and strategies for trading, given the models. Virtually all the literature speaks of examining price changes with standard statistical tests. Are price changes the "raison d'être"? Looking at price changes is like cutting up a cat into sections, examining its tail, and concluding from that what the other sections must look like! Academicians simply are not modeling price behavior well yet, nor are sophisticated trading strategies being tested.

Both sides err. The investing public uses crude techniques and academics don't build proper price models and trading strategies. Neither seems to wish to learn from the other, either.

THINK SUCCESS

There *are* instances of huge success in commodities, however. Many of the better known had typical, all-American, Horatio Alger rags-to-riches experiences, too. W. E. Cutten, a turn-of-the-century trader, and perhaps the greatest commodities speculator of all time, was a grain expert who continually entered and left the market moving prices his way (such was his influence). He started out as a clerk, became a floor trader for one of the brokerages, and made millions by in and out scalping. In 1925 he made $10–15 million in wheat and was said to be worth $50–100 million at the height of his career. For another intriguing tale, see "Prince of the Pit" [General, 5][1] in the bibliography.

Jesse Livermore, king of the speculators in the stock market who made and lost more than $4 million, wrote "anyone who is inclined to speculate should look at speculation as a *business* and treat it as such and not regard it as a pure gamble as so many people are apt to do." He believed in following rigid rules of calculations and decisions based on the "pivotal point" system for timing trades [Trading Methods, 19].

MUCH ADVICE ABOUNDS

There certainly is no lack of advice on the way to trade successfully. Almost every pamphlet issued from a brokerage office, articles in business magazines, books galore, and the friendly chum who just came in off the street to watch the boards will gladly proffer the gems of wisdom to

[1] Specific references from the bibliography in Section 7 are referred to in brackets by category and number.

willing persons. Typically, some will tell you to stick to a certain stock or commodity, a particular timing system, or time of the year. Another may instruct you to "cut losses short, let profits run." (Seems like very sage advice—but how do you specifically do it?).

Some advise having the right personal circumstances and characteristics first before even considering whether to trade. Cash funds for trading must be genuinely "risk" capital. If such is not the case, market judgment could be adversely affected.

You must have the temperament and willingness to take losses. Even the most successful traders do take losses, even strings of losses, before net gains push the account into the plus column.

The trader should have an objective temperament, to be able to evaluate ever-changing facts in a situation without regard to preconceptions and without regard to his position in the market. He should not needlessly worry or lose sleep because he is holding market positions, or, as a saying goes, "liquidate down to the sleeping point."

A speculator should decide on a method of operation and stick to it. Even if losses occur early and the account seems to be going nowhere, he should hold onto it. If it has been intelligently and logically constructed, he should not rationalize himself into discarding it to justify a losing market position.

However, he should keep an open mind and have his plan or timing methods flexible enough to adjust to changing market conditions. He must be able to see quickly when his opinion of the market has been wrong, admit it, and act accordingly.

One colloquialism is "When in doubt, stay out—do not feel you have to be in the market all the time" (it could lead to whipsaw losses, for one). Another tells us not to overinvest—you need sizeable reserves for these loss periods, which happens with every method.

"As far as increasing commitments," another adage goes, "do not add to your position unless the last previously acquired contract shows a profit. But also make sure to not add more contracts at any one time than the number of contracts in the original commitment" (this prevents "inverted pyramiding" or the chance that most of the gains or losses result from the last traded price, not the first or most successful one).

"Trade with the trend, not against it," runs another headline. "Don't anticipate or prejudge the end of a trend, lest losses mount on a continued trend, against your new position." This means not buying on dips with big bargains in mind. Or "average" against the trend, on the theory that the average cost of purchases made in an uptrend will simply cost less (the trend may be changing or have changed).

"Also," say commodity market followers, "you should consider selling short" (most casual public traders think only in terms of buying low and selling high, not the reverse, selling high and buying lower—which is a short sale). Many times there are good, long-term trends of commodity prices on the downside. For instance, the grains are often in long, steep declines.

Many market practitioners admonish investors not to trade in more markets than they can follow. This stems from the fact that their analyses are probably incomplete or markets are difficult to follow simultaneously (due to human limitations).

Don't trade in thin or inactive markets, as prices for completed trades are apt to be poor (disadvantageous to the trader) due to poorly executed transactions.

Out-of-the-way or abnormal conditions may provide special opportunities for a trader. For instance, looking for good odds—where the profit potential is huge in comparison to the loss potential—may come at a time when a commodity is selling at or near a historically low price and prices seem to be bottoming. Likewise, when there is evidence of a sudden profit surge, like several limits in a row in the trader's favor, these windfall profits should be taken.

"As in the stock market," say some commodity pros, "buy bullish news, and sell (close out) the position when the news or rumor become fact." Take a potential grain sale: since the market tends to "build—the news into the market price," this advice would tell the trader to buy on the first piece of news or rumor and sell out when the sale was actually consummated.

Certain specialized methods have been ferried about. Some successful traders trade the divergence from normal or what is expected. If traders in general believe the market is headed higher and the rally fails, it's usually a good sell signal, especially following government reports. One millionaire waits for market traders to lean one way and then turns a trade in the opposite direction.

Some veterans look for key breakouts through trendlines. Using bar charting, if a price breaks through a trend line and 50% trading occurs outside of the trendline for two or three days, it's usually a good signal that a reversal in trend is coming.

Still others wait for retracements of a current move. Prices have tendencies to react or retrace up to half of a recent trend move, and then move in the direction of the trend again. This spot (50% retracement) represents a good place to initiate or reinstate a position with the trend.

Fast in-and-out traders often sell when prices get near the top of a channel of current prices in hopes that prices will go back toward the middle or other end of the channel. This approach is particularly useful in a trading market or a well-defined, enclosed trend (not highly varied between highs and lows).

Others might watch the magnitude of price changes or ranges. When a market is moving lower but the daily price ranges or close-to-close changes are tightening up, this may be a signal that the market has bottomed and an uptrend may shortly be in the making.

Certain chart formations have real meanings to technical afficionados. Some look for congestion areas (tight ranges of price successively) to indicate a trend has slowed. A breakout of prices in the direction of the trend means a major continuance of the trend, whereas a breakout in the other direction means a reversal or change in trend. Many place tight stops above and below the congestion area to quickly jump aboard any (supposed) price move when the breakout occurs. Also, the lower that prices stay in the congestion area, the greater will be the subsequent breakout move from that area.

Key reversals are of special importance to chart followers. A major reversal of an uptrend is usually indicated when prices make new highs or high volume and then price erosion during the same day causes a lower close than the previous day's close. A *two-day key reversal* happens when on the first day the move is into new high ground and a close on strength near the high of the day, followed the next day by an open near the previous close, and then a close sharply lower, indicating a downtrend is at hand. An *island reversal* is formed when prices gap into new highs on one day, then gap lower the next day, flashing a green light for a new downtrend.

A head–shoulder formation has special significance for many commodity traders. This formation, physically resembling a head with right and left shoulders, usually means that prices are topping out (headed lower). Similarly, "M" chart price pictures indicate sell (downtrend) signals. Triple tops or bottoms are an extension of this concept and indicate even more that a top has been formed and more surely that prices should soon plummet. Finally, many market technicians watch volume of trades and open interest (total number of long or short positions held currently) for clues to price movements. When prices and volume (and/or open interest) go up strongly together, it is an indication that prices will continue to remain in that direction for a considerable move.

TOWARD A COMPREHENSIVE TRADING PLAN

Despite the proliferation of do's and don'ts of trading rules, there certainly isn't any cohesive system of methodically trading for profits. The rules are rather vague, to say the least, and defy explicit, unequivocal application. What is a "W" formation to a trader? It probably is different for each investor. Likewise, how much reserve capital should you keep? Are there any ways of correlating size of reserve with expected account size volatility? How can you explicitly and uniformly (for all time) time trades to catch expected price moves the same way whenever they occur? Given a timing technique, what explicit growth and volatility can you expect in the account? How does a trader best diversify among commodities? How much money should be traded, one commodity versus another? Are there set rules for disciplining yourself to follow trading program rules exactly and continually?

This book attempts to apply to the investment arena management-science techniques that have been used successfully in general business applications for corporations, the federal government, and municipalities for some time now. Hopefully, systematic, scientific treatment of commodity (or stock) trading can result in a clear, useful methodology for successful investing.

2 A Systematic Approach to Commodity Trading

Man, more than any other living creature, is a systematic entity. Not only is he physically the most complex creature, but his habits, routines, and variety of modes of operation are the most complex. Perhaps it is because of his great capacity for extending continually beyond current frontiers that he must be well organized to undertake these new endeavors and achieve the results.

Systematic, methodical ways of operating are an integral part of modern life. From the simplest spinning top as a toy for a tot to a lunar laboratory for working physicists and engineers, rational, disciplined ways enter our daily lives. We drive complex, systematically run vehicles to work; push buttons to watch people miles away on television; see microscopic life; and as Marshall McLuhan might say, "we extend ourselves beyond our capabilities." The objective of this chapter is to "extend ourselves" to explore what constitutes meaningful questions in commodity trading and then to formulate an overall approach.

The past sixty years have probably seen more technological progress for man than in all the rest of the centuries combined. Moreover, the rate of progress is accelerating; the next ten years will probably see more progress than in the past sixty. We have seen the development of new

15

and better consumer products, computers and their application, and space travel. These improvements have come about because of technological and scientific innovation. But these innovations are a direct benefactor of increased knowledge—better education and further research.

The March 15, 1967 issue of *Forbes* magazine featured an article on the future of home communications in general and home entertainment in particular. The cover of the issue showed each member of a family viewing his favorite shows on separate, individually oriented television sets. The article itself took a broader approach. Projections were made for even more sophisticated equipment for the home; videotapes, wall screens, and even computers or computer hookups were envisioned for the future. The applications could be quite startling: selecting groceries by video in the home, movies from some central video bank to your home at your selection and convenience, books, magazines, newspapers, and yes, commodity and stock information from a central data bank.

This concept of the electronically oriented home of the future is not only exciting but probably is an understatement of things to come. However, lest we get carried away, we should realize that it takes many small grains of sand to build a castle. We need to build a prototype, a first step toward the idealized commodity-trading system.

Great progress has been and will continue to be made in technological and scientific areas. Moreover, important steps are being taken in human-activities research. The sciences of mathematics and statistics are being applied to market research and surveys for business, human-factors studies for defense and nondefense environments, and public-opinion polls for consumer products and political surveys. A growing interest on the part of our governments, institutions, and industries has been shown toward the still-young science of economics. One portion of economics has been gaining much favor recently, and that is the application of mathematical techniques to economics, or econometrics.

INTERPLAY OF ECONOMIC FORCES

Much attention is being given to the interplay and effect of general economic forces in the national economy (macroeconomics) and to the interactions and effects of individual firms' actions on other firms or on the particular industry. Very little scientific theorizing, however, has been done to explain the forces and their effects that influence the nation's security and commodity markets. Occasionally, articles appear in the *Journal of Operations Research, Econometrica, Management Science,*

Journal of Business, and a few other scholarly periodicals, but the research is small and scattered.

We need a total systematic approach to trading commodities to blend the various components—money, commodities, computers, investing techniques, and the investors—together and operate most efficiently toward making profits.

SYSTEMS METHODS

Systematic approaches are used by most people to solve at least one problem or another. The barber in town may play the horse with the best average running time or else has an inside tip on a long shot. The systems analyst in a research firm attacks a warehouse inventory and scheduling problem with the use of flow diagrams and mathematical formulas.

An investor doesn't trust his intuition or subjective judgment and places all his funds in the top five mutual funds as a way of optimally investing his money. Likewise, one chooses an out-of-the-way set of secondary roads to commute to work each day, rather than travel the crowded, slow main highways; ever so often, however, he may have to change the pattern of side roads because many other commuters have found the same system of roads to be optimal, and the system then becomes as clogged as the main highways.

Probably the area of endeavor in which the greatest percentage of people use systematic approaches are the securities and commodities markets. Fundamentalists are somewhat akin to the barber in town: whichever stock shows the best (earnings) form in its industry or relative to the market is picked for the best performance. Or he might pick up some insider information (tips), and invest expecting a subsequent technical move.

VARIETY OF SYSTEMATIC APPROACHES

Technically oriented investors do much the same except that charts and mathematical calculations aid their analysis. They use charts as the systems analyst would use flow diagrams to present a picture or history of a commodity or stock. Likewise, chartists employ graphical and reasoning tools to this picture, as the systems analyst would use mathematical and computer aids to solve the problem represented by the flow diagram.

The number and variety of systematic approaches for stock and commodity investing are quite large, as evidenced by the great number of well-known ones. Since these represent only the visible (published part) of the iceberg, one can imagine the proliferation of divergent methods. The bibliography gives just a peek at the above-surface portion of the iceberg.

Why all these systematic approaches? Better yet, why any systematic approaches? The answer to these questions, from philosophical and statistical viewpoints, could probably fill several volumes. At the risk of oversimplifying, I believe the first situation arises from the sheer numbers of people, all with divergent interpretations of market actions. The number of approaches have been compounded by the fact that no one system seems to have accumulated wealth for more than one practitioner of the method, leading one to believe that most techniques are quite subjective and preeminently useful for only the original user, if that. This has meant that most investors either develop their own subjective approach (hunches) or employ systematic strategies.

CONSISTENCY IN INVESTMENT

Because very few individuals can rely on subjective considerations to make profits (as they can for small bets in horse races where losses are usually small and are considered as entertainment costs for the evening and profit is not a serious goal), they must turn to more reliable methodology to obtain consistent investing profits. Essentially, this is the answer to the second question; investors employ systematic approaches to obtain consistency and reliability in their investments.

Consistency in investment performance enters the picture because the investor hopes to achieve a continual growth in capital, a pattern of upward growth. It is important, moreover, that the pattern be reliable; a greatly variable (zigzag) trend does not lend confidence to the investor that the ultimate end of the pattern will result in much, if any, capital growth. A trend of excess heads over tails in a series of coin tosses may be consistently above a zero line and display some sort of upward growth, but it cannot reliably continue upward (see the coin-flip example in Chapter 22).

A systematic approach, because it is objectively constructed and adhered to, will help eliminate human subjectivity. An investment strategy that delineates the choice of the five best performing mutual funds on the first of the current year leaves no room for investor flexibility;

the investor cannot subjectively choose the few funds whose prospecti
he first sees on entering his brokerage office on any given day during
the year. Although the latter is a system, it is inherently subjective and
subject to the mood and eye-focus pattern of the investor for a day
choice and a prospectus choice. He might as well use the same system
and play the horses and obtain as good results.

INVESTMENT DISCIPLINE

Likewise, a systematic approach promotes an investment discipline. It
forces the investor to act when disconcerting facts make him waver and
lose sight of a clear-cut opinion. It will not allow the investor to add to
or subtract from the procedures and data specified by the methodology.
In effect, it enforces a uniform response to similar investment situations.

Moreover, it has a psychological advantage over human-based approaches. The systematic method tends to reduce psychological strain
on the individual by minimizing subjectivity and promoting consistent
and reliable investment events.

The systematic approach, because it is based on nonsubjective procedures, improves the average investor's capital growth by providing
consistency of growth, reliability in the intermediate and final outcomes,
reduction in human subjective investment judgments, and investment
discipline, which in turn reduces the psychological strain on the investor.

AN INVESTMENT STRATEGY

What sort of system should the commodity trader employ to maximize
his profits? As previously mentioned, the literature is full of general and
customized techniques. Most, however, are concerned with timing entrances and (sometimes) exits in the market. Although this sounds adequate on the surface, since the trader merely wants to have his capital
grow, most methods are only useful parts of a complete trading system.
This means that the trader must consider everything from capital requirements to coordination of trading programs for maximizing profit
over time and hopefully minimizing psychological problems. It is important to the trader to choose a system that maximizes his capital growth
rate with acceptable risk. For instance, the investor should have ways of
determining adequate starting capital, to be prepared for any adverse

luck. He will need to carefully screen the list of commodity futures and select those that represent good trading mediums.

Naturally the trader will require a good timing technique for opening positions in every commodity selected. He will also need to know what are good stop losses to employ for those commodities to safeguard his position and increase his profit.

These are two natural components of a trading system—enough capital and a good timing technique. But what else constitutes a necessary part of the system?

Some reflection should be cast on *defining* the problems faced by commodity and stock investors and the tools available for solving them, to ferret out other needed components of the trading system.

Defining Problems

In any of the scientific or engineering disciplines, great importance is placed on the definition of terms and formulation of questions. It has been said, especially by those in the business of operations research, that once a problem is properly posed and formulated, assuming the existence of a solution, half the work is done. This may be overstating the importance of problem posing and formulation, but most would agree that much insight can be had from well-posed problems.

There are many aspects of a question that can be emphasized. The question as to what can be investigated relative to commodity investing can be analyzed with emphasis on "what" or "can," and thus the question becomes two questions: what types of questions should be examined and which of these types it is possible to answer. These are not trivial distinctions; a question such as "Can you predict tomorrow's May potato future price with ninety percent accuracy?" is a properly formed "what" question in that it is a type of question meaningful to commodity investors. It appears that the second part, "can," will be answered in the negative from a theoretical viewpoint (because of extreme price variability from day to day due to crop news, government action, buy–sell demand, general news, etc.). Hence any efforts made to construct a predictor will be in vain. The following posed questions are representative types of importance to commodity traders.

Question 1: What about predictive devices?

This question is probably uppermost in the minds of commodity price analysts and theorists and, of course, would be of utmost importance to all investors. Everyone would like to know or "predict," with a given accuracy, what price or price range will occur at some specified time in the future, given that certain price changes and levels have occurred in the past.

As an example, a price break in May potatoes occurred after January 13, 1967, and prices fell (with two brief rallies) after that. The price started at $4.80 per hundred pounds and plummeted to about $1.90 per hundred pounds. It would be nice to know the price a day or week from then; whether it continued the trend (which was four-year potato futures low) or stayed at the same level; or reversed and dramatically went upward. Certainly, no one knew for sure. Just as the huge January 13, 1967, drop caught most by surprise, so did the last course perplex most observers (the fundamental and technical positions seemed to be at odds). In this situation (before the contract expired), one would have very much liked to predict with a certain degree of accuracy, the next day's or next week's price level.

One of the most used predictive tools in science and engineering comes from the discipline of mathematical statistics. The tool, regression, essentially states that there is a formula that relates tomorrow's price, say, to data from today and other past days and has a certain degree of accuracy. Two examples of regressions are:

multiple linear regression

$$P = a \times A + b \times B + c \times C + d \times D + \ldots +$$

and the linear predictor

$$P(i) = \sum_{n=0}^{N} P(i-n) \times K(n)$$

where

$K(n) =$ a difference of exponential functions,

$P =$ the price (closing) or price range on day i,

$P(i-n) =$ the (closing) price or price range $i - n$ days ago,

$A, B, C, D =$ previous (day $i - 1$ or previous) price closings, price bands, high, lows, volume, open interest; changes, accelerations of previous prices, and so on.

$a, b, c, d =$ factors or multiples of A, B, C, D, and K.

Question 2: What about indicators?

Probably everyone knows of at least one index used for financial gauging. Popular indexes include the Dow Jones Averages, Standard and Poors 500-stock composite, various moving averages, new highs and lows, Bureau of Labor Statistics' Commodity Price Index, and many others. Generally speaking, an investor uses an index to do the obvious: indicate or foretell a change in the general investment climate. More precisely, he hopes to tell on a day-to-day or period-to-period basis whether a reversal in an indicator's trend is imminent. The index has preceded or at least paralleled past price movements with some degree of accuracy, and so the investor hopes to time his purchase or sale in line with an index move.

The index does not predict a future price level, as do predictive devices like regressions. Rather, it foretells a directional movement, and hence probably enjoys a greater degree of success, since its information need not be so precise and its knowledge of the future so exact. The following methods are sometimes used to divine the direction of indicators.

Commodity investors use ten- and twenty-day moving averages in combination with current price movements to determine the direction of the underlying trend. Hypothesis testing, composed of parametric and nonparametric testing methods, is an area of mathematical statistics that has been used for a large number of economic, scientific, and engineering applications. Tests have been used to determine whether an average per acre yield of wheat for one year was essentially the same as the previous year's average yield or whether it was significantly different. Also, sequential tests are used in production control to sample manufactured parts from an assembly line. This determines whether the quality is good or whether the whole batch needs examination. Hypothesis testing might be applied to popular indexes or price and volume movements to test whether the current statistics are in line with the general (or latest) trend. If they are not, a significant change is indicated, and the investor should buy or sell, depending on the new direction.

Question 3: Is it a minor or major trend?

This question is a continuation of Question 2; once a change (in prices, etc.) has been detected, it is natural to ask how significant the new trend is (called *trend-strength analysis*). Action taken by the investor on a minor trend will yield him nothing—only commission charges. A major trend, however, by definition will yield him more than enough to pay commission charges—although how much more will vary with the definer and whether 5%, 10%, 20%, or more increase or decrease in price, and so on, delineates a major trend.

The investor, then, would like to foretell, once a change in trend has been noticed, whether the current trend will progress far in the new direction. Again, trend-strength analysis does not predict a specific price or other level for a specific date, but merely gauges the strength of a trend. The difficulty of gauging the strength of a trend lies between that of pinpointing a trend change and that of predicting specific levels for specific dates. Even if only this question could be answered, most investors would be able to take advantage of occasional major trend changes and take profits with the use of stop losses or limits.

Several analytical approaches appear to offer hope for arriving at an answer to the question. By using hypothesis testing, you can ascertain whether a change in prices, for instance, is strong enough by relating the change to other significant changes in the past. Likewise, the rate of change, or acceleration, of prices, could be statistically compared with those of previous major changes. Comparison of price slopes, accelerations, and of the general new trend line could be made with those immediately preceding the change, and statistical tests construed.

Question 4: What is the basic, underlying trend?

Most investors become perplexed, at one time or another, by a commodity's seemingly erratic price behavior. One day it may be going up, the next day down or sideways, and then up again the following day. Many times this occurs within the day's action. Also, it may be impossible to tell at a glance from a chart whether the commodity is basically moving up or down (because of many fluctuations) and, hence, an average (sideways) movement is assumed.

The investor would like to know the basic or predominant trend for the current period. In effect, he might want to know whether a systematic or mathematical treatment of the data could produce a line or curve or set of lines or curves to adequately describe recent past action. If he had such a line or curve, the investor would be in a position to project into the future a continuation of a price movement's recent past, as shown by the line or curve, or by comparison with historical movement ascertain that a different line or curve will describe the immediate future. The line or curve could thus become a projection aid to the investor.

Probably the most useful mathematical–statistical methods for determining such lines or curves are simple linear, quadratic, or curvilinear regression techniques. These lines or curves can be expressed as:

$$P(t) = a_1 t + a_2$$
linear regression

$$P(t) = a_1 t^2 + a_2 t + a_3$$
quadratic regression

$$P(t) = f(t)$$
general nonlinear or curvilinear regression

where

$P(t) =$ the price of the commodity or indicators at time t,

$t =$ time (usually days, so t would be an integer; i.e., $t = 1$ would mean day 1, etc.),

$f(t) =$ any general nonlinear function of t,

$a_1, a_2, a_3 =$ coefficients (constants) to be determined from the specific data in question.

Question 5: How long in one direction?

Once a trend change has been noted (Question 2) and a major or minor trend ascertained (Question 3), the investor would probably be interested in knowing how far it might go in one direction before changing again. For example, the January 13, 1978 sharp downward movement in May 1978 potato prices might have been adjudged a major trend change, and now it must be ascertained how far it might go or at least how to recognize when it has finished running the course of a bear plunge.

Many investors use stops to close out a position that is starting to reverse, so as to take profits or accept losses. It is no easy task, however, to determine what constitutes the start of a reversal. This is, in effect, the same as trying to determine whether the reversal is a major or minor trend change.

One possible approach is to determine at what point (statistically or otherwise) the trend has stopped growing in a fast manner, will start to grow more slowly, and will soon level off to the top of the trend. Essentially, it is at the point where the rate of change of prices goes from positive to negative that the price growth begins to diminish. This point is called an *inflection point* in mathematical applications. It is not, however, the same as the top (peak) of the trend but is closer to the middle of an ascent or descent.

Question 6: Prices—continuous or clustering?

Many a trader has watched and wondered about price occurrences at certain numbers and has observed transactions occurring together rather than at spread-out, even-increment intervals. How preponderant is this phenomenon, and how does it affect larger, trend-like movements? Are trends accentuated one time and dampened another because price transactions tend to cluster? Most of the clustering effect for stocks occurs within day periods [Price Models, 19], and not from day to day, week to week, and so forth. The investor would thus like to know how long-range and trading, or intermediate, trends are affected by clustering of stock and commodity price transactions, and what implications for trading can be derived from such information.

Question 7: What time increments?

A stock article [Price Models, 6] suggests that students of financial analysis have been studying the wrong time intervals for price transactions and have been led to erroneous conclusions concerning stochastic descriptions of the stock (and by inference, commodity) market.

When an analyst, trader, or investor studies price movements, he uses (assumes) the fact that the price records, usually showing high, low, and close, occur at equal time intervals of a day, week, month, or year. Some even break a day's high–low–close price into a complete, moving history of the day's transactions, thus capturing the upward, downward, and sideways movement for every transaction.

Others do not directly use time-recorded price transactions but prefer to record only when sizable price movements have occurred (point-and-figure method). Time is indirectly a factor, however, since monthly notations are made, presumably so that the investor can determine whether he is making a good profit with respect to time. It is not good enough for an investor to say he doubled his money—if he only performed that feat over a twenty-year period.

Choosing a time interval is important for two reasons: (1) it enables the investor to critically view his stock or commodity's performance over a period of time, hence obtaining a percent-per-time index; and (2) it enables the analyst (and ultimately traders and investors who depend on his advice) to center on the significant time interval over which price movements can be characterized and trends determined. Of interest to the investor, then, is determining which time intervals are significant and which are related to the various trend analyses.

Question 8: What is the effect of news?

Every investor probably has his favorite story about how a sudden bit of news helped or hindered his investment. News affects all investments to some degree; crop news, weather occurrences, government price support and loan actions, foreign and domestic buying (cash market) . . . all affect a given commodity (and sometimes many simultaneously) to a considerable extent; on the other hand, Federal Reserve members bank reserve requirements and interest-rate raising or lowering, company earnings, Near East news, British unemployment statistics, political events, and yes, even the lunar tides, probably affect all stock prices, each to a greater or lesser extent.

The investor would like to know what (quantitative) relationship, if any, can be construed between news and a general market index, and individual stock or commodity price movements. For example, what connection can be made between a particular bit of news (e.g., rain of 1.2 inches in the eastern part of Kansas during the wheat-growing season) and the present trend of a wheat contract? If the price trend were up, how many (if any) points will the wheat price fall?

The problem is further complicated by the fact that an extremely wide variety of factors could conceivably affect, to some degree, every commodity futures and stock price. Part of the solution lies in the application of multiple and partial correlation coefficients between prices and the different types of news items. With careful application investors should be able to separate out highly relevant types of news items that display a high correlation with the price movement under consideration. Thus the prime news influence could be discovered.

But the use of correlation coefficients can give wrong conclusions. For instance, it could be shown that there exists a high correlation between the rising crime rate and the rising literacy (education level) in the United States. This would lead to the conclusion that the more educated the citizenry becomes, the more heedless of law and order it becomes.

Question 9: What constitutes a trend?

Question 4 asks whether an underlying trend can be described, and if so, how. This question is more basic; it asks whether there is a trend and how an investor goes about finding out if it exists. Essentially, the trader is interested in knowing whether present price moves are random or systematic. If random, does it mean the movement is basically sideways, and if a trend, is it strong or weak, up or down?

When viewing a graph of the price of a stock, market indicator, or commodity, the trader often subjectively superimposes a trend line over the chart action. The superimposed trend line may be derived by linking together closing highs of all previous minor and major upward movements, or closing lows of all previous minor and major downward movements. It might be done by drawing a line through the data, so that it hits as many of the closing prices as possible. Two lines, one representing a line above which no data occur, and one below which no data occur (called *channel lines*), may help to "box in" the data so that a funneling effect is created and a general direction of movement is indicated. Whichever method the investor uses, however, implicitly assumes a manner of identifying or describing a trend. One method may show a trend one way, whereas another may show no trend, or even an oppositely directed trend. Obviously the method used (trend-identifying procedure) impels the investor to one action or another, and since each investor tends to have at least a slightly different, if not radical, trend-identifier approach, a multitude of investor actions results with every price movement.

From the field of statistics one might be able to employ random testing (parametric and nonparametric) procedures to ascertain whether a price movement were a trend continuation or alteration.

Question 10: What basic relationships exist?

Questions 1–9 could be presented as natural outgrowths of this question. Basically, the trader would like to know the relationship between a closing, high, low, or open price on day i and

- the price (closing, high, low, and open) on previous days $i - 1, i - 2, i - 3$, and so on,
- the volume on previous days $i - 1, i - 2, i - 3$, and so on,
- similar statistics for other commodities or stocks, and the news (as explained in Question 8) of the commodity(ies) or stocks of previous days.

These are the essential reportable facts about any commodity. It seems reasonable that today's price should depend to some degree on yesterday's price and other factors, as noted in the preceding list. What is not obvious, however, is *how much* it depends on yesterday's facts, and if it does, which variables are most important and how they relate to today's prices.

In exploring what constitutes part of an overall commodity-trading system, and in getting into basic questions, one comes across misleading, incomplete, or untrue concepts or actions that must be examined and discarded lest they become detrimental to the trading system.

Illusion or Reality

"Some analysts derive money from the infantile impulse to play with feces. Ferenczi, in particular, calls money 'nothing other than odorless dehydrated filth that has been made to shine.'" (Marshall McLuhan, *Understanding Media: The Extension of Man.*) This might be considered an overstatement. However, men are eager to make money. And in pursuit of the easy dollar do market traders delude themselves?

For example, an article [General, 10] suggested that one of the greatest hindrances to having a profitable trading record was the trader himself, because certain psychological traits prevent many traders from objectively using fundamental or technical trading methods.

Certainly a trader with significant psychological aberrations cannot hope to trade as successfully as one who minimizes these aberrations and steers close to a rational approach. Of course, there are exceptions; people who "know the sense of the market,"—the Livermores, the Loebs, and the Goulds, who consistently profit, using (seemingly) subjective analysis.

Most of us, however, realize that there are few who have that sixth or seventh instinct, and hence we must rely on objective indicators and methods to fathom the market's sense. Further, even if we overcome psychologically created illusions, there is the problem of determining from an objective viewpoint how good a given trading system is.

Illusions about Trading Records

Traders can cash in on their ignorance or lose badly, by drawing too many conclusions and/or by being led to draw too many conclusions from advisory services' records.

The Securities and Exchange Commission (SEC) currently requires stock-investment advisories to list complete records after one year's operation. This requirement, however, is quite minimal. The commission does not require proof that a prior recommendation was made for the entrance (opening) of a trade for precisely the day referred in the record list, nor does it require proof of the prior recommendation for the date of closing of the same trade. Also, it does not require a detailed explanation of how the prices of trades were arrived at. Should one assume the trades were made at the open, low, high, close, or average price?

Even more misleading, however, is the implication that if the profits of the trades listed were averaged, a representative profit per trade could be obtained, and that if the time spent in these trades were again averaged, an average trade duration could be obtained, and by compounding the average trade, a yearly capital growth rate.

A number of stock and commodity funds and advisories employ this device to infer what a trader would have done over some extended period of time. For instance, one might show a hypothetical initial investment of $10,000 on August 1, 1950. Then its value as of September 22, 1967 grows to $170,000! What was not said, however, was what would have happened if the same investment had been made on November 28, 1950 and accounted for on December 18, 1967. The capital may have grown by then to only $110,000, a 70% difference with a slightly different (by three months) starting and end points. And had the hapless investor put his $10,000 into the fund on May 13, 1959 (perhaps a higher water mark in the fund's growth) and accounted for it on October 10, 1966, the capital may have *diminished* to $8,000!

This type of statistical inference, however, is by no means limited to funds and advisories. Federal administration officials use different bases for general price indexes to prove or disprove the fact that the general cost of living is relatively up or down. Enormous differences in interpretation have resulted, depending on the base year used.

Yearly Performance

The answer to the preceding fund-performance dilemma is to determine how the fund has performed over time intervals of varying lengths and starting from arbitrarily specified starting points in time. By averaging the yearly performances of these myriad combinations, one could assess an overall average per unit time profit-percentage performance. This would make the question of the "right" investment entrance (and exit) time of secondary importance.

Investment advisory records, however, are even more difficult to analyze. The mere listing of the precise record of all completed trades does not in itself indicate how one would have fared, on the average, using the advisory's recommendations over the time specified.

The fund's actual capital performance record, notwithstanding the aforementioned objections, is in black and white. The trader, however, must make additional decisions when presented with recommendations by an advisor. Should he accept them all? How much capital should he put in each recommendation? The trader then is in effect his own investment manager and must make decisions. Some of the recommendations will be correct, some wrong. Some of the traders will profit by certain combinations of trades that they have chosen from the advisor's list. Many, however, will not—and this is mainly why there is always a heavy turnover of customers for almost all advisories. The customers are in effect making the final decision as to how to exactly allocate their funds to recommendations.

If, on the other hand, the trader rigidly followed the advisor's advice and allocated equal amounts to each recommendation at the time the recommendations were being made, he could better evaluate the advisor's performance.

Even then, however, it is nearly impossible to determine the effectiveness of a list of completed recommendations. If the trader invested in consecutive trades, his capital growth would not correspond to the arithmetic averaging of the profits of the recommendations. Degradation of the recommendations' profit average would also occur if (and most likely) losses come more rapidly, on the average, than gains.

Likewise, without a sufficiently large sample of recommendations completed, the trader cannot have any statistical confidence in the average profit for the list as a predictor of future results. The following paragraphs elaborate on these points. The train of thought is expanded, to include illusions about a trader's evaluation of his techniques.

Illusions about Consecutive Trades

Traders will often examine an advisory's record or that of their own research and dwell on the arithmetic average of profits and losses. By noting how many trades were made in a year's time, or by projecting the results of a few trades, the trader would calculate the yearly growth rate by multiplying the average profit per trade, by the number of trades in a given commodity. Or he would simply add the total profit percentages and subtract the total loss percentages, to obtain the yearly percentage growth. By doing this he would be fooling himself about the actual yearly growth rate.

For example, suppose he actually or theoretically made successive trades resulting in a gain and a loss of 90% and 50%, or vice versa, in pork bellies. Suppose his initial capital were $10,000. The trader would think he averaged $(90-50)/2 = 20\%$ per trade, and would end up after the two preceding trades with an approximate 50% increase in capital, a little over $14,000.

But he actually lost 5%, or $500, over the two trades! This is because, in reality, the trader made 90% on the first trade. This meant that his capital stood at $19,000 after the first trade. However, he lost 50% of the reinvested capital ($19,000) during the second trade and hence was left with $9,500 after two trades.

Comparison of Profits and Losses

Although this is a simple case, it illustrates the fact that bare percentage profits and losses can not be compared without knowing whether the trades were consecutive or simultaneous. A simultaneous gain and loss of 90% and 50% on half the initial capital each would have made the capital growth 20%, to $12,000, after the two trades, as compared to the 5% loss with the same, but consecutive, trades. The same phenomenon results when a trader inspects a fund's performance record. Consecutive yearly profits and losses cannot be compared without knowing whether the or cumulated, analogous to the simple example in the preceding paragraph.

Illusions about Loss–Gain Parity

Another illusion traders suffer under is the belief that equal consecutive or nonsimultaneous loss and gain percentages cancel out each other. This reasoning is fallacious for two reasons. First, it is a fact of mathematics (real analysis) that can be applied to demonstrate that equal gains and losses taken in a string, regardless of order, always produce an overall loss. For instance, a 50% gain followed by a 50% loss produces a 25% loss. Likewise, even equal small losses and gains produce losses; a 5% gain and a 5% loss results for one investment pile in a very slight loss. On the other hand, the larger the two respective equal gain and loss, the larger will be the resultant loss. In fact, greater weight must be given to all losses than to gains when consecutive trades are made. Second, losses and gains cannot be on an even parity because of slippage from a theoretical arithmetic average, due to the fact that losses are taken on the average earlier than gains. Even if a trader diversified in a number of simultaneous trades, losses would come before gains on the average. This means, effectively, that the trader would make more trades than he had expected (if he employed his now available capital, after an earlier than average trade duration). If his method's success percentage (number of profitable trades divided by total number of trades) were less than 50%, he would run the risk of incurring more losses, and possibly a slow erosion of his capital.

It is even quite possible that continual erosion due to faster loss trades than gain trades could diminish the capital investment piles considerably and leave the trader with all gaining open positions. He then would have to hope that these presently gaining positions can bring his capital back to the starting point and, hopefully, ahead.

Illusions about Research and Actual Experiments

A number of articles have appeared concerning the performances of certain trading techniques. Alexander [Price Models, 1] used a percentage filter method to take positions in a price-swing direction when the swing exceeded a certain percentage, and to reverse the position when an opposite swing of the same size occurred. He tried a number of different percentage swing sizes as different methods. Only in a few cases, however, did the number of trades reach 200 or more, not enough in most cases to place any significance in the results, from a mathematical statistics viewpoint. Moreover, he used the methods on the Dow Jones Industrials and the Standard and Poor Average. These indexes cannot be used to assert what one would have done with a randomly selected or a specific portfolio, however.

Heiser, Gitomer, et al. [General, 10] compared their composite method to both the Commodity Research Bureau's (CRB) and a ten-day moving-average technique. The total number of trades for their method, however, was only sixty-five. The CRB method was used for 202 trades, and the ten-day moving-average approach was used for fifty-seven.

However, it is doubtful that these samples are sufficient to allow valid conclusions. Statisticians, when drawing samples from corn fields to determine the effects of certain chemicals, fertilizers, or pesticides, must choose a sample large enough to accept or reject a hypothesis made on the effect of the chemicals, fertilizers, or pesticides on the corn. Not only must the sample be large enough (several hundred samples are considered a minimum), but the samples must be independent of each other.

Cochran gives a formula [Testing Methods, 2, pp. 74–75] for determining the proper sample size to determine specific proportions in a population for two different characteristics, given a desired degree of precision. Assuming that one might be interested in determining what sample size is needed to verify a success percentage to a given technique for projecting into the future, the formulas on these pages would indicate a minimum of around 400 samples, using a zero proportion corresponding to a zero profit.

Further, traders should realize that samples should be representative, so that conclusions drawn from the sample could be projected to all commodities over all time. This means a sample might include a large selection of commodities (all active ones, currently around 20) over several years. In addition, the sample should be taken over periods in which little price movement occurred ("still waters") and in periods in which large price movements occurred. The ratio of these two periods should be in the same proportion as that over all modern or significant history of the commodities in question and what the trader expects to occur in the future (and therein lies the rub). The Heiser, CRB, and ten-day moving-average technique tests, however, do not meet any of these sampling requirements. Hence, significant valid conclusions cannot be drawn from these tests.

Edmonds [Trading Methods, 8] similarly researched a moving average approach. He essentially tried hundreds of combinations of these approaches on a small set of commodity data. Aside from being a perfect example of hindsight selection of a best technique on some data, without testing the same on a future set of data the method(s) suffer from lack of testing on an adequate sample.

A test of a trading system should include an adequate sample. It must be large enough, have independent samples (not closely related contract months or possibly interdependent commodities, such as some grains), be representative of a sufficiently large and broad spectrum of commodities, and be representative of "still-waters" periods as well as ones of large price swings (and in the proper ratio, representative of all or a significant part of previous history).

Illusions about the Theories of Methods

Even more damaging to a trader's chances of having his capital grow is the case where his method is not based on any theory, economic or mathematical. For instance, the popular moving-average approach is not based on any economic theory. It essentially dictates taking a position when the current price(s) touch below or above a moving-average line. Some have added a filter to this approach, calling for a trade when the current price(s) move a certain distance above or below the moving average.

This mechanical technique is based neither on a supply–demand law or some other econometric theory nor on estimation, prediction, testing, sampling, or any other mathematical statistics formulas. There is a connection to electrical applications, wherein data on charts and oscilloscopes are smoothed to filter out noise and leave the main signal. The idea transferred to commodity prices is that there is (it is assumed) some "main signal" or "trend," and moving averages will remove the random price moves to reveal it. It may be closer to mechanical rules of chance than to economic laws. There may be times, of course, when the moving-average technique signals a trade when an unknown economic one would also have done this.

However, without the benefit of knowing the economic laws that describe price movements, traders are forced to subject their moving-average approaches to a large amount of testing. This is because they wouldn't know how much in the long run their moving-average technique coincided with a truer economic description of the price movement.

This means the trader with a moving-average approach must subject his technique to at least 400 samples (completed trades), probably more, to assure that this method will coincide sufficiently with the unknown economic laws governing the price movements to account for enough profit. It also means other random signals given by his method but not in consonance with economic law will not yield an exorbitant amount of losses.

Likewise, the trader may make arithmetic mistakes in his computations. Even if he manually calculates his method for a good set of data and generates more than 400 trades, he runs the chance of having made enough calculation mistakes to completely change, or significantly alter, his overall profit per trade average. Moreover, he may have subjectively ignored, altered, or omitted some calculations or signals in his anxiety to produce a good trading system.

The solution to this problem is to automate, or computerize, the method. Computer programs, when completely debugged, don't lie. The trader will receive a quite objective answer as to whether his technique is any good.

A Model for Optimum Trading Intervals

Another problem that pops up often and defies solution is how often should one trade to maximize growth in the account. Obviously much of the answer depends on capital available, market conditions, and the ability to be there and make a decision (perhaps within the day even) for ceasing the current investment, expanding on the size of it (pyramiding), or doing nothing.

The following study examines the possibilities for maximizing account growth with four variables at the disposal of the trader to manipulate: the number of trades over a period of time, the amount invested in each period of time, the price rise chosen for each (pyramid of) trade, and the number of new contract positions initiated each period. The example assures somewhat idealized conditions, too.

The following involves the use of simulation or system modeling, which is one of the techniques from operations research. In effect, the application aids the speculator, trader, or hedger in maximizing his profit over an anticipated long-term, upward, or downward trend. More than likely, the commodity speculator has as his goal maximization of the ratio of total return to total investment over a given period of time. Many will not even have a precise duration of time in mind but are flexible (to some extent) as to how long it will take to achieve a satisfactory ratio. This "goal" can be represented mathematically in the following manner, where the objective is to maximize the net capital to invested capital ratio, CR,

$$CR = \frac{C_N}{\sum\limits_{n=1}^{N} I_{n-1}} \qquad (1)$$

where

$I_{n-1} =$ the initial or additional investment at the end of period $n-1$,

$C_N =$ the value of the investments as of the end of period N.

Now C_n can be formulated in the following manner:

$$C_n = T_{n-1} \times MIN_{n-1} + k \times r_n \times T_{n-1} - c_n \times T_{n-1} + (C_{n-1} + I_{n-1} - T_{n-1} \times MIN_{n-1}) \qquad (2)$$

where

$k =$ the dollar rise or fall per point rise or fall for each open contract,

$T_{n-1} =$ the number of open contracts initiated and/or maintained at the end of period $n-1$,

$r_n =$ the number of points the contract price rose or fell by the end of period n (a positive number for contract prices rising, negative for prices falling, if the position held were a long; vice versa for a short position), that is, the price rise or fall increment for period n,

c_n = the commission charged per contract for each round-turn transaction at the end of period n.

Equation (2) assumes the investor reinvests (plows back) his earnings C_{n-1} made during period $n - 1$, in effect trying to "pyramid" his capital. Note that he could retain, rather than pyramid, part of his capital at the end of period $n - 1$ by letting the invested capital I_{n-1} be negative. Now T_n must be an integer, since only integral contracts are traded on the exchanges. Also, T_{n-1} is constrained by the amount of cash available for investment at the end of period $n - 1$. Hence

$$\text{maximum } T_{n-1} = \frac{C_{n-1} + I_{n-1}}{MIN_{n-1}} \tag{3}$$

where

$[x]$ = the integer (whole-number) portion of x,

MIN_{n-1} = the margin required per contract at the end of period $n - 1$,

N = the number of periods selected (note further discussion).

Equation (2) is arrived at by representing C_n as the sum of:

$T_{n-1} \times MIN_{n-1}$ = the total margin requirements (dollars) of T_{n-1} contracts invested at the end of period $n - 1$,

$k \times r_n \times T_{n-1}$ = the total (dollar) return on T_{n-1} contracts invested at the end of period $n - 1$ (held through period n),

$c_n \times T_{n-1}$ = the total (dollar) commission charges for T_{n-1} contracts closed out at the end of period n,

$(C_{n-1} + I_{n-1} - T_{n-1} \times MIN_{n-1})$ = the total (dollar) value of the uninvested portion as of the end of period $n - 1$,

I_{n-1} = as previously explained.

Equation (2) can be consolidated and now becomes

$$C_n = C_{n-1} + I_{n-1} + (kr - c_n) \times T_{n-1} \tag{4}$$

Further, there may be constraints on some of the variables in the system. Specifically,

$$\sum_{n=1}^{N} r_n = R \tag{5}$$

$$\sum_{n=1}^{N} I_{n-1} < I \tag{6}$$

Equation (5) states that the sum of price rises or falls will equal an anticipated long-range (total) price rise or fall of R; fundamental analysis, for instance, may show that wheat prices over the next year or so will move upward, such as by 50¢ a bushel, because of steadily decreasing government surplus stocks; or, R or each r_n may be a random or stochastic variable. Equation (6) states that the speculator, hedger, or trader has a maximum amount I that he is willing to invest in the commodity over the given time duration (N time periods).

Before continuing, it should be noted that there are essentially four decision variables at the disposal of the speculator: N, r_n, I_{n-1}, and T_{n-1}. In other words, he can control the number of transaction periods (N), choose what he hopes will be good price rise (or fall) increments (r_n), choose the outside capital he will invest at the end of period $n-1$ (I_{n-1}), and determine the number of contract open positions to take at the end of period $n-1$ (T_{n-1}).

For example, suppose he initially invested in one long potato contract position with $300 margin. Call it an initial investment I_0. Suppose further he waits for a 30¢ rise in the potato price; at the end of the first period he realizes, using equation (4),

$$C_1 = 0 + 300 + (5 \times 30 - 25) \times 1 = 425$$

where

$C_0 = 0$ since no capital was realized at the end of the initial period, only an outside investment I_0,

$I_0 = 300$,

$k = \$5$ per point rise or fall in price,

$r_1 =$ a 30-point rise in potato prices,

$c_1 = \$25$ commission charge per round-turn contract transaction.

At the end of the second period

$$C_2 = 425 + 0 + (5 \times 30 - 25) \times 1 = 550$$

Here, no new investment (I_1) was made at the end of the first period. Table 1 shows the effect of continued price rises on the total capital of the speculator for five periods.

At this point one might ask what would happen if the trader manipulated some of the four decision variables previously mentioned. Specifically, suppose the following simplifying circumstances were to occur: (1) the speculator ascertains from fundamental considerations that the price of potatoes will rise seasonally from the present time (summer) to a point later next year (spring) a total of 210 points; (2) the commission charges during that time will remain constant; (3) the price change will come about fairly smoothly (no whiplashes possible for him); (4) he will trade at constant (equal) price rises, and (5) his initial investment of $300 will be his only outside investment. This means that $c_n = \$25$ for all periods:

$$r_1 = r_2 \cdots r_N \qquad (7)$$

$$R = \sum_{n=1}^{N} = 210 \qquad (8)$$

$$I_0 = 300$$
$$I_1 = I_2 = I_3 = \cdots = I_N = 0$$

TABLE 1   Return on Capital for Five Reinvestment Periods.

Period	Total capital available, end of period (C_n)	Return on open contracts, plus margin, end of period $(MIN_{n-1} \times T_{n-1} + k \times r_n \times T_{n-1})$	Price-rise increments for period (r_n)
Initially	$ 300	—	—
1	425	$ 450	30
2	550	450	30
3	675	450	30
4	925	900	30
5	1300	1350	30

The speculator has only one decision variable at his disposal: N, the number of trading periods. A choice of N small would mean that he will trade after a large price rise has occurred, and a choice of N large would mean that trades will occur after small price increments have happened, since $r_n = (210/N)$ from equations (7) and (8).

Tables 2–7 show the effects of trading at different price increments under the preceding assumptions. Figure 2 shows in graphical form a plot of net capital: invested capital ratio (CR) versus different price-increment values and summarizes the results of Tables 2–7.

It is evident that neither the extremes of trading on every small-point price rise (10 points) or only once for large gains (210 points) give the maximum return for the same initial investment. In fact, the greatest net gain apparently occurs somewhere near the middle, between price increments of 35 and 65 points. It should be pointed out, however, that more trading risks are incurred if the investor increases the number of trades from one.

The Five Components of the Commodity-trading System

The last few discussions digressed somewhat from the subject at hand, namely, what constitutes a viable commodity trading system. The intent,

TABLE 2   Return on Capital for One Reinvestment Period.

Period	Total capital available, end of period (C_n)	Return on open contracts, plus margin, end of period ($MIN_{n-1} \times T_{n-1} + k \times r_n \times T_{n-1}$)	Price-rise increments for period (r_n)
Initially	$ 300	—	—
1	1325	$1350	210

TABLE 3   Return on Capital for Two Reinvestment Periods.

Period	Total capital available, end of period (C_n)	Return on open contracts, plus margin, end of period ($MIN_{n-1} \times T_{n-1} + k \times r_n \times T_{n-1}$)	Price-rise increments for period (r_n)
Initially	$ 300	—	—
1	800	$ 825	105
2	1800	1650	105

TABLE 4 Return on Capital for Four Reinvestment Periods.

Period	Total capital available, end of period (C_n)	Return on open contracts, plus margin, end of period $(MIN_{n-1} \times T_{n-1} + k \times r_n \times T_{n-1})$	Price-rise increments for period (r_n)
Initially	$ 300	—	—
1	600	$ 625	65
2	1200	1250	65
3	2400	2500	65
4	2800	3000	15

TABLE 5 Return on Capital for Six Reinvestment Periods.

Period	Total capital available, end of period (C_n)	Return on open contracts, plus margin, end of period $(MIN_{n-1} \times T_{n-1} + k \times r_n \times T_{n-1})$	Price-rise increments for period (r_n)
Initially	$ 300	—	—
1	450	$ 475	35
2	600	475	35
3	900	950	35
4	1350	1425	35
5	1950	1900	35
6	2850	2850	35

TABLE 6 Return on Capital for 11 Reinvestment Periods.

Period	Total capital available, end of period (C_n)	Return on open contracts, plus margin, end of period $(MIN_{n-1} \times T_{n-1} + k \times r_n \times T_{n-1})$	Price-rise increments for period (r_n)
Initially	$ 300	—	—
1	375	$ 400	20
2	450	400	20
3	525	400	20
4	600	400	20
5	750	800	20
6	900	800	20
7	1125	1200	20
8	1350	1200	20
9	1650	1600	20
10	2025	2000	20
11	2325	2100	10

TABLE 7 Return on Capital for 21 Reinvestment Periods.

Period	Total capital available, end of period (C_n)	Return on open contracts, plus margin, end of period $(MIN_{n-1} \times T_{n-1} + k \times r_n \times T_{n-1})$	Price-rise increments for period (r_n)
Initially	$ 300	—	—
1	325	$ 350	10
2	350	350	10
3	375	350	10
4	400	350	10.
5	425	350	10
6	450	350	10
7	475	350	10
8	500	350	10
9	525	350	10
10	550	350	10
11	575	350	10
12	600	350	10
13	650	700	10
14	700	700	10
15	750	700	10
16	800	700	10
17	850	700	10
18	900	700	10
19	975	1050	10
20	1050	1050	10
21	1125	1050	10

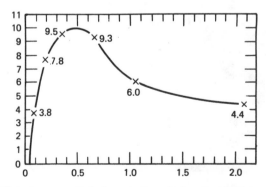

Figure 2. Plot of net capital: invested capital ratio (CR) *versus different price-increment values.*

however, was to show that many components *could* be incorporated in a general trading system: continuous testing mechanisms for trend determination, maximization of contracts invested, and so on.

From these explorations, however, come at least five basic components of an effective commodity trading system:

1. enough genuine *risk* capital—to initiate and undertake all possible trades signalled, and to withstand periods of erosion in the trader's account,

2. optimal *selection* of commodities for trading candidates, to optimally utilize available resources in the best payoff areas,

3. efficient *timing* of buy and sell points for the trades, to make individual trades most profitable,

4. proper *management of capital;* initial capital requirements, allocation to each candidate trade, the maintenance of proper money reserves in the trading account, and proper evaluation of account growth statistics to best ensure smooth growth in the trader's account, and

5. the maintenance of good *disciplinary actions* on the part of the trader, to ensure the continued and complete follow through of the trading system program.

The following sections will separately discuss in depth the five basic components of a trading system identified previously. There surely may be other components or subcomponents that the reader can bring to mind. Hopefully the following discussions will touch on them.

SECTION II

---

3 Risk

The first component of an efficient commodity trading system is to have enough capital, and it must be genuine risk moneys. These requirements are needed to ensure that the account can survive periods of capital erosion due to losses, in order to continue trading all signals that occur and in the amount of dollars required for each trade. Moreover, moneys placed in the account must not be subject at some later date to another use because the trader has no alternative (an emergency, perhaps). He could then no longer follow the plans for trading, which defeats the purpose of a systematic approach.

PEOPLE RISK MONEY

People are funny, as Art Linkletter would say. Some risk money to get more money, which is the standard attitude. But many risk money for other reasons. Some consider going to the horse racetrack as an entertainment and the net losses experienced over the long run as the cost of having fun. Others might risk money for masochistic reasons—they feel guilty about having made or taken money from others in their business or profession. Still others think of an altruistic act—someone (the winner in a state lottery) more deserving needs the money. Yet some may have fatalistic motives—we are all dust sooner or later, they say, so why not gamble for one big payoff, the one that could make this miserable life heaven for a moment. And there are those who even believe in a personal, benevolent interest on the part of an omniscience—a pot of gold will surely come his way if he risks a quarter in the rainbow stakes. Addiction for risking money, like drug or alcoholic addiction, can incapacitate or ruin investors. There was one fellow who kept losing more and more money in commodities, and kept at it, even though he knew he was using losing methods. He didn't like it, but was unable to stop himself from calling each day *and* placing orders with the broker.

A Kaleidoscope of Influence

Where and how much money is risked depends on many personal attributes, such as an individual's job status, own psyche, general geographical location (city, countryside, etc.), sex, age, financial position, education, and attitude.

Women generally are more cautious and less risk taking than men are. The fair sex is seldom involved in commodity trading and other more risky areas. Curiously, gals seem to gamble at casinos and racetracks as much as men do, perhaps because of the entertainment and limited loss value at these places. It's possible that the traditional home chore of budgeteer still strongly influences their risk-taking attitude.

Younger people tend to be bigger risk takers and have an even larger dollar risk: financial circumstance ratio. That is, younger ones want their usually limited resources to grow much more than do older, more financially secure people do and hence will take larger risks for the larger reward. And why not—youngsters just out of school with little family responsibility can afford to risk everything, because they have little to lose and few financial commitments.

Individuals with college education are more apt to have risk funds, for several reasons. They tend to have higher incomes and hence more disposable money for risk ventures. Higher education also tends to give a person greater capability for understanding the complexities and alternatives in risk investments.

Financial circumstances play a large role. A millionaire can afford to place $5,000–$10,000 with a broker to let him play with it, and not really experience serious risk taking because a total loss would be equivalent to an average income earner losing a $20 bet at the racetrack.

Geographical and cultural factors can influence an individual's risk-taking preferences, too. A farmer with a family history with the soil might be less disposed to taking an investment risk in Polaroid stock than would a city factory manager whose firm produces metal plates for cameras as one of its products. Moreover, first-generation Italian-Americans might be less interested in trying commodity futures or stock options then using spare, hard-earned money for investment in their or their children's education or job-skill building.

Also important is an individual's occupation or profession. An engineer, with his intellectual curiosity about mechanistic workings and orderly paths, might be more intrigued and challenged by a quantitative problem (how to get rewards out of risked moneys). He is also generally more affluent then the average worker and can more readily grasp the concepts and mechanics of risk and return.

Religion may also play a hand, though perhaps less so than any other factor. Certain faiths prohibit gambling and generally discourage modern investments and prefer for their members the use of extra funds in more traditional forms, such as farmland.

Probably the most important factor influencing a potential risk taker is his own, personal characteristics—in short, his *attitude* about risk. An older person with not great financial circumstances lived in a rural setting and acted like a wild speculator. Likewise, some scientific colleagues, though young and professionals with good incomes, would not touch commodities with a 10-foot pole.

Risk Attitudes

When an individual opens a managed account with me I often send him an investment attitude questionnaire. The questions are designed to find out his attitude about risk—whether he is basically conservative, moderate, or speculative when it comes to commodity trading. I use it to tailor the amount traded to fit a client's risk outlook. The following details the questions and possible answers.

Question 1. Which of the following best described your risk taking in commodities?

a. Conservative.

b. Moderate.

c. Speculative.

Question 1 asks just that—whether he is a conservative, moderate, or speculative risk taker in commodities. Questions 2–10 are designed to determine whether his answer is true and if not, to ascertain which apellation fits.

Question 2. Which is more important to you?

a. Setting a dollar-loss cutoff point on your account.

b. Setting a percentage-loss cutoff point on your account.

The answer to this will tell us whether he is risking a set dollar amount or comparing it to another investment area, to check which one is losing/gaining more percentage wise, with the idea that he may shift funds to the better-acting one in the future. It may also show a conflict with the answer to the first one: if he says he is basically a conservative investor (Question 1) and yet answers this one with setting a dollar-loss cutoff point *and* specifies the dollar loss of $3,000 on a $4,000 account, then we know he is *not* conservative, for that level of money, at least.

Question 3. Which of the following would you be more comfortable with?

a. The possibility of an 80% gain or a 40% loss on your account (over several trades lasting several weeks total).

b. The possibility of a 40% gain or a 20% loss on your account (over several trades lasting several weeks total).

This question tries again to determine whether he is speculative or more conservative in trading commodities. Answer (a) is more speculative than (b) and indicates that the trader will take on more risk for trying to get higher returns and is not as concerned as to whether the account has a higher volatility.

Question 4. Which of the following would you be more comfortable with?

a. A loss of 40% on one trade on your account.

b. Losses on several trades totaling 40% on your account.

Is it the size of a drop in a customer's account equity or the suddeness of the drop that makes him nervous? Some people don't mind a sudden loss but with potential for quick, large gains soon thereafter, as opposed to a longer period of small losses adding up to a sizable loss. Of course, a third answer, "either," might indicate that he doesn't care and is only concerned with "the bottom line"—how much has been gained or lost. Some people, however, fool themselves and *are* genuinely concerned with a large drop. To them, it represents a sharp rise in the overall risk in the account: similarly, large drops could happen more frequently and then the account is in danger of becoming inoperable. A longer series of small losses may just mean a stale, unprofitable time in the market, and it's just a matter of time before profit moves occur. Losses on several trades also means some diversification has been done, to further reduce risk but also reduce individual trade gains.

Question 5. Which is more important to you?

a. A long series of small gains and losses over the years slowly accumulating to a sizable growth in the account (e.g., 40–60% per year, better than the stock market).

b. A short history of spectacular gains (100%) and large losses (50–60%) to your account resulting in large ups and downs in growth, but equal to a large sum at one point in the near future (hundreds of percents' rise, like a growth from $25,000 to more than $100,000).

The intent of this query, long-winded though it is, is to determine whether the trader is interested in spectacular growth potential *and* is willing to risk good size losses to achieve it, or whether he is more conservative and would rather have a more stable, albeit less spectacular growth (really competitive with an alternative investment, though), giving up huge growth for less risk. This is another way of determining whether he is basically conservative or speculative.

Question 6. Which do you feel you could stand more, before a rise in the account started again?

a. A long series of small losses over a period of time (months or a year or more) cumulating to a sizable loss in your account (e.g., 50–60% or more).

b. A few large losses in a short time (days or a week) adding up to a sizable loss in your account (e.g., 50–60% or more).

Can the trader stand the heat of the fire for a *long* period, or can he only show limited patience and stay with the trading system a short time?

Neither situation is pleasant (both lose half or more of the account), but the trader is pressured to pick a slowing, waning loss rather than a quick one.

It is meant to test whether the individual has a stubborn, World War I trench attitude (bitterly dug in) and can withstand long periods of drought in the account, or whether his patience, and thus ability to continue trading a system, is short lived.

Question 7. Which is more important to you?

a. Smoothness in the account growth, not how steeply it grows upward.

b. How far or steeply the account rises, regardless of how smooth the growth is.

Many of these questions appear similar in content (they are), but are phrased differently (true, too). If the trader answers each one with a preference for reducing risk at the cost of less growth and is patient with long losing periods, then he is basically conservative. If, on the other hand, his answers are sporadically split between risk-taking and risk-averting, then that is a danger sign—he is inconsistent about investment approaches and probably would not follow a systematic trading approach well, if at all.

Answer (a) of this question would indicate the person is a risk averter, and answer (b) would delineate his preference for growth at virtually any cost.

Question 8. Which applies more closely to your situation?

a. All my account monies are speculative: I will risk every dime until the account is not tradable, assuring that risks taken do not allow for a deficit account.

b. Only part of my account monies are speculative: I will set a loss cutoff point to stop trading.

A little different twist is represented in this one. The trader is really asked whether he is putting up his account and offering that to the broker as his risk moneys, or only a *part* of the account. Some people keep reserves for losing periods, margins, and so on, in a *separate* place. Many traders fool themselves by setting a cutoff limit at which point they'll quit trading, for they are really only risking a *portion* of their risk capital. If that is the case, if he sets a cutoff point of $2,000 on a $5,000 initial account with the intent of calling it quits after it loses $2,000, he might as well realize he is dealing with a $2,000 account in the first place, not a $5,000 account risk. He may as well put up only $2,000 and put more in to meet margins at times and if needed and gain interest on the other $3,000 in the bank. He is also fooling his account manager—the poor devil thinks he has a $5,000 account under management, when he really only has a $2,000 one. I'm sure he would trade a lot less or in smaller amounts if he knew he had less than half of what he thought he was trading!

In sum, the trader is doing a disservice to himself and his account manager when he answers (b) and has a *real* risk objective different from what his account size indicates on the face of it.

Question 9. Which of the following is more fair (reasonable) for you to expect?

a. A series of gains sprinkled with a few losses, from the start of trading and thereafter.

b. An unknown mixture of gains and losses, possibly even a string of losses, from the start of trading and thereafter.

For the unsophisticated investor this question is a trap and an eye opener. Anyone who has traded in any of the variable risk–return investment media (stocks, commodities, real estate, etc.) knows that gains and losses are rather randomly mixed together because of the nature of the markets. It is not realistic or reasonable to expect an (virtually) unending string of gains, or even a smooth pattern (two gains, one loss, two gains, one loss, etc.) of gains and losses. Just as with flipping a coin, the sequences of heads and tails are not uniform. This question, then, tests the traders investment sophistication (and later on his ability to believe and follow real results). Circling of answer (b) shows he acknowledges that all sorts of win–loss strings can occur (even losses at the beginning, just as with buying a stock mutual fund at a recent peak). Answer (a) would mean that he is naive, and the odds are he'll be a loser.

Question 10. Which best describes your reactions to uncertainty?

a. I can stand mixtures of gains and losses, even if the account seems to be going nowhere or down, or not growing as fast as I wanted. And I do not change my goals (loss cutoff or gain goal) at any time.

b. I like to review my loss cutoff objective when the account seems to be going nowhere or down over a long period of time.

The last one is a real dilly. Answer (b) seems realistic on the surface, until one reads answer (a) and realizes the consequences of following the policy implied in (b).

If the trader answers (b), he is exercising an escape valve for getting out of a trading system for any reason or host of reasons he may suddenly cook up. This constitutes a concession to fear and nerves, and is the worst possible way of running a trading program as a response to risk (losses). It enables the trader to react to every risk (loss) situation that arises. He is thus overriding everything in the trading system—the amount of money risked changes from what it was originally set out to be, which in turn affects the next trade(s), the amount put into it, and the selections of commodity to trade (probably keeping away from feared risky commodities). The timing of the trades is also affected (by hesitating to take a possible risky trade, or finally, not taking any), and ultimately, the trading system itself is overridden, since parts of it have been altered.

In truth, the trader is fooling himself; if his loss cutoff point is variable, so is his entire concept of risk for his account, and neither he nor the manager really know at any one time whether he is speculative or conservative in risk taking. Hence the account manager doesn't really know how to standardize or fix the trading program for the trader. In short, because of a potential revaluation of risk, the trader is not following a system anymore. For variable risk taking, the trader is getting uncertain (and in the end losing for sure) trading results.

RISK VERSUS REWARD

People will accept more risk in return for greater return on investments. The investment spectrum discussed in Chapter 1 gives some support to this. In fact, you can derive return: risk ratios for most of those investments. For instance, a typical bank interest might be 5% per year, with very small risks or a fraction of a percent. For real estate, rewards are typically 10–20% per year, with average risk as high as 5%. Stocks can go higher, perhaps 20–30% per year, but risk (losses) is (are) higher, too, perhaps 10–20% per year. Commodities can gain an individual 100–200% a year, but losses of 50–100% are not uncommon (for the average public trader).

However, the return: risk ratio for higher risk mediums, albeit higher rewards are present, seems to drop. Brealey [Risk Models, 1] notices this in stocks: from conservative to speculative stocks a drop in return: risk ratio seems to prevail. I believe this is also true for the span of mediums—for instance, stocks pay off inherently less in return per dollar risked than do government instruments and savings.

ADEQUATE RISK MONEY FOR COMMODITIES

In addition to all the other factors that influence risk taking, there is one that is permanent: adequate capital to undertake investments. Enough capital is needed to take care of margins for each commodity for all the commodities covered and reserve moneys for anticipated possible losses.

Commodity margins, or deposits required to trade a commodity, currently range from as low as $200 for 1000 ounces of silver to over $5,000 for coffee. The trader must have at least that for each commodity contract candidate. Likewise, he needs to keep perhaps two or three times the total margin dollars for all commodities contemplated for trading, as reserve for losses. The reserves will enable him to continue trading the commodities he has selected.

If he is thinking of trading several commodities in the low–middle margin requirement category, then he may need $5,000–$10,000 in his account to begin an even moderately effective trading program.

In-depth treatment of initial capital requirements for commodity trading follows in Section 5.

4 Selection

Perhaps one of the most agonizing and frustrating problems facing a stock investor is to choose candidate stocks for buying. Since there are securities numbering in the tens of thousands traded on the major exchanges and over the counter, you can imagine the problem even a computer might have, let alone an individual trader. Fortunately, there are only a couple dozen or so commodities on the major futures exchanges. This cuts down the problem a bit!

Most people feel selection is of somewhat subsidiary importance—timing comes to mind as the first one. But consider this: whatever timing method is used, it needs to be applied to a likely candidate. If one generated a buy signal at 10:30 A.M. and bought soybeans instead of cocoa, the results would be quite erratic and random. In the stock market, selection is not quite as crucial. If the investment manager gets a buy signal on the market as a whole, he can afford to buy across the board or equally representative industry securities. He may not catch the optimum stocks, the high flyers, but at least he'll catch the general market investment and profit from that. Because about 70% of a stock's price movement is due to the general market momentum [Risk Models, 1], he can afford to diversify to catch the general market move and turn in a good performance for his portfolio.

In commodities, however, it is quite important to know each commodity future and its potential performance. Some are big, liquid markets. Others are thinly traded and represent hazards for the trader (poor execution and exaggerated gains and losses, and sometimes dead markets mean no profit or loss realization).

A sprinkling of commodities have good trading potential all the time, whereas others are highly erratic or have sporadic, infrequent trends. A few regularly display seasonal tendencies, whereas others are dependent on sudden events primarily. Some have huge trend potentials in relation to prior history, and others traditionally act rather calm and have only moderate potential.

Occasionally there are special situations—a government edict or weather events that present abnormal trend possibilities. Then, too, there are definite areas to avoid or lessen possible commitments. Catastrophic events may provide windfalls for a lucky few but total ruination to many other hapless souls. In rare instances there has been a total market movement—panic selling across the board due to extreme, overextended price moves in one direction, leading to disaster for many long traders in all commodities.

Finally, it is not clear whether automatically diversifying in as many commodities as possible really is best for the trader's account. Putting more money in a more select group may return more money per unit dollar invested and still yield acceptable account growth risk and variation.

Ideally, one would like to invest in numerous big, liquid markets that have steady, multiple trend possibilities all year long and year in and year out, act smoothly (do not have streaks of limit moves, lest the trader get caught but once in the wrong direction), produce no catastrophic cases, and have each commodity act independently. Sounds like Santa Claus just arrived.

No, there is no such perfect package of commodities. But by analyzing each commodity by itself and groups of related ones, the trader may be able to arrive at a good substitute for the ideal system of commodity candidates.

The following discussions delve into each of the major commodities and examine each with respect to the preceding criteria, with the hopes of coming up with a good list of trading candidates at the end.

The use of the preceding criteria is not intended as a rigorous mathematical means of optimizing portfolio selection. Econometric model development for commodity portfolios is still in its infancy (see bibliography). Rather, this exercise is meant to help the investor both reduce the risk in his portfolio and also increase the return, by leaning on the experience of the author and others. Specifically, candidates will be scrutinized and chosen or rejected (as determined from past history) on the basis of: liquidity of market; smoothness of price moves; and most price movement per unit time and per margin, relative to other commodities. These criteria are probably the most important factors to allow most timing approaches to do best.

THE GRAINS

Without a doubt the largest business in futures trading is done on the Chicago Board of Trade, and mainly in the grain pits (silver is another mainstay, too). Corn and soybeans vie for the lead, but the number of contracts traded and left outstanding (open interest) is stupendous. On Wednesday, November 21, 1978 over 27,000 soybean contracts were bought and sold. Since most speculators deal in only a few contracts, the number of participants can be seen to be quite voluminous.

Soybeans

The soybean market is a huge, speculative market. The ultimate trading, according to many traders, is in "beans." Price moves abound all the time. Large or limit moves are frequent, even when the general news is vapid. Margins are high but commensurate with price changes.

Seasonal tendencies used to be prevalent (lower near harvest—the end of summer—and higher in the winter and spring), but don't too seriously enter the timing picture now. The triple threat of inflation, Russian grain demand, and bad weather shot all seasonalities to pieces in 1973–1974, and regular price patterns have not fully recovered yet.

Figure 3 depicts weekly-basis price moves of beans for the past since 1969. Some huge price moves have occurred, primarily in the triple threat year 1973–1974. Margins varied between $0.50 and $1.00, so potential returns were quite large. Many people using technical systems (especially moving averages) did quite well during this period, but have done poorly lately due to the tightened markets (lower price levels and ranges).

Vicious price reactions and long sideways moves do happen with beans, however. Few timing methods do universally well in this medium.

Surprisingly, prices of soybeans can go into the doldrums. The first quarter of 1976 saw a very tight price range in beans (see Figure 4), with sometimes only a few cents' daily price range. Only with true patience could a trader expect to weather or stay out of beans until a big move came along (almost five months later), and some other commodi-

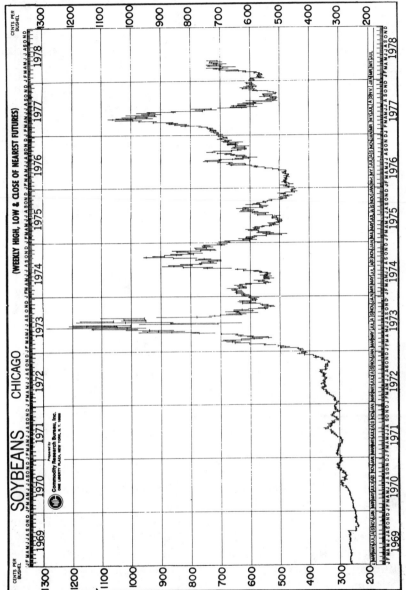

Figure 3. Weekly-basis price moves of soybeans since 1969.

55

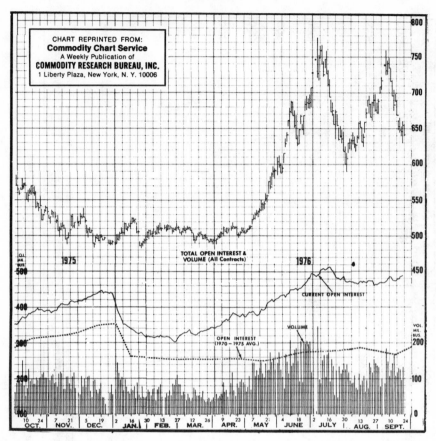

Figure 4. Soybean price range for November 1976 contract.

ties are like a pressure cooker: the more heat applied, the more the boiling potential, until it bursts outward in a spasm.

News events can drastically affect beans. The monthly federal government crop report probably is the biggest influence. Every time the reports stated less soybean stock carryover available for the rest of the year, 1973 contracts prices rose more and more feverishly.

Unfortunately, the huge, major price moves to or about new levels in beans *and* wheat and corn come once in a blue moon. The three long-term (past forty years) charts are shown in Figures 6–8 (short-term, in Figure 5). There were really only two important price bulges in the past forty years: right after World War II and during 1973–1974. The rest of

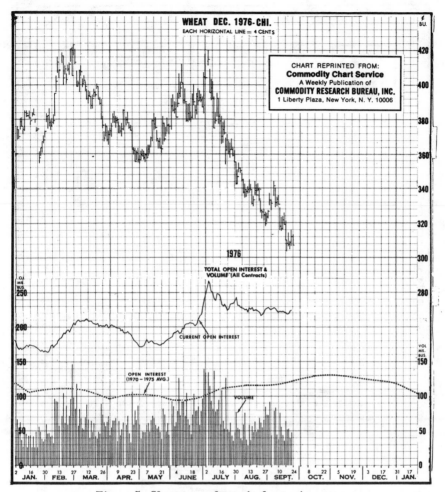

Figure 5. Short-term chart of wheat price moves.

the years were spent in small perturbations about the latest price plateau (after World War II and 1973–1974). This means long droughts in profits for long-term trend-seeking methods (like moving averages), despite lower margins—but with compensating higher rates of return.

If a timing method can adjust from wild price moves to tight sideways markets, beans represent a real, powerful potential area for trading. Place this commodity as one of the highest on a candidate list.

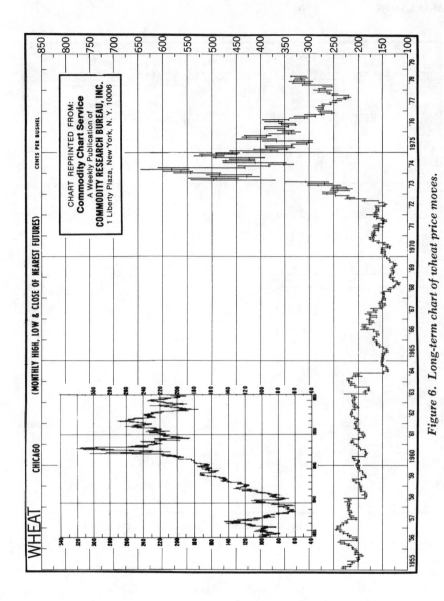

Figure 6. Long-term chart of wheat price moves.

58

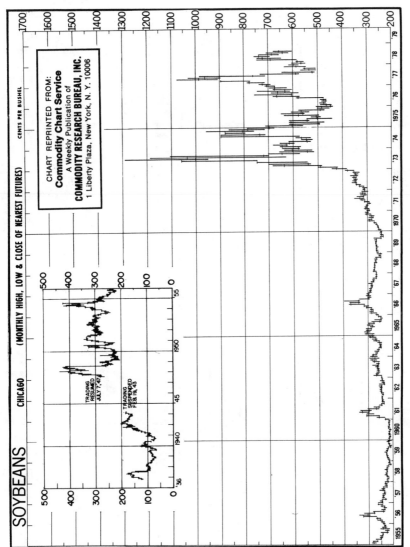

Figure 7. Long-term chart of soybean price moves.

59

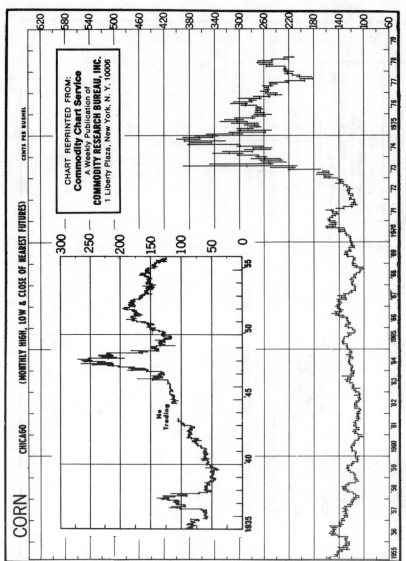

Figure 8. Long-term chart of corn price moves.

60

Wheat

Wheat acts much like beans in that price moves can be considerable once started, but are unlike beans in that moves don't extend as far, re-actions are less vicious, and it tends to trade in much smaller daily price ranges. If a trader had to choose only one of the grains to trade, he might consider wheat. It has much of the price-move potential of beans (espe-cially considering comparative margins or deposit requirements) with relatively less price volatility, to minimize risk in the account.

Like beans, sudden weather or government reports can drastically alter the price picture. We are all reminded of the 1972 Russian wheat purchases, which lifted wheat prices from the $1.50-per-bushel area around which prices had been fluctuating for years, to over $6.00 per bushel, a fourfold increase! But such moves do seem to take time to de-velop, not like sudden freeze effects on orange juice in Florida and coffee in Brazil.

Wheat prices can also show trending tendencies even when the other grains (corn and beans) might be in doldrums (see Figure 5 for first-quarter 1976 price action, compared to that for beans and corn in Figures 4 and 9). Long-term wheat is shown in Figure 6.

Again, wheat rates very high in a trader's commodity candidate portfolio.

Corn

The most stable (pricewise) of the grains, corn, can be thought of as the little old lady of commodities. Price levels, trends, and ranges are much smaller than for wheat or soybeans, even accounting for somewhat smaller margins.

Corn can be horribly dull (check the first quarter of 1976, Figure 9), and money spent in it can be considered almost idle funds for much of the time. Many traders use this medium for short-term trades, with only a few cents' profit objective.

The price structure over many years can be exceedingly flat and bar-ren in appearance. Figure 8 shows an especially tight-ranged period (many years only 10¢ in price range), from the early 1950s to late 1960s.

Corn should be placed lowest on the list of grains for trading, to be used only if no other signals or trends were available in the other grains and one had surplus cash in the account not being used or intended for use in the near future.

For portfolio considerations, however, the trader must realize that

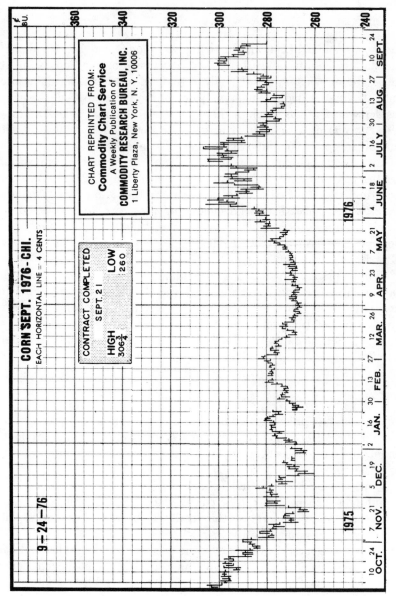

Figure 9. Corn price range for September, 1976 contract.

62

the grains tend to go together in price direction (not extent, though), and so no real diversification benefit (lowered risk) is achieved by dividing monies among the three grains for trades. As a rough estimate, the same price direction correlation figure (70% or so) exists between a grain and the general grain complex as does between a stock and the stock market in general. One major reason that a trader compels to diversify in the grains would be if he had a timing method that examines abnormal temporary conditions in each particular commodity and plays that situation for a limited gain.

Other Grains and Products

Oats and rye, flaxseed, and rapeseed constitute four other grains. Unfortunately, volume of trading is low in all of them (oats are not too bad), making it difficult to get good executions and find smooth price movements. Flaxseed can be especially treacherous. I was just trying to cover my small (8000-bushel) position one day in 1973, and my trading constituted about 30% of the day's entire volume of all flaxseed traded!

Soybean products, oil and meal, are heavily traded. One is used for cooking oil and other food uses, whereas meal is a prime ingredient of livestock feed. Although they are viable trading mediums, their price charts will often just duplicate that for soybeans (demand for beans will lift bean prices and a by-product or two, since it is for the by-products that soybeans are crushed). Sometimes, however, oil and meal will go separate ways, reflecting strong demand for one of the products and no change in the other.

Because of the low volume of trading for these grains and the fact that soybean products mostly duplicate price moves of soybeans, they probably should not be included in a trader's portfolio.

THE MEATS

Second only to the grains, meat (cattle, hogs, pork bellies, and iced broilers) futures are also traded in the thousands of contracts each day. Cattle traded to the tune of more than 17,000 contracts on November 21, 1978. Again, most traders deal in one or two contracts at a time, which means thousands of individuals buy and sell hoofers each day. A very big, liquid market.

Like the grains, there is a certain amount of market comovement, perhaps due in large part to their mutual substitutability for each other as meats to eat in the consumer's mind. If cattle prices go down, most of the time hog and pork bellies will too, to a different extent. This means not too much diversification benefit is achieved.

The meats have not been traded too long (compared to the grains) so the long run price patterns are not clear. However, in the brief ten years or so they have been traded actively, they have established a reputation of liquid markets with steady, nonseasonal trending characteristics.

Cattle

The cattle market, the largest of the meat markets, has displayed good-sized trend moves but with many sideways markets thrown in. Figure 10 shows the steady oscillation between 35¢ and 55¢ per pound price range over the past three or four years. Each 3¢ or less means a 100% gain potential on margin put up, so the large profit potential is there. Daily price changes are moderate, there are few limit moves, and trends take time to develop (good for trend-following methods).

Seasonal trendedness or changes do not seem to be existent or pronounced in cattle; rather, there may be a cycle over several years.

Methods used in this market should be sensitive to major trend changes but not too sensitive to be whipsawed in sideways markets. Moving-average techniques had trouble with cattle in the past few years.

Cattle should be rated as a major consideration for your commodity candidates, because of its liquidity, steady trend potential, and smooth price changes.

Iced Broilers

Iced broilers constitute a relatively new market and do not have much volume of trading (several hundred contracts per day). Moreover, the trend potential of this market is small. Only once (in 1973; see Figure 11) did it move considerably in price, and then only because all other commodities did so. Furthermore, it tends to follow grain prices, acting as a price follower. Many traders should not include this on the trader's list, for the preceding reasons.

Hogs

The movement for hogs is a little different from that of cattle. Prices tend to fluctuate more daily, and trends or drifts in prices tend to extend fur-

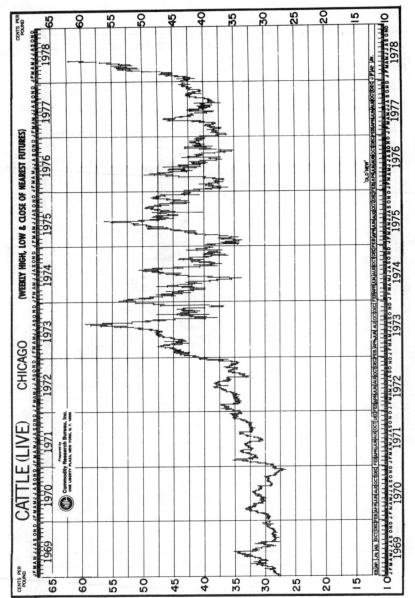

Figure 10. Weekly-basis price moves of cattle since 1969.

65

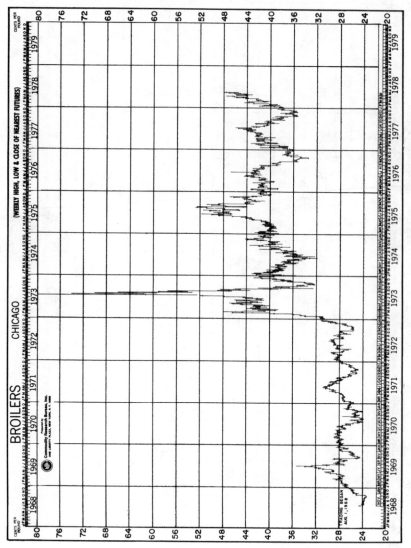

Figure 11. Weekly-basis price moves of broilers since 1968.

66

ther than cattle. Tight trading ranges (but also wide daily price ranges) also frequently occur. The liquidity is good but not as good as with cattle. Limit moves happen somewhat frequently, so price erraticity is not unknown (see Figure 12).

If a trader needs to spread out or diversify his money in the meats, he should do so probably with cattle and hogs.

Pork Bellies

Along with soybeans, pork bellies are considered the premier speculation. And with good reason. Moves of 30¢, 40¢, and higher occur almost every year (even though its futures history is short), and many a day's trading is marked by limit moves. For those intent on pyramiding or losing a fortune quickly, this is surely one of *the* commodities to consider. In fact, it is one of the few futures mediums that has more speculative, as opposed to hedging and trade, interest. It is surely Las Vegas in the Midwest. Prices often gallup up or down a full cent in minutes' time. A trader leaving his broker's office or the Chicago Mercentile Exchange floor thirty seconds before the closing could come back after a coffee break and find a 0.5¢ gain for the day turn into a 0.5¢ loss in the closing seconds!

Liquidity is generally good but is accented by very erratic price hinges due to a large speculator or two influencing the immediate prices. The past two or so years have seen greatly diminished volume (only a few thousand contracts a day traded) compared to around 10,000, and at one time the largest number of any commodities, several years ago. It appears the wild, almost daily moves have disenchanted many a speculator and disenfranchised many more from their stakes.

In pork bellies, there are, as in hogs, many longer-term trends (see Figure 13), but the trader's method must catch trend changes almost immediately (within the day) to assure not being trapped in the wrong direction on a bunch of limit moves and unable to get out. On the other hand, if one can watch almost every tick, have a line to a floor broker, then day-trading bellies may be this trader's cup of tea.

Tight trading ranges for days and weeks generally do not occur in bellies: prices usually career straight up or down, or so it often seems.

Like cattle, bellies can and are affected by cold storage reports, especially quarterly ones. One can almost watch the reaction and take a trade in the reaction direction right after a major report, except that often much of the report's thunder has already been discounted and the trader is in for a little surprise—not much will happen (maybe even a

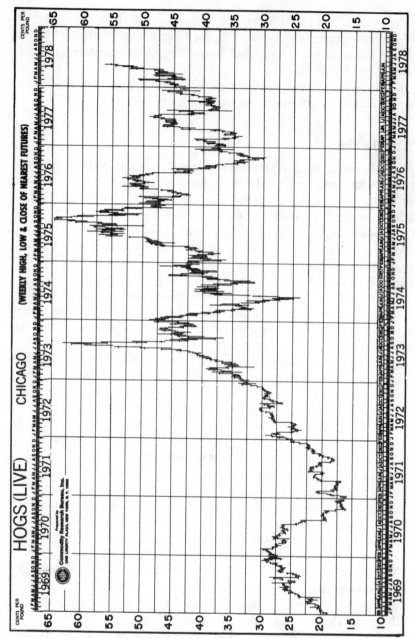

Figure 12. *Weekly-basis price moves of hogs since 1969.*

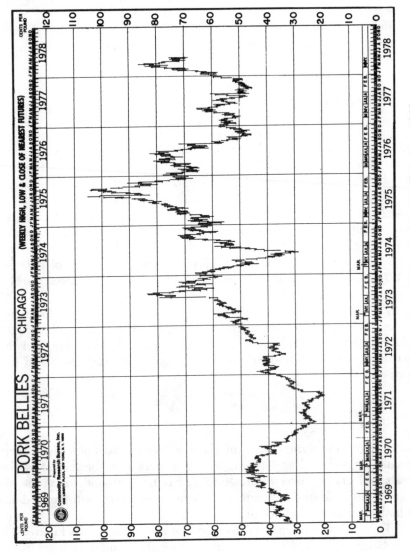

Figure 13. Weekly-basis price moves of pork bellies since 1969.

wicked reverse, even on the day after the report, after prices initially go one way).

Bellies, however, should probably be the last to be included from the meats for diversification and for long-term accounts.

THE METALS

All that glimmers is not gold. But try to tell that to the enthusiastic mid-America floor broker and their customers when they had a special midnight, candlelight inaugural trading session in gold futures in the first day of 1975. Americans were beset by horrendous inflation (past tense?) and desperate to hedge against it and have "something of intrinsic value," and so many bought heavily at $200 per ounce (a great value, so they reasoned, since it had climbed from around $35 per ounce a year or two earlier). By late 1976, however, the cautious hedger's bubble had burst. Gold now sold at around $100 per ounce. The return of inflation in 1978 brought the gold bug fever to a pitch again, and prices reached a new record of $250 per ounce.

The bulk of traders, however, play these commodities for trend moves that many touts and speculators long for. The continual lurking of inflation, the use of gold as a hedge against currency volatility, and the increasing volume of trading makes this a good candidate for trend following methods.

Silver

Surprisingly, this lowest price of the *precious* metals holds the largest speculative and trading interest. As big a market as the largest of the meats and grains, silver futures trading has been around for about ten years as a viable trading medium. It is big and liquid, with large doses of both speculative and hedging interests.

Trends, however, are very sporadic in appearance (see Figure 14). Only twice in the past ten years have meaningful, long-term large trends developed. One occurred right after the United States government stopped supporting the $1.29 conversion rate (1967–1968), when prices more than doubled. And again in the inflational markets that hit all commodities in 1973–1974. Between, before, and after those two instances prices have bounced, chopped, and wiggled in relatively tight trading ranges.

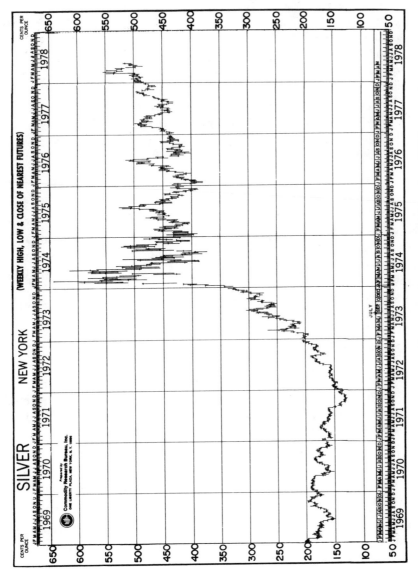

Figure 14. Weekly-basis price moves of silver since 1969.

71

This kind of market has been murder to most trend following techniques. Whipsaw losses have become the rule and good-sized moves and profits, the exception.

Although long-term trends are infrequent, intermediate-sized moves (30–50¢) are fairly frequent and represent fairly regular opportunity for 50% and 100% returns on an investment in a week or so.

Also, daily trading ranges are consistently wide, which gives day traders ample chances for quick, 5¢ profits with lower trading costs (day-trade commission rates). This commodity should be included in a trader's portfolio, but only short-term, limited profit objective or day-trade methods should be used.

Copper

Copper has had a long history of futures trading, due primarily to large trade or hedging interest. It also has had longer, smoother, and more frequent trends than its cousin, silver (which is obtained primarily from copper ore extraction processes) (see Figure 15).

As expected, longer-term trend following methods have done well in this medium. Day trading is almost nonexistent because of regularly small trading ranges within the day. Trading for limited profit objectives can be quite profitable, too, as copper frequently goes into tight trading ranges.

Liquidity is very good in copper. Trading volume is large, and limit moves (which could trap an unwary speculator in the wrong direction) are relatively rare. When they do occur, a speculator can often still transact (close out his old, or initiate a new, position) at the limits.

I would recommend copper for methods that detect long-term trades and that look for limited objective, intermediate-sized moves.

Gold and Platinum

Gold is a relatively newly traded commodity on American exchanges. Its price history, however, is legendary. From ancient Egyptian and Roman times gold has come to symbolize the international embodiment of wealth and security. Even in recent times Europeans and Arab interests hurriedly place their holdings in gold when currencies fluctuate in value and inflation rears its head.

Even though its price history on American exchanges is short (see Figure 16), both trendedness and trading, volatile markets are evident. Trading volume is heavy (quite heavy in 1978—almost 50,000 contracts

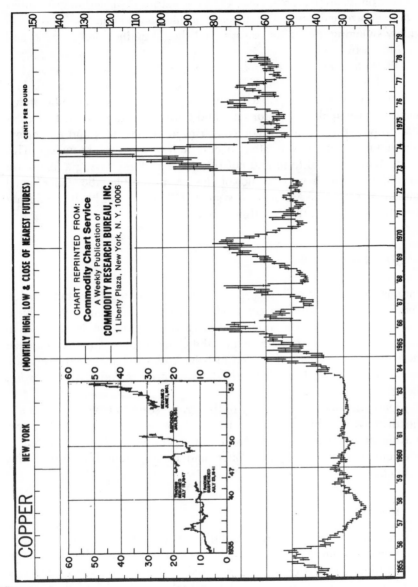

Figure 15. Long-term chart of copper price moves.

73

per day on all exchanges). Also, the very nature of uncertainty in international currencies and the recurrence of inflation is bound to keep prices widely swinging. For these reasons gold should be included in trend and trading portfolios.

Platinum, the most precious of the metals, has a very sporadic history. It has been trended in 1968, 1969, 1974, and 1978 (see Figure 17). In between, prices have acted erratically. From a fundamental viewpoint, its principal reasons for rises and falls would depend on two areas —its proposed use as a catalytic converter in automobiles and its narrow production capabilities located in only a few spots in the world. This metal should appeal to in and out traders or to those taking a long-term position based on news or rumor of changes in the two above-mentioned fundamental factors. Mechanical systems followers most likely would not want to include it in their portfolios, however.

FOODS

Various other commodities, conveniently lumped together and labeled "foods," represent another commodity area and different geographical trading locale than the grain and meat trading, which is situated in Chicago. Except for eggs (traded on the Chicago Mercantile Exchange), these everyday staples are traded in New York, and many have separate exchanges. They do have distinctly different price making characteristics, though.

One price mechanism many of this group seem to have in common is the distinct possibility (almost frequent occurrences) of limit moves starting after a stable period from just a simple weather or (foreign) government pronouncement. Coffee and cocoa admirably display this distinction.

Eggs

Egg trading is very seasonal, with little real price activity occurring generally between midwinter and late summer. Even during the more active period the volume is not large compared to the meats, grains or metals. With this in mind, it would be detrimental for a speculator looking for long-term trends or possibly even good-sized intermediate or limited profit objectives, to trade in this market.

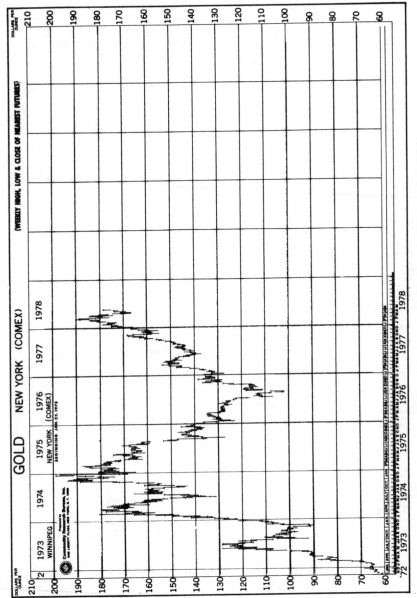

Figure 16. Weekly-basis price moves of gold since late 1972.

75

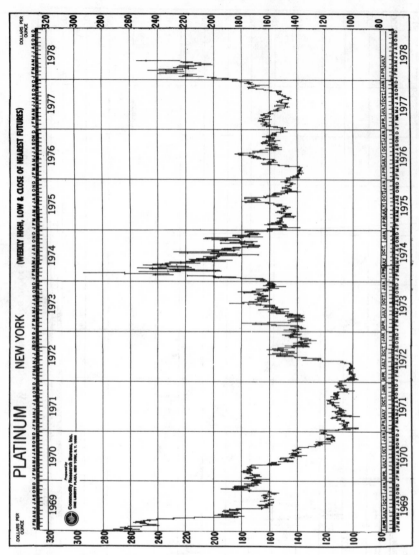

Figure 17. Weekly-basis price moves of platinum since 1969.

Maine Potatoes

Trading volume has been large over the years, and good-sized trends (especially the past three or four years) have been in evidence (see Figure 18). There are some parallels with pork bellies, in that this is a market dominated by speculators or hedgers who also speculate. The 1976 potato scandal involving some unsatisfied contracts at the expiration of May contracts had temporarily torpedoed trading until new regulations were instituted.

The same comments regarding pork bellies would also apply here. Potatoes should be lightly traded for long-term possibilities only. Limit moves, especially in early spring, are a commonplace occurrence. This medium should be studiously avoided for intermediate term profits or small, limited profit objectives, as limit moves in the wrong direction could lose far more for the trader than a lot of small gains could accumulate.

Sugar

Sugar futures trading is a brisk business, one of the largest of "international" commodities markets. Long-term trends can and certainly have occurred. Most people remember the torrid rise from 3¢ or 4¢ per pound to over 65¢, a gigantic increase on a margin of a fraction of a cent. Figure 19 depicts the past forty year span of world sugar futures prices. A somewhat regular pattern of price spurts every five to seven years has criss-crossed the chart.

This medium is good for long-term trend seeking methods but poor for day trading and short-term moves. In addition, the account should be well capitalized, especially if prices start moving limits often. The trader should also be aware that much of the supply influences on price is due to relatively small places in the world (e.g., Cuba). It is not always good to place a meaningful portion of capital in a heavily influenced medium.

Cocoa

Cocoa should be considered in the same category as sugar, in that volume is heavy but fundamental factors are affected greatly by weather and governmental influence in developing countries like Ghana. Good-sized trends can and do occur often, but the trader should not put much (5% or so) of his funds in an area like this. Only well-capitalized ($100,-000 or so) accounts should trade cocoa, and only in conjunction with

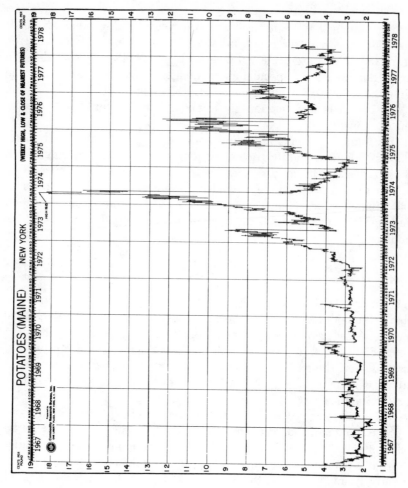

Figure 18. Weekly-basis price moves of potatoes (Maine) since 1967.

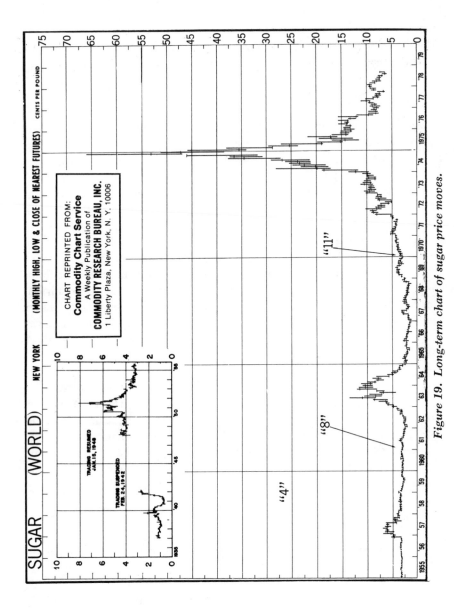

Figure 19. Long-term chart of sugar price moves.

long-range trend-finding methods. Even then there are times when considerable sideways activity occurs. One must be patient to get long-run
profits here and in many other "internationals."

Coffee

Events in Brazilian and a handful of other South and Central American
economies are the major influence on coffee prices. One event—a crop
freeze in Brazil—really shook prices a couple of years ago. When news
of the damage reached the United States, initial estimates placed crop
damage at 50% or more. Prices skyrocketed many limits before stopping
for a breaker. Fortunes were made (and *lost*) during a few weeks'
period!

Coffee-trading volume, though increased over initial years' volume
substantially, is still not in a league with the grains, meats, metals, or
even sugar or cocoa. Unfortunately this is still a speculator's speculator
market—like bellies but not as solvent. Moreover, it is predicted on basically only one event—crop freeze down under. The commodity trader
should place even less a percentage of his funds in coffee than in sugar
or cocoa.

Orange Juice

Orange juice is even more specialized than coffee. It is strictly a weather
market, dependent on either a crop freeze in Florida or a hurricane disaster. The volume traded is somewhat small, and a not very liquid
market results. And to add a third coup de grace, the hurricanes and
freezes occur only between August and December! Very few traders
should even speculate a tiny bit of their capital in this medium.

Financial Markets

Prior to several years ago there were no such markets as currency, Ginnie
Mae, or Treasury Bill futures. Marketers at the Chicago Mercantile Exchange and Chicago Board of Trade decided to introduce insurance
media for the broker and financial media so as to protect those buying
and selling goods in foreign currencies from price erraticities in the near
future. At that time most European countries had decided to "float," or
let the market decide, the relative value of a Japanese yen versus the
British pound. A year or so later the same ideas were extended to United
States financial instruments—the Ginnie Mae (government mortgage)

instrument and the U.S. Treasury Bill, to protect banks and other users against prices (which they might have to pay) of the bill and mortgage note from future fluctuations.

U.S. Treasury Bills and Ginnie Maes

The Treasury Bill and Ginnie Mae are catching the eye of the banks and other hedging institutions—the futures market seems to fulfill a genuine need for insurance against wobbly prices—but speculators still have not come in droves. Although the histories of these two are small, they do seem to project long-run trends, reflecting general interest rates and inflation trending tendencies in the economy.

Trading volume and both hedger and speculative interest is rapidly building, to the tune of several thousands of contracts per day traded in each instrument. The pace seems to quicken in proportion to inflation's rate of change.

Although the exchanges' price history is short, there is enough potential for trend following portfolios to include these commodities.

Currencies

Currency futures do have trends but are very susceptible to many limit moves and (due to currency revaluations by foreign governments) have relatively small trading volume, but it is picking up. This can also be a speculator's *real* nightmare. Devaluation can cost a speculator virtually everything he owns. Take Mexican pesos, for example.

In the early part of 1976 there were rumors that became louder and more persistent as the year wore on, that the Mexican government would devalue the peso for the first time since 1954. Estimates varied between 10% and as much as 40%.

There were, however, many people who believed it would not devalue. I had one customer who kept buying and taking small profits. As time went on, I became more and more nervous about the possibilities. And the possibilities were quite awesome and terrible. The exchange margins then were $4,000 on an approximately $80,000 contract, and the spot month price of pesos was a shade or two under 8¢ to the dollar.

In July I told the customer we could not allow him to trade pesos any more unless he was willing to put up a good portion of the contract's value as margin (about $30,000 or so). He chose not to trade any more through us, but went to a large stock brokerage to trade at a lower margin.

Figure 20 shows the horror story that occurred in September of that year. The Mexican government did devalue the peso, and it amounted (a free float) to about 40%. This means the contract's value dropped from about $80,000 to under $50,000. If the customer put up only $4,000 as a deposit, he lost more than $25,000 over and above his initial deposit. Of course, he is required by the customer's agreement to make good the difference, but the broker stands to make up the difference if the customer can't. In this case a lot of brokers had to dip into their pockets.

Traders should utilize currency futures for purely speculative positions or lightly trade the larger economies' currency (e.g., Britain, Germany, Japan) for trends, at this time.

Woods

Lumber and plywood futures are closely tied to building trade general health, interest rates, and the general economy.

Longer-term trends can and have developed, but this general area is susceptible to many periods of sideways, churning markets, much to the curse of trend followers (see Figure 21).

Volume of trades can be adequate but often is small (a few hundred contracts traded a day, meaning lower liquidity). Sometimes while placing orders for buying or selling only a dozen or two, prices have jumped or dropped by a dollar or two while my trades were being consummated.

These two markets should be suited to in/out or short-term traders, or for those placing a very small percentage of committed capital into them, for longer-term results.

Cotton

"King cotton," as it was once known, commands an ever-growing interest and daily trading volume. Although it is only a pale shade of what it was before World War II (it did larger dollar volume than all the stock markets combined!), cotton contracts change hands at the rate of several thousand a day, a respectable size.

Only lately, however, has it seemed to come to life (trendwise, that is). Prior to 1972 trends were almost nonexistent, volume was low, and speculators despaired. Since then trends have occurred during the inflation year 1974–1975 and afterward as a kind of afterwash, it is perhaps too soon to treat it as a permanently trending-potential medium. I would again place only a very small amount of money committed to longer-term situations, to cotton (see Figure 22).

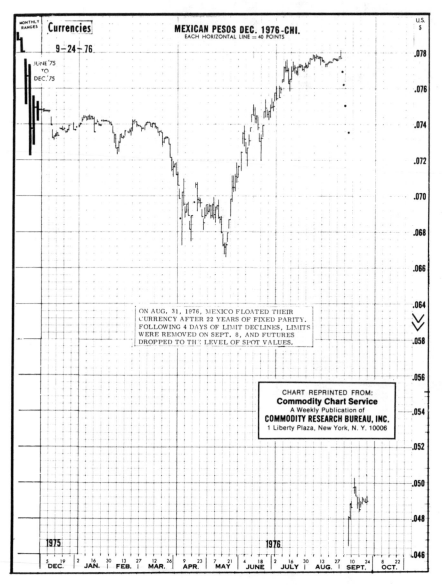

Figure 20. *Mexican peso price chart for December 1976 contract.*

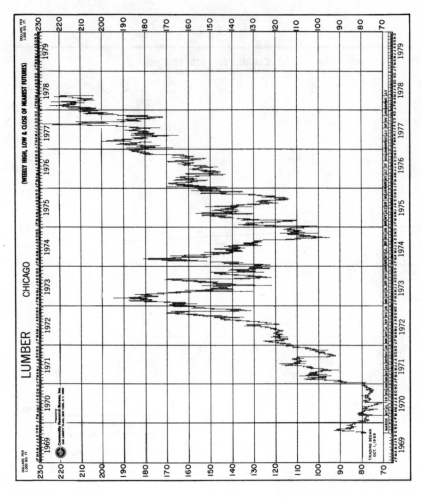

Figure 21. Weekly basis price moves of lumber since October 1969.

84

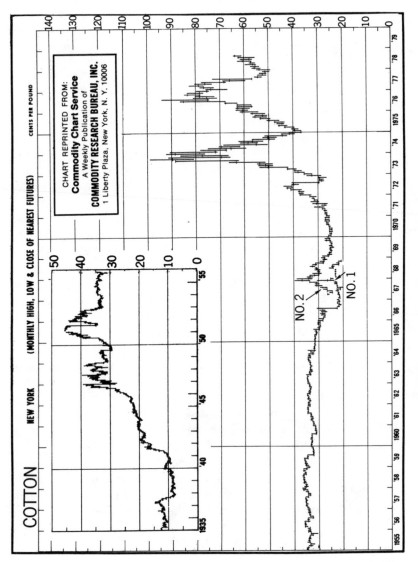

Figure 22. Long-term chart of cotton price moves.

CONCLUSIONS

Not all commodities should be considered for inclusion in a portfolio. Some should be lightly considered (very little capital invested in these situations), and some should only be candidates for long- or short-term trades (long trends or limited profit objectives).

It is a moot point as to whether an investor's funds should be diversified to be able to catch all big trends that come up in all viable commodities, or whether he should concentrate his funds in a limited number of commodities that have historically been constantly trend producing or have simply produced the best overall trading results for the trader and his approaches.

In the first case, complete diversification, the trader can count on getting most all of the trends in all the commodities. But the account will grow slower, with less strong spurts up and *maybe* down, and with less general (average) growth, than by concentrating on a select group of sterling performers. The latter strategy will produce a stronger average growth, and possibly even as good or better volatility (losses) as with complete diversification. It is possible, however, that account drops could be more severe than with complete diversification, due to less diversification alone; or the few commodities diversified in could display a lot of comovement, as happened in late 1973 (mid-August), when all the grains, meats, metals, and sweets—virtually everything—went down limits for several days, due to huge panic selling by grain and meat speculators (prices had climbed too far too fast).

With these points in mind (the three criteria of liquidity, price smoothness, and historical trendedness), I would favor a smaller group of efficiently productive (profitable) commodities to follow rather than a herd of mixed-performance ones. For each dollar committed, I would rather aggressively seek higher growth potential and seek ways of mitigating sizes and sequences of losses among the few followed.

SUMMARY

Each of the major commodity areas was scrutinized for inclusion in various portfolios. For the systematic trader with mechanical technique, however, three criteria were used to judge each commodity: trading volume as a measure of liquidity (the ability to trade when one wants to); smooth price behavior to minimize erraticity in trades (minimize losses, make gains larger); and most price movements, to maximize gain potential.

Using these criteria, the trader should stick to the grains (wheat and soybeans), meats (hogs and cattle), metals (gold, copper, and silver for short-term objectives), and possibly one or two international commodities (e.g., sugar, cocoa, or cotton) or one of the financial instruments for larger accounts. It is a limited list, but a very practical, high potential one.

TIMING

5 Schools of Timing

Perhaps no other aspect of commodity trading commands the attention and even fervor of the speculator as does the timing of buying and selling. All engage in passionate pursuit of the silver chalice atop the highest pinnacle of trading success—the perfect timing technique.

Almost every trader you talk to will agree that timing is the main—and often only—ingredient in commodity success. It is very important, but not necessarily *the* most important part of a total trading approach. If the trader does not understand the basics of risk and how much an account can vary in value, especially on the downside, or if he cannot stick to a prearranged, systematic approach to trading (discipline), then no matter how great the timing is, he will end up losing. Likewise, if he doesn't have enough initial capital to withstand periods of initial losses, he will lose.

But we cannot detract from the importance of timing the entrances and exits of trades. Without properly buying low and selling high prices, the speculator cannot make money. Refer to the bibliography for a lengthy list of articles or books on trading (timing) methods.

This chapter serves as an introduction to the section on timing. Each general type is described, contrasted with others, and examples are given. All the timing methods generally fit in one of the schools of timing

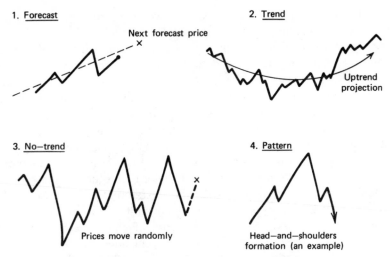

Figure 23. The four schools of timing methods.

described here. The great bulk of techniques fall under the trend following school, however.

There are essentially four main schools of timing techniques: (1)
forecasting prices, (2) detecting or projecting trend direction of prices,
(3) testing for prices abnormal in random (no trend) movements, and
(4) detecting significant price patterns. The four are graphically depicted in Figure 23.

FORECASTING PRICES

There are many quantitative forecasting methods for determining prices
in the future. The advanced, scientific applications occur in industry,
business, and government. Chemical engineers at Texaco might use them
to forecast octane content of certain blends of gasoline. Military analysts
project in war games attrition rates on battlefields given strengths of the
armored, supply, infantry, and other units and ditto for that of opposing
forces. Colgate Palmolive forecasts a new toothpaste's market effectiveness based on a sampling from a test market.

In commodities and stocks, forecasts fall into two categories. One
deals with using data fundamental to a company's vital statistics (cash
flow, industry trends, competitors, last five years' earnings, etc.) or
supply–demand data in commodities (carry-over stock, last government

monthly crop report, weekly exports, weather projections for the next five days, etc.). This is the "fundamental" approach.

The other concerns mathematical or procedural means of forecasting one or two price periods or data ahead, given so many previous data. By far the more used by the trader of the two, the mechanical approach assumes prices will continue to move in the latest direction by the amount forecast from the last period to the next. The techniques run the gamut between simply drawing tangent lines on graphs to nonlinear filter predictors. The more sophisticated methods assume that prices follow a curving growth pattern, like sinusoidal. Forecasts, of course, all have errors, and the major problem is determining how big a risk to take when prices are out of line with the next forecast. The trader doesn't really know if that represents an opportunity (bargain prices) or an ominous turn in direction. The purpose of the forecast is to tell the trader when prices are considerably different now from the next forecast —which situation represents "bargain" prices. He usually will buy at the bargain price and hold until the forecast price has been met, and then will sell. Fundamental approaches (Chapter 6) and the adaptive forecast method (Chapter 19) are two examples of this school.

TREND FOLLOWING

By far the most popular of timing techniques, trend following, and detecting methods have been around for many years and have thousands of advocates.

The federal government uses trend-following techniques quite a bit. Most people hear about general economic trend indicators—such as the price index, cost-of-living index, and percent unemployed. But methods of analysis for these indexes are pretty crude—two months of changes in a row typically (to the government official) foreshadow a major change in direction.

Trend-following methods range from drawing lines through the core of price moves or drawing lines that touch succeeding bottom prices, to mathematical formulas (like moving averages) to represent the current trend. A new set of trend-detecting methods, some of which are described within, use mathematical statistics to test whether current prices are really different from the prior trending direction of prices. These methods tend to look for events or sets of events that tip the direction of commodity prices.

Forecasts take no interest in the current drift in prices—in fact, assume no drift—but rather are concerned with whether prices are outside of the channel (errors above and below next forecast) and thus are bargains for purchase or sale.

Trend-following and -detection methods, however, predicate price buying and selling opportunities with regard to starting and stopping (and often reversals) of major trends or drifts in prices. Moving averages (Chapter 8), breakout methods (Chapter 12), and statistical testing methods (Chapter 16) are diverse applications in this area.

NO-TREND OR RANDOM MARKETS

Academics (especially a school of thought located in Chicago) love to conduct voluminous studies to show that price changes are not predictable from prior price changes. They stress that these changes simply discount events that randomly impinge on the marketplace each day. This effectively shoots the trend-following school of thought, for randomists claim there are no causal trends (one set of price changes leads to another in the same direction), so it is of no use to utilize trend-seeking methods in the first place.

The best one can do under these circumstances is to take advantage of abnormal prices outside or near a channel of prices, that is, to sell prices near the top of the channel and buy back near the bottom, in anticipation that prices will return to the middle of the channel and perhaps lower. In short, sell strong rallies and buy strong dips—in anticipation of a reversal of prices to more normal prices. This insinuates that the strength of the rise or fall has no economic meaning. The only thing a trader can count on is that prices will fluctuate, and if one has enough perseverance and capital, prices will eventually come back to his position entrance price and probably better.

The contrary-opinion approach is one offshoot of this school of thought (Chapter 9), along with the oscillator method (Chapter 10).

PATTERN DETECTION

The fourth school of thought involves pattern recognition in prices. Certain price configurations (resembling, pictorially, heads and shoulders, pennants, tops, saucers, etc.) presage major events—a major trend starting up, or a lull period, for example, in charting methods (Chapter 7).

Pattern recognition is a recognized branch of electrical engineering in industry. It is used to detect the basic underlying "pulse" or rhythm in currents on oscilloscopes, for instance. Military strategists sometimes use it for analyzing photos from aerial reconnaissance.

In stocks and commodities, however, the state of the art is still not scientific, and great reliance is placed on the individual analyst's ability to "see" shapes and forms in the charts.

The remaining chapters in this section present and analyze a number of specific, different, and popular timing methods for buying and selling used by commodity traders.

6 Fundamental Approaches

The following method describes a general approach used in both stocks and commodities, has a long history of use, and belongs to the forecast school of timing.

Perhaps the major difference between fundamentalists and other technical method traders is the data used. The former use primarily supply and demand statistics over longer periods (years, typically). The latter utilize only price information, and usually only over the past few days, weeks, or perhaps a month or two.

Methods of analysis vary in fundamental analysis from simple rule of thumb or personal interpretation ("the supply data are up compared to last year, so prices will be lower this year") to more sophisticated statistical methods like correlations, and, a step further, forecasts from regressions.

Unfortunately, most analysts, private and governmental, write articles concerning forecasts of corn prices without ever getting around to forecasting specific corn price or even supply–demand totals for the upcoming period. Most simply list prior year totals for these two categories and mention new factors or changes in old ones that will influence this year's supply–demand balances. But rarely do they say how *much* the amounts will be, and even rarer still, what resultant *price* can be predicted.

One of the most cognizant and well-known fundamentalists is Charles Keltner, who has been forecasting grain prices for over three decades and is well respected as one of the leading experts in grain analysis.

THEORY AND OBSERVATIONS

The fundamentalist tries to predict futures prices for a later point in time using basic factors generally known as supply–demand statistics of the past, and estimates of the future. Given price predictions, he then will establish a position based on whether current prices are well below the forecast (a bull or long position), or well above (a bear or selling position). The position is then held until the predicted price has been met. Some traders might add to the original position from time to time, as profits accrue, or if prices move lower and present buying opportunities with higher forecast prices later on.

The first step in arriving at good forecasts for the grains, according to Keltner, is to separate out the important factors influencing supply and demand.

The most important simple factor that determines the price of a commodity is the supply–demand balances, that is, the difference between available supply and consumer demand. Government statistics (USDA figures) are the most reliable and should be compared on a crop year (usually end of summer for most grains) basis.

Three data elements comprise the supply side of the equation: the new crop, old crop, carry-over (left over after consumption and reserve stocks held by government and others), and probable imports. On the other side of the equation, two categories compose utilization (demand): domestic and export use. Under domestic usage are such subcategories as food, seed, industry, and feed.

One must subtract out supply that is kept by the government reserve, owned or used as collateral as loans to farmers and to be sold only at a certain price or higher. This figure will then be the net supply available. If the current and prospective prices are well above government sale prices, then almost all of the supply can be considered available to meet demands and must be included in the equation.

On the demand side, domestic requirements and the portion of exports one believes will be filled from free (nongovernment-held) supply stocks are added together to arrive at total net demand.

Net supply less net demand gives us the (estimated) balance of grain left over at the end of the crop year. If this figure is low relative to other years, a "squeeze" may develop and prices zoom up considerably before the end of the year (soybeans have a knack for doing this often). Keltner outlines four basic market factors that would influence prices greatly:

1. An indicated significant supply scarcity, is the most bullish of all situations. The trader should not sell short until prices have advanced to a sufficiently high level to discount the bullish interpretation. The fundamental analyst, however, has no real way of fixing a ceiling or top price on the price move upward. If other factors (e.g., general inflation in the economy) are present, the extent of the price advance will be even more exaggerated.

2. An indicated substantial supply surplus would alert the trader to generally sell and not buy until prices go substantially below government loan rates.

3. Crop-scare situations can result in sudden bull moves. This is particularly true if supply is only moderately larger, because the market would then be sensitive to any sudden developments, weatherwise, or man-made (government pronouncements, etc.). The scare more usually extends further than warranted, because of publicity and exaggerated reports. Short positions are particularly vulnerable during this type of season, especially if the net gain crop surplus is not well estimated, it is early in the season, or it is a critical growth period (e.g., August) for corn.

4. Inflation can itself be a bullish influence (note 1973–1974 grain prices in comparison to general inflation rates), so that in forecasting high and low prices, forecasts should be adjusted for the general commodity price trend and level.

5. There are normal seasonal price tendencies that can have anywhere from a modest to major influence on price. Mostly, seasonal tendency gives the fundamentalist a "flavor," or slant of direction to aid him in biasing trades to the long or short side.

HOW TO APPLY FUNDAMENTAL ANALYSIS AND ARRIVE AT TRADING POSITIONS

The method Keltner uses examines three basic factors—the net supply–demand balance figure just described, the seasonal price tendency, and price level, in that order.

Under the supply–demand balance the trader should first determine whether there is a scarcity or surplus. Then he must determine how much of this surplus could be drawn off by the government, or how much supply made available by it in the case of a scarcity, to arrive at a surplus or scarcity figure after government influence. As a sidelight, the trader should determine what premium over loans or discounts under the loan to farmers has been necessary in past seasons to cause similar impoundings or redemptions.

Next, consider seasonal tendencies. Determine whether prices should logically follow the established tendency (if all other influence factors previously mentioned are dormant or normal this season) or not (weather reports are giving rise for possibility of major crop damage). If so, then decide whether to take a position immediately or wait for a better buying or selling opportunity.

Positions against the general seasonal tendency should be established when "excellent reason exists, such as a distorted seasonal problem or when the market is being dominated by a factor of a special nature [General, 12, p. 183]."

Finally, observe the price level. If the prices are low relative to similar conditions in other years, then buy. Current prices may be already too high, with the result that events and the analysis have already been discounted in the prices; vice versa for a bearish situation.

If the price level shows that the normal seasonal tendency has been distorted by, say, an advance during a period normally showing seasonal weakness, then look for another counterseasonal move to follow, irrespective of situation.

STRENGTHS AND WEAKNESSES OF FUNDAMENTAL ANALYSIS

The fundamental approach to trading has four strong points that come to mind:

1. Relatively little time and effort are needed to obtain the initial facts, relate them, and make up a broad strategy for buying and selling. The fundamentals should not change much, except for sudden weather changes, for example. Major changes in influencing factors generally happen only a few times a year, at most.

2. Fundamental analysis gives the trader the satisfaction of knowing why prices have moved the way they did and hence can give him

more confidence to follow his analyses in the future. Similar to picking a sports team to win because of its strengths, and not because of a nice name or team colors, fundamental studies can give more assurance to the analyst that sound approaches will yield more profits over a long period of time than will a hit-or-miss system, such as acting on tips, broker's advice or throwing darts.

3. Large profits can result from sound, long-range analyses. Anyone attuned to the imbalance in demand caused by the 1972 Russian wheat purchase and possibility of somewhat smaller wheat crop prospects for the 1973 harvest could have reaped a fortune by buying even after the Russian deal became public knowledge, especially if profits were reinvested (positions added) with the knowledge of a forecast for a huge increase in wheat prices to unheard-of levels.

4. Even if the fundamental forecast has a great deal of error possibility (as all forecasts do that look far into the future), knowledge of the *direction* of price change can produce advantages for the trader. Unwarranted dips in price could be seen as bargains, in the light of some upward adjustment over the course of the season.

Unfortunately, there are a number of weaknesses in relying solely on fundamental analyses for trading commodities:

1. Foremost, the rules for developing and applying fundamental analyses, no matter how clearly Keltner promulgated them, are simply too vague and general to assure uniform success for every practitioner. No hard-and-fast quantitative yardsticks or methods are indicated. Determining whether prices have discounted a bullish supply–demand balance figure is, to say the least, heavily interpretative. Much of the comparisons and determinations are strictly judgemental, and hence the trading results depend largely on the skill of the analyst.

2. It takes a long time to adjust fundamental supply–demand equations to reflect new facts, and the fundamental trader could be taking a beating or losing much of any profits he had before new facts became available and confirmed. For instance, bad weather could induce a panic buying market in fear of crop damage. Not until the government surveyed and estimated the damage could the pure fundamental analyst act. By then limit moves could have cost him a bundle had he been short.

3. In part because of the potential for large losses before adjustments in positions can occur, the fundamentalist can become very disillusioned, having to wait out great changes in equity before the trade and season is completed. Lack of confidence can chase many a trader away from perfectly good (long-term) positions and good operating plans.

4. Because of the wide variation in equity due to holding on to the position, the trader must keep huge reserves, in case he had to put up more margin to support a long-term position that his studies show will eventually work out.

5. Fundamental analyses have no timing strategies inherently built in—to either enter or exit a position—and thus much of long-term profit potential is left open to a gamble that at the end of the seasonal cycle profits will be optimum.

7 Charting

Perhaps the most glamorous and artistic of the timing techniques is charting. Advocates of the form see important stories developing in an ensuing epic of gigantic proportions. Many see it almost as wars of two opposing armies—one composed of bears and the other, bulls. Marches are made up and down (pricewise) the battlefield, with many a minor skirmish, once in a while a major battle (long-term trend—bulls or bears giving way to an upward or downward onslaught by the other side), and, finally, a conclusion of a war at the end of the contract's life. This particular technique falls aptly under the general school of timing called *pattern recognition.*

One of the better-known chartists in commodities, William Jiler, editor of the Commodity Research Bureau chart services, sees considerable value in using chart interpretation for timing buy and sell prices. The following figures give examples of chart formations.

An offshoot of the normal form of charting that uses bar charts as the means of displaying important price movements, is the school of point and figure. The main difference between the two is that bar chartists will chart every price that occurs, whereas point and figure people will filter out minor movements and record only the major changes and the cumulative extent in each direction. This can be thought of as a way of smoothing the wrinkles in choppy price actions, for the purpose

99

of obtaining the grand picture—the major moves. Frequently, a point and figure chartist will describe his school as more sophisticated than ordinary bar charting, since he ignores meaningless wiggles.

Bar chartists, however, counter that every tick recorded is meaningful; often the longer it takes prices to move in one direction or stay trapped in a sideways market has important repercusions for the immediate future. The longer a commodity dribbles slowly one trend way or sideways means a pent-up, long-lasting, and extensive move in a new direction may occur.

Even though the methods of obtaining data are somewhat different (but not greatly), the techniques of analysis and trading are almost identical. The following presents the principal chart formations encountered by both bar and point-and-figure chartists.

THEORY AND APPLICATION

The art of forecasting using charts depends on the "proper recognition and interpretation of formations that are associated historically with a subsequent movement in a particular direction." Jiler [Forecasting Methods, 13] believes there are about a dozen formations, described here, which gives the trader a clue and signal to take a position or close one out.

Trend Lines and Channels

The greatest dream to a commodity chartist is to discover the beginning of a new, long-lasting trend. Jiler holds that prices in a trend tend to hold very close to an imaginary straight line. Three points, A, B, and C in Figure 24, form lines when A is drawn to C and constitute uptrends, downtrends, or sideways trends, depending on the start of the line. Jiler finds it hard to clearly identify a trend until it is well on its way. This probably stems from ambivalence on which tops or bottoms to connect. Examples of some trends are shown in Figure 25. It is obvious the chartist must take some license in choosing which bottom to connect together, as Jiler did not choose any bottoms until August 21, even though three or four other bottoms had occurred prior to that date.

Channels, in which prices are apt to move back and forth, are formed by adding another line well above the uptrend line, usually connecting outstanding (intermediate) high prices. This gives an informal measure of how far up the trend may proceed at its highest move.

One common trading rule is to climb aboard the trend once it is

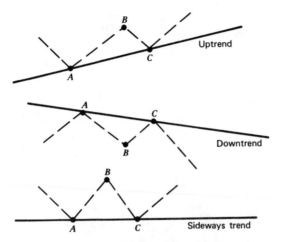

Figure 24. General trends in charting.

recognizable (when one can draw a basic trendline in one direction), and then reverse when current prices go through the trendline by at least 3%. Jiler feels this formation is one of the most frequently appearing on charts and is perhaps the most reliable to follow and use.

Head and Shoulders

Often at the top of an uptrend move a formation resembling the head and shoulders of a person appears. An example is depicted in Figure 26. This

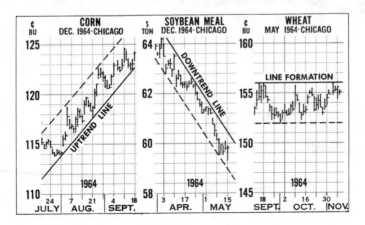

Figure 25. Examples of trends and channels.

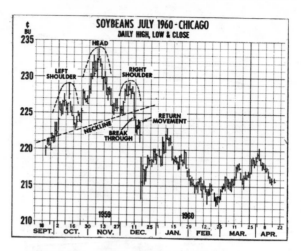

Figure 26. Head-and-shoulders formation.

can signal a downtrend. The left shoulder is recognized as a rally and decline of equal proportions. The head is formed by a second rally carrying beyond the first rally, but the subsequent reaction carries back to where the second rally started. The right shoulder occurs when a third rally falls short of the second rally in extent and a subsequent decline occurs that carries below the stopping points of the two previous reactions.

This formation heralds the start of an oppositely directed trend, and the trader should reverse or initiate a position in the direction of the new trend (downward in Figure 26). Some traders hold that a move extent equal to the second decline, from head to neckline, can be anticipated.

Triangles

Prices that move into ever-tightening ranges are referred to as *triangles.* Several examples of these are displayed in Figure 27. Again, tops and bottoms are connected to form the triangle, which comes about as price movements narrow toward the apex of the triangle, and buying and selling become so balanced that a minimum of extra force can upset the balance. Subsequent breakouts from the tight range often bring about a return move to the trend line, and this second move then can become the critical signal. The ascending type of triangle often points to a breakout move upward, and the descending triangle means a decline may be in the offing.

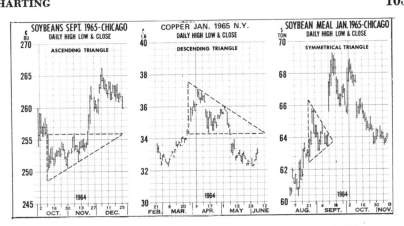

Figure 27. Triangles.

The trader can then buy when breakouts above an ascending triangle occur and sell when declines below descending triangles happen. As a general rule, the move should carry at least as far as the vertical distance in the triangle. However, Jiler feels the "most positive assertion about triangles is that they portend significant moves," although the directions (up or down) and extent of the move are not well determined. Triangles may well be the beginning or just part of other formations (e.g., a head and shoulder).

Rounding Tops and Bottoms

Trends often do not end sharply and reverse, but rather selling dries up in a downtrend, and a rounding bottom results, with prices slowly edging upward as tentative buying comes in (see Figure 28 for an example of a rounding bottom). According to Jiler, rounding formations are very reliable and imply that a move of major proportions is imminent. The more time prices spend near the end of the trend, the larger the subsequent new trend move can be expected. Again, connect lows for testing for developing bottoms and highs for possible developing tops.

When the old trend has stopped and is gradually turned around so that enough of a curve or hook has developed, the trader should then change or initiate a position in the direction opposite to the old trend.

Double Tops and Bottoms

In some cases prices form an "M" at uptrend tops or "W" at downtrend bottoms, rather than a sharp turnaround (a "V") or rounding tops and

Figure 28. Rounding bottom.

bottoms. Intermediate tops and bottoms are noted by the trader to test whether a double top or bottom is forming (see Figure 29 for one example). The extent of the new trend, after a double top or bottom signals a change in trend direction, can be quite large, as with other important formations. The trader notes intermediate tops and bottoms for possible double top or bottom schematics.

Flags and Pennants

Flags and pennants resemble triangles in many ways, in that prices tend to wind into narrower and narrower trading ranges over a couple of weeks' time. But the main difference between triangles and flag/pennants is that flags occur after the current trend has just made an impressive move. It may represent consolidation before a continued onslaught in the current trend direction occurs again.

Lines are drawn connecting intermediate highs and lows to arrive at the flag or pennant shape (Figure 30 displays two examples of the formations).

A trader would take a position in the current trend direction when the flag or pennant has been completed. His profit objective might be to make as much on the move from the point he got in as had occurred

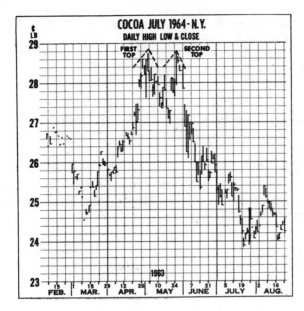

Figure 29. Double top.

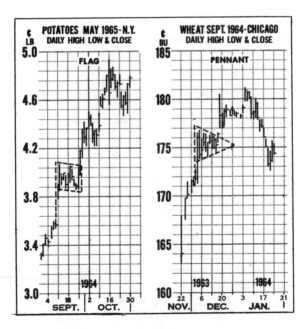

Figure 30. Flag-and-pennant formations.

from the beginning of the trend to the price where the flag developed.
In other words, the flag is halfway in the total move of the current trend.

Gaps

Gaps are exactly what they seem to be—blank spaces on a chart where
no price transactions have occurred. An upside gap occurs when the
lowest price on one day is higher than the highest price of the preceding
day.

Four major types of gaps are shown in Figure 31. The first, a common gap, occurs on April 29, but is quickly filled by May 3 as prices
declined and spanned the gap left on the 29th. The breakaway gap, appearing after a formation is complete, occurs early (February 24),
whereas runaway gaps happen twice near the end of the trend, when
panic buying by short sellers and late-entering longs join to accelerate
the buying urge. Finally, an exhaustion gap occurs at the end of sugar's
tumultuous move, a day before a complete trend reversal and collapse.

Breakaway gaps can be used to initiate positions in the direction of
the gap, as they portend extremely active trading interest in the trend's
direction. After prices start galloping, however, and the trend has made

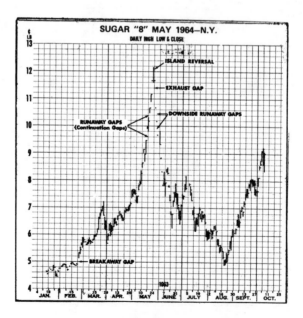

Figure 31. Gaps and reversals.

a huge move, care should be exercised not to enter into new or add to existing positions in the current trend direction, as a reversal and collapse of the trend becomes increasingly probable.

Reversals

Reversal of uptrend days occur when prices, after making new highs for the uptrend move, suddenly turn around and close lower than the previous day's close (see Figure 31). This could signal a reversal of the trend, especially if the price range is wide and volume heavy on the day of the price reversal. In this case, the trader should strongly consider reversing his position or initiating a new one contrary to the old, existing trend. Many substantial, quick moves have resulted after reversal days.

CHARACTERIZATION AND CONFIRMATION

Jiler points out that certain commodities display one or more chart formations more regularly than others do. Thus the chart trader will come to look for certain ones rather than others and will find the reliability of these better than others that don't appear as frequently. For example, soybean charts display many triangle formations that more regularly foreshadow major trend changes than others do. Wheat charts show many heads and shoulders, and cotton has shown many rounded tops and bottoms in its history.

Several contracts of the same commodity and often longer-range charts should also be used to see if the trader's commodity signal is *confirmed* by other months. If it is, this indicates a general movement in the commodity in question, not an isolated event in one contract month, which might be influenced heavily by a few traders or hedgers on a particular day or few days.

VOLUME AND OPEN INTEREST

Many traders will append a supplementary analysis to their chart studies and wait for additional confirmation of buy/sell signals from volume and open interest action.

In brief, if volume of trading is rising (and especially strong) when one of the chart formations signals a trend change or an additional move in the trend, then the signal is especially strong. More volume with higher, strong prices means more people are willing to buy up (and overcome sellers) and strongly force prices higher. Lower volume may give the trader a second thought—the price formation he just witnessed could have been a fluke—panic covering by isolated shorts.

When open interest increases, new positions are being established. If prices are rising, this means buyers are more aggressive and are overcoming selling and shorts are entering the market. This also means there will be more potential buyers from the ranks of new sellers if prices continue to move strongly up, creating a bull market situation that might feed on itself. In this instance chart formations signaling new or continued uptrends should be taken seriously, and buying should be initiated also by the chartist.

If open interest falls, chart formations signaling a bull or bear market should be looked at with suspicion, since traders are covering their positions, and no additional push should be made on prices other than to just get out. Price moves could be moving quite randomly and resemble (by chance) some significant chart formations.

ADVANTAGES AND DISADVANTAGES
OF CHART TRADING

There are three distinct advantages to using charting procedures for trading commodities:

1. Vertical line charts and drawing lines and configurations are easy to construct and maintain. The rules for obtaining, interpreting, and trading on chart formations are easy to follow.

2. Charting techniques have been used for a long time by many traders who swear by them. Because of the large number of followers alone, the great use of chart methods tends to confirm subsequent price events due to chartist influence. When chartists buy, prices will most likely go up, just as they anticipated (but only for charting considerations).

3. All the various price actions and tendencies are displayed and must be taken into account. No price (and perhaps volume and open interest) information is missing or unaccounted for in a chartist's interpretations. If his analyses are half decent, he'll catch most of the important moves that show up before major trends begin.

However, there are at least three valid criticisms of this broad approach to trading.

First, the rules for construction, interpretation, and use of chart formations are vague and left wide open to individual interpretation. Jiler refers to charting as an art form, which is probably an accurate description about an inaccurate subject. It is left open to the trader whether he should connect exactly the succeeding high prices or to ignore some. In ignoring some he is subconsciously altering his game plan for formation construction, probably to supplement it with an emotionally held attachment to a previously held notion about where prices are headed. Likewise the amounts needed for neckline penetration in a head/shoulder formation, for instance, or what really constitutes a "rounding" bottom (some bottoms are lumpy, some square, some firm or straight up) is left up to each practitioner.

Second, there is no real economic or mathematical modeling justification for using chartists' approaches. There is no economic reason why the top of an ascending triangle, drawn differently by different chartists, will prove to be a price level of sufficient selling to stave off buying waves, just because they drew a line. Likewise, when a line is drawn connecting lows in a supposed "trend," there is no economic reason why prices must behave in a straight line—why can't selling and buying waves distort the growth—move prices sideways, up fast, down far, but drifting on balance upward? Why must growth be linear, or straight? The world doesn't act that way—life is full of ups and downs, but progress has been made.

Third, the facts don't support the claim of success of charting. No long-term record of results by a number (not just one) of chartists has been offered or verified. A study by Robert Levy [Trading Methods, 18] examined in depth almost all the important chart formations in chartist theory. The model tested the results of positions taken when a breakout from the chart pattern occurred, until a certain time after the position was initiated. A five-year daily price history of over 500 stocks was tested, with the result that none of the thirty-two possible patterns used separately or otherwise, and for many positive holding times, showed any evidence of profitable forecasting ability in either bullish or bearish direction. Whereas this is only one study and not all possible combinations (including other contract confirmations and linking of volume to the chart patterns) were tested, and the study concerned stock data and not commodities, its exhaustiveness and the absence of hard evidence of profitable results by chartists casts doubt on the profit validity of chart pattern methods.

8 Moving Averages

The moving-average approach is also a popular one among "technical" practitioners in the stock and commodities markets. It is an easy one to formulate in quantitative terms and is less open to many interpretations than are other methods. It can be easily tested and manipulated on computers. For this reason many serious analysts use this method to develop portfolio approaches to investing: computer-simulated track histories of a moving-average strategy can tell the analyst portfolio account values, growths, risks, and general market influences, on even a day-to-day basis. This method, one of the trend-following school of timing, has legions of followers. Perhaps it is little wonder that many of the other major techniques are also trend following in nature, differing from the following method only in means.

Many individual traders use this method for timing buys and sells. Each one seems to use slightly different parameters in the equations, as if to personally characterize them as his own. Stock and commodity brokerages and advisors with weekly sheets are also numerous in their use of moving averages. Perhaps the longest, most widely followed guru of the method amongst advisors is Richard Donchian, for over twenty years a devotee of the art. The largest user probably is Pro-Com, a mutual fund in commodities that started with around $7 million in its portfolio in the early 1970s.

110

THE THEORY

The basic assumption of the (arithmetic) moving-average approach is very similar to that of the trendline method from charting (see Chapter 7): the growth of a trend is essentially linear (i.e., straight). The two strategies don't agree much beyond this, however.

The trendline method assumes that the growth line of a trend is determined by the first batch of prices just after the trend begins. It is thought that these prices are closely representative of future prices later in the trend. The moving-average method, however, predicates the trend's growth line on the latest prices, not the very first. This means it assumes that the growth line may change and is only related to the latest prices. Moreover, the trendline technique gives weight in the growth line determination to only those (two) price points that form the two tops and bottoms in the price series. The moving-average method gives equal weight to each price used in determining the growth line.

The two methods do agree in application, however. Whenever the growth line of either method is violated, an opposite position or a closing out of the current one is signaled.

Briefly, the theory is that the moving-average line of current prices represents the current growth line of the trend. If the actual prices diverge significantly from this growth trend, such as to below the line in a bull trend or above the line in a bear trend, the current trend itself is then suspect, and a change in the actual prices to a new, oppositely directed trend has probably occurred.

The analogy with an assembly-line process is appropriate here. If too many of the sampled products on the assembly line (too much of the price series) are defective (violate the trendline), the conveyor belt and production process (current primary trend) are halted (trader closes out or reverses his position).

Figure 32 shows the essential use of the moving-average method. In example (1) a bull trend is in effect until the moving-average line *a* is intersected at price *A* by the actual prices. A bear trend is considered in effect from that point on. Example (2) is just the reverse of (1). A bear market was in effect until actual prices cross over and above the price *B*, indicating the probable birth of a bull trend.

APPLICATION

The construction of a moving-average line is quite easy. The line is like a price series and is generally plotted on the same graph with the same

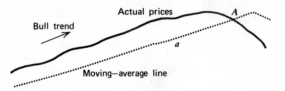

1. Moving–average line *a* is violated when the actual prices cross
the line at price *A* and signal a possible reversal in trend from
bull to bear.

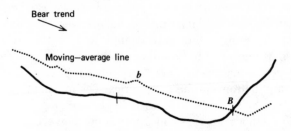

2. Moving–average line *b* is violated when the actual price series
crosses the line at price *B* and signals a possible reversal in trend
from bear to bull.

Figure 32. Basic idea of trend violation in the moving-average technique.

size and time scales as the actual prices. A different color or dotted line
differentiates it from the actual prices.

HOW TO CALCULATE
THE MOVING-AVERAGE LINE

The trader first specifies how many prices he wants in his average. If he
stipulates a larger number (e.g., 100), the moving-average line so generated will be conservative; he believes the growth line is probably
slowly varying and is small in slope. This means the growth doesn't
change with one or two price changes, only with a large number, over a
long time. Also, the rate of growth is fairly small and probably reflects
an annualized growth rate.

On the other hand, if he specifies few (e.g., 5 or 10) prices in the
average, he believes the growth line is volatile and depends on almost
day-to-day price-making events. Likewise, the growth rate is assumed
high, reflecting the short-term impact of a momentous single event (e.g.,

radically different government crop report, bad weather, volatile national or international situation).

Of course, this description is relative: if the time basis (measure period) is monthly and not daily, a few prices reflect a long-term growth line, not one dependent on day-to-day actions. But the concept is still valid; the large number of points averaged represents a relatively conservative average, reflecting the impact of the long-term index. The small number of points average represents a relatively short-term index.

Once he has specified the number of prices (e.g., N) in the average, the trader plots a moving-average figure for each date. The figure is arrived at by dividing the sum of the closing price for that date and the previous $N-1$ closing prices in succession, by the number of prices (N). The growth line is constructed by simply drawing lines connecting each of the moving-average figures graphed to date.

ADVANTAGES AND DISADVANTAGES

This technique in theory is a reasonable, workable investing tool. The idea of approximating the prices' trend by a flexible growth line that adjusts to current price movements is a sound one. But it, too, suffers from not always being able to tell the difference between normal reactions to a trend and the beginning of a new trend. In practice, the moving average is often violated, and then crossed again, back and forth, creating a lot of small, losing trades, more popularly known as "whipsaws."

For example, refer to Figure 33, which displays hog futures prices into 1976. Through much of early 1976 (until late June) prices wiggled, waffled, wavered, and wandered between 40¢ and 44¢ per pound. Moving-average approaches, whether short-term (N small in the computation denominator) or long-term (N large), brought nothing but grief and sorrow to the commodity trader. If he had strong faith that prices would eventually move into a long, trended state, and thus held on through the torment of January to June, he would have been amply rewarded from then on.

But the trader will always have this problem: will the current no-trend or sideways, vicious markets pass on and long, smooth-trended markets return soon? Unfortunately, the trader could be out of capital by the time that occurred. There seems to be no end, at times, to the *number* of whipsaw traders in a row.

To circumvent the "whipsaw" problem, some traders adjust for this by rendering the moving average much less sensitive to current reactions

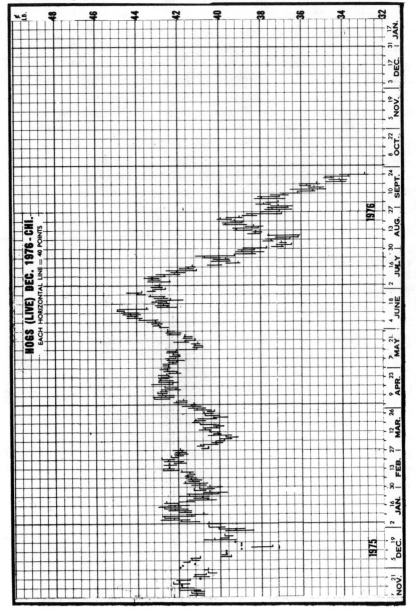

Figure 33. Price chart for December 1976.

to the trend (by increasing the number of prices in the average, equivalent to including prices from way back in time). However, this many times also renders the moving average less sensitive to real new trend changes, and great profits may have washed away or losses in positions arisen because the trader got in too late.

Traders with access to computers try to optimize the profit per trade by balancing the moving-average line somewhere between being too sensitive or insensitive to current price movements. This, however, can lead to "curve fitting," or the unconscious setting of hindsight profits. Only by subsequently testing the exact same method on a future period, in addition to past periods, will hindsight be removed.

9 The Contrary-Opinion Method

Perhaps the most starkly different method—in assumptions and calculation procedures—from the main drift of techniques, the following adheres to the no-trend or random-price-movement school of timing methods.

A novel approach that, ironically, may have more profitable application in commodity markets than in stock markets for which it was formed, contrary-opinion techniques are used by some analysts and speculators who don't accept conventional philosophies of trading. This method has its early roots in stock-market trading and traces its start to some observations made by Robert Rhea, a turn-of-the-century advocate of Charles Dow's theory on stages of growth and decay in the stock market.

According to Rhea, there are "three phases of a bull period; the first is represented by reviving confidence in the future of business; the second is the response of stock prices to the known improvement in corporation earnings, and the third is the period when speculation is rampant and inflation apparent—a period when stocks are advanced on hopes and expectation."[1] Bear periods have three similar phases marked by some hope, good earnings, and speculation and deflation.

One other possible technique to determine when trends are changing is to discover when a bull or bear trend is in its final stages. According to Rhea, this is when speculation and rampant inflation or deflation occurs. In a bull market, this would mean when the trend was experiencing its greatest growth. The irony is that when the market is experiencing its best growth period, bad times are near at hand.

This is the heart of contrary-opinion theory: "Contrarians observe the psychological status of the crowd and then take an opposite approach."[2] An intelligent (contrarian) trader, then, would wait until speculation is rife, prices soaring, and the vast herds of average investors have unhesitatingly bullish attitudes; at that point in time he should sell his holdings (and possibly go short).

The object of contrary thinking is to "challenge generally accepted viewpoints on the prevailing trends in politics, socioeconomics, business and the stock market. . . . The contrarian's purpose is to contest the Popular View because this view is usually untimely, misled by propaganda, or plain wrong."[3]

James L. Fraser, a prominent stock advisor, attributed the contrary opinion theory to H. B. Neill, who bases his theory on four "laws" of sociology and psychology:[4]

1. A "crowd" yields to instincts that an individual acting alone suppresses.

2. "Herd" characteristics make people follow group impulses instinctively.

3. Emotional motivation makes people in a crowd more susceptible to hope, fear, and greed.

4. Obsessions of the herd are substituted for sane, individual reflection.

As a result of these herd-like mannerisms, the crowd, or the public in general, act in unison in the stock market: when the market is up, the crowd joins in and buys; when the market plummets, the crowd sells. Fraser infers that the crowd acts against the better interests of its members because of these impulses. Of course, because of its collective influ-

---

[1] Greiner, Perry P., "The Dow Theory—An Anthology," in *Encyclopedia of Stock Market Techniques,* Investors Intelligence, Larchmont, N.Y., 1965, p. 108.
[2] Fraser, James L., "The Neill Theory of Contrary Opinion," ibid., p. 650.
[3] Ibid., p. 663.
[4] Ibid., pp. 658–659.

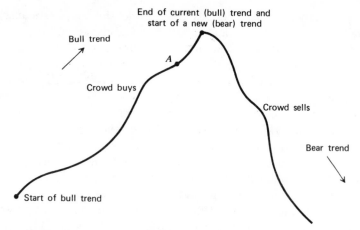

Figure 34. The "crowd," or public in general, buys and sells at the wrong time in trends. A contrarian will try to sell at price A when it appears the (bull) trend is ending, whereas the crowd waits and sells when the new (bear) trend is well under way.

ence, the crowd's behavior further accentuates the market moves. Because of its influence, it is often right in its choice of direction.

"The public is probably right more of the time than not. But the public is right only during the trends and wrong at both ends—usually wrong when it pays to be contrary."[5] This means that the public would lose money over the long haul, were it not for inflation. Most people have a bullish attitude and hence tend to accentuate purchases rather than sales. In the long run, prices will rise and their bull positions may more than offset short positions or sales of long positions and commissions. And this is why most people do lose money in commodity markets, which has *little* inflation!

The ones who profit most, says Fraser, are those who, unlike the crowd or public in general, can be right at both ends of the trends. That is, financial rewards go to those who know when a trend is ending, rather than when a new one is starting. This sounds like the same thing; the end of a current trend signals the start of a new trend. The timing and price of a new position however, are different.

Figure 34 capsules the tenets of the contrary-opinion approach. The "crowd" or public in general buys well after the start of the (bull) trend and doesn't sell until well after the start of the new (bear) trend. The contrarian, however, tries to determine when the current (bull) trend is ending, and hence sells or sells short at price A. He is not always

[5] Ibid., p. 663.

able to choose the exact end of the current (bull) trend, but the price is much closer to the start of the new (bear) trend than the crowd is able to obtain later on.

APPLICATION

Unfortunately, Fraser does not mention, let alone subscribe to, explicit, quantitative formulations of the contrary-opinion theory. We'll have to take the liberty of translating his thoughts into concrete instructions.

As mentioned in the introduction to this method, one possible technique determining when the current trend is coming to an end, and thus when primary trends are changing, is to discover when a bull or bear trend is in its final stages. According to Rhea, this is when speculation is rife and rampant inflation or deflation occurs. In a bull market, this speculative stage represents the bull trend's greatest period of growth. This approach is labeled "version 1."

Version 1

One obvious way to determine when the greatest period of growth in a bull trend would be is to examine the past history of growth rates within bull trends.

Figure 35 breaks down part of a bull trend into subintervals of time, and corresponding growth rates are labeled for each subinterval. For instance, during the time from point 3 to point 4 the bull trend will have grown at a certain growth rate (GR), say, of 7% (see (1) in Figure 35, the sequences of growth rates in a bull trend).

If we collect these growth-rate figures for this and all other bull trends and plot the numbers of time each growth rate occurred against each size of interval, the graph would appear like the one in (2), Figure 35. We could compute the average of the growth rates and other statistics.

One statistic that could be computed from this graph and would aid in determining when to reverse or close out a bull position would be something called a *percent cutoff point* for the growth-rate size.

HOW TO DETERMINE THE
PERCENT CUTOFF POINT

The actual 90% cutoff point is arrived at by examining the actual distribution, or the aggregate of frequencies of all the growth-rate sizes, and

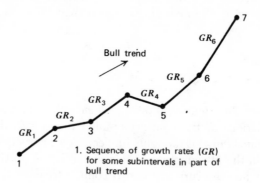

1. Sequence of growth rates (GR) for some subintervals in part of bull trend

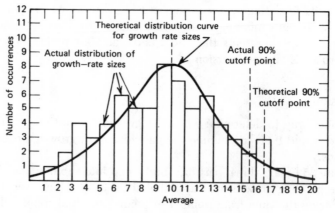

Growth rate size (GR), in percent, for subintervals of all bull trends

2. Graph of the number of occurrences for each growth—rate size subinterval

Figure 35. Growth-rate sequences in a bull trend's subintervals, and a graph of growth rates, for all bull trends.

determining where the lower 90% of the number of growth rate sizes occur. In an example, 90% of the growth rates are less than 13% in size. This could mean that only approximately 10% of the time in the future could we expect growth rate sizes of 13% or more. The assumption in this strategy is that an unusually large size occurs at the end of the primary trend (Rhea and contrary-opinion theory), and we should use this occurrence as a signal to reverse or close out the position.

We could get fancy and search for a theoretical distribution that best fits the data and use it to determine the theoretical 90% cutoff point (called *critical confidence level* in statistical jargon). However, without more assumptions and a thorough testing and good choice of data, we could not determine this information. Then, to make it frustrating and somewhat laughable at the same time, we would have to pinpoint what percentage cutoff might bring a large difference in growth-rate size (e.g., from 13 to 20%).

Instead, we can approximate the results of a theoretical distribution by having a large number (more than 20) of growth rates recorded and graphed. The more the better.

As a practical matter, we should calculate growth rates over daily or weekly intervals. Daily intervals, however, are sometimes too short and reflect the viscissitudes of very short term news and market-making affects. Monthly measurements are far too long, as many trends don't even last that long.

Version 2

Another way to determine when a current trend is or should be coming to an end is to examine the history of the total extent of each trend's move. That is, from discovering how long a trend has been in the past, we might expect that if a current one is approaching a length nearly equal to the longest ever recorded, it shouldn't go much further, if it follows past history at all. If it shouldn't go much further, this means the trend is nearly at an end, and we should close or reverse our position, a la contrary-opinion theory.

Figure 36 depicts the information needed for this strategy. Example (1) shows an alternation of five bull trends and four bear trends, with accompanying lengths (sizes of moves). The second part is devoted to graphs of the numbers of times growth-rate sizes occurring for each size of interval. For example, there were two bull trends 1–10% in size: bull trend 3 (3%) and bull trend 4 (5%). There was one bull trend (5) that was between 20–30% in size (actually 25%).

HOW TO CONSTRUCT PERCENT CUTOFF POINTS

As with version 1 growth rate graphs, we can construct 90% (or whatever)-sized cutoff points in the graphs in Figure 36. In other words, for the bull-trend graph, 8% of the trends (four of five) in the past (and graphed here) were less than twenty percent in total length (size). Similarly, 75% (three of four) were less than 10% in size for the bear trends.

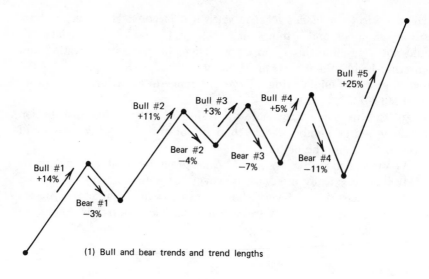

(1) Bull and bear trends and trend lengths

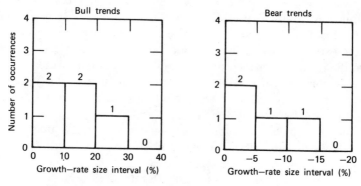

(2) Graphs of number of occurrences for each growth rate size interval

Figure 36. Hypothetical bull and bear trends, trend lengths, and graphs of the trend lengths.

This means we might expect only one of five (20%) bull trends in the future to be equal to or greater than 20% in size. And one of four (25%) of bear trends in the future to be equal to or greater than 10%.

The 90% cutoff point, then, is arrived at by first arranging the growth rate sizes in order of size and determining which size separates the 10% largest sizes from the other 90%

Figure 37 diagrams the two contrary-opinion versions for trading.

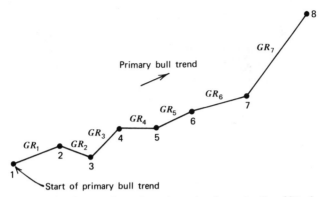

Version 1. Wait for growth rate in an interval to be greater than 90% of those in past history (here GR_7); take a short or close out bull position.

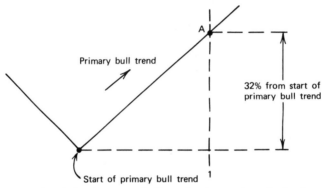

Version 2. Wait for the current (bull) trend to become larger in size than 90% of those in the past history (here 32%), then go short or close out bull position.

Figure 37. Two versions of going short or closing out a bull position using the contrary-opinion method.

The first example is version 1. The trader waits for the growth rate in an interval to become larger than the appropriate (here 90) percentage of similar trends in the past. If and when this occurs, he takes a position opposite to the direction of the trend (at or after point A). In example (1) the trend is a bull market, and so the trader takes a short (or just closes out his bull position) after detecting the exceptional growth rate (GR_7 in this example).

The second example is version 2. Here the trader waits until the net growth of the whole trend has equaled or exceeded trend sizes of the appropriate percentage (here 90%) of trends in the past. In other words,

90% of the (bull) trends in the past were less than 32% in size. When this critical trend size has occurred, he takes a position opposite in direction to the current trend or closes out his current position.

As a note, we should measure growth rates and trend sizes or extents using daily or weekly closing prices only.

GOOD AND BAD POINTS

The contrary-opinion approach is the most unique and one of the least used of the techniques discussed. It is probably also the most difficult to formulate and adhere to. The theory has certain appeal to those who like to be different and those who think they are one step ahead of the "crowd," or the public in general. It makes the investor feel very individualistic and able to make sound judgments superior to and as a result usually different from the crowd.

However, it lacks conciseness and definition. How does one judge when the crowd's psychological status is overwhelmingly bullish or bearish? Open-interest figures? Daily volume? These certainly are some possibilities, to augment or even supplant price studies alone. A psychological status and overwhelming feelings would indeed be hard to measure, let alone determine when they were abnormal or excessive. Since a trader could not interview or test each actual or potential investor all the time, let alone once, he would have to rely on indexes of some sort. Then we're back to the problem of the Dow theory: we become general practitioners monitoring the patient's health, and not surgeons or biologists determining the patient's well-being.

The main criticism, however, is of a practical nature. Ideally, the contrarian tries to determine when the current trend is about to end. Two ways of relating the psychological status of the crowd to the end of the trend are to determine (1) when the trend has entered a frenetic, speculative, inflationary period (overwhelming psychological status of the crowd) or (2) when the trend itself has grown much too large, in comparison to normal size ranges from the past—another indication that the crowd has pushed the prices as far as they will go.

When the contrarian then takes a trading stance opposite to the prevailing trend and overwhelming status of the crowd, he is taking a calculated risk that prices will soon reverse because of the heavy imbalance of demand (supply) in the direction of the trend. However, this is quite a gamble. Not only could the heavy imbalance and extreme psychological status of the crowd continue, but events could accentuate or prolong the imbalance. The results for the contrarian could be quite devastating. Prices might tend to move even more speculatively, faster, and act almost like the beginning of the same trend all over again (and this happens often in commodities).

Not only would his position be losing money fast, but the contrarian really couldn't get out of it, using his rationale, until an opposite trend favorable to his position occurred. Only when the trend favorable to his position began to reflect a heavy imbalance of demand (supply) in the direction of that trend could he then take a position opposite to his current one. This involved set of rules ironically leaves much room for huge losses and locked-in positions.

10 Oscillator Method

The oscillator method has recently become an attractive alternative to moving averages or contrary techniques per se. This term has been given to a family of indicators that measure price change rather than price level. This type of method is believed by many to indicate, as contrary opinion does, periods when price action has sown the seeds of its own impending reversal. Because its principal "raison d'être" is to detect or sense an impending reversal of prices, this technique should properly be thought of as belonging to the no-trend or random-price-movement school of methods.

According to Tewles, Harlow, and Stone, traders believe if prices are continuing up but at a slower rate than hitherto, they might surmise that the market is tiring and that a decline is imminent. The whole trick here is to counterbalance some of the better virtues of moving averages and contrary opinion.

If prices acted smoothly, we could almost "see" where to buy and sell: buy when prices stopped dropping and settled to no change (because prices would resume an upward course, since prices were smooth and would not resume a downward trend again); sell when prices reached and stayed at a plateau. "Buy low, sell high," as they say.

However, prices don't act smoothly, which is why they must be smoothed to obtain an approximate representation of trend drift. Once

that is done, the trader can look at the smoothed curve and decide to buy
after a bottom has formed and sell after a top has occurred, using a slight
extension of contrary opinion. Only here he is cheating, or hedging, a bit.
He won't take a chance that the smoothed curve has reached a peak or
trough; he'll wait for it to actually happen. And he should have plenty
of time to still catch the actual prices' tops and bottoms—the smoothed
curve should indicate a topping out before actual prices permanently
head down. So he hopes, anyway.

THEORY AND APPLICATION

Actual daily closing prices are shown in Figure 38. A three-day average
of these prices is plotted on the same graph. The smoothed prices lag in
representation what has actually occurred—real prices start new trends
and bottom out much faster than do the smoothed averages of actual
prices. But if the smoothed prices accurately reflect the trends inherent
in the actual prices, then methods that test for tops and bottoms in the
slopes or price changes of the smoothed curve *will* catch the actual
prices' tops and bottoms, since tops of slopes of curves occur much before tops of the curves themselves. In other words, smoothed prices lag
the real prices a little, but tops and bottoms of derivatives (slopes) of
the smoothed curves precede the smoothed curves a little, so we're back
at base zero: we can find the actual prices' tops and bottoms.

In Figure 38, a three-day average is constructed to represent the
trends in the actual prices. Tops and bottoms of the smoothed curve lag

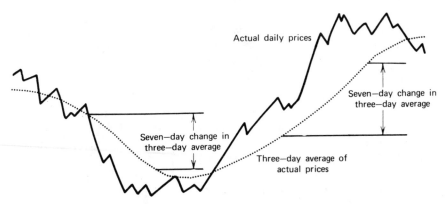

Figure 38. Seven-day oscillator: seven-day change in three-day average.

the same for actual prices. A seven-day change in (slope of) the three-day smooth curve is taken (not graphed, though). Call this the "oscillator." The changes will top or bottom out before the smoothed curve will top or bottom out. Hence the tops and bottoms of the seven-day change (or "oscillator") are close to (but not exactly) the tops and bottoms of actual prices.

A moving-average method would wait for actual prices to cross over the smoothed prices' curve before reversing positions. The direction of current prices, compared to the old trend (represented by the smoothed prices), has dramatically signaled a new trend. This is conservative, but the trader waits for the real bottom to have occurred.

A contrary approach would tell the trader to buy when the moving average was dropping hard (buy short dips) and to sell when it soared high (sell strong rallies). Here the trader buys before the bottom. Sometimes this strategy enables him to buy right at the actual bottom. Often, however, prices keep dropping a lot before a bottom is reached, leaving the trader with a big open loss.

This method combines the two: buy sharp dips, after leveling, and sell strong rallies, after turning, in the smoothed prices. That is, when the oscillator becomes so large negative and then becomes less negative (turns), the trader should buy. Conversely, when the oscillator reaches a strong positive and then slackens (becomes less positive), the trader should sell.

The trader must test three parameters for each commodity to optimize the use of the oscillator. From testing past results he should find the best price smooth (e.g., three-, five- or ten-day), the best change (e.g., three-, five-, seven-, or ten-day change) in the best price smooth, and the best value for strong positive and large negative oscillator values.

For example, for soybeans he may find that a five-day average of prices in combination with a seven-day change (which change defines the oscillator) gives the best representation for picking tops and bottoms of the commodity under study, and a 10-point oscillator value for new positions.

As an illustration, suppose the trader has constructed charts like Figure 38, with the five-day average plotted along with actual prices. He would construct on the same graph or in tabular form the seven-day changes in the five-day average (he subtracts the five-day average, seven days back, from the current five-day average). Then, when the seven-day change in the five-day average has turned up enough (enough is figured from other times the real bottoms in prices have occurred) from its own bottom, he takes a long position in the market. As one example for a stop, he might close out his long position when the seven-day change figure has reverted to below its current bottom (which may then indicate the real bottom has yet to occur).

Table 8 gives a specific application, using a strategy of waiting for the seven-day change to turn by a predetermined amount, to initiate a position. Using a three-day average of actual prices and a seven-day change in the three-day average (columns 3 and 4), the trader can now evaluate when to buy and sell. If we assume he has chosen, from past data, a value of 10 for a turn in the seven-day change to be significant for initiating a new position, he would go long on day 15, as the seven-

TABLE 8   Application of Oscillator Method

Day	Actual price	Three-day average	Seven-day change in three-day average	Action
1	688			
2	692			
3	696	692.0		
4	702	693.33		
5	700	696.0		
6	680	697.33		
7	662	680.67		
8	646	662.67		
9	633	647.0		
10	622	633.67	−58.33	
11	612	622.33	−71.00	
12	603	612.33	−83.67	
13	595	603.33	−94.00	
14	588	595.33	−85.34	
15	582	588.33	−74.34	Go long
16	577	582.33	−64.67	
17	573	577.33	−56.34	
18	570	573.33	−49.0	
19	568	570.33	−42.0	
20	567	568.33	−35.0	
21	567	567.33	−28.0	
22	568	567.33	−21.0	
23	570	568.33	−14.0	
24	573	570.33	− 7.0	
25	577	573.33	0	
26	582	577.33	+ 7.0	
27	588	582.33	+14.0	
28	595	588.33	+21.0	

day change value rose to −74.34, a change of almost +20 from the bottom of −94.00 on day 13 (a decrement of 10 from a high plus value of the seven-day change value would tell him to go short). The trader might have chosen his value of 10 for the seven-day change by going back over old data, picking out significant turning points (in his estimation) in the actual prices, and then noting what least change in the value of the seven-day change picked all the tops and bottoms, without getting caught choosing "false" bottoms and tops.

Of course, there will be times in between tops and bottoms when "false" signals occur—values exceeding this least value, but no real trend change occurring. This leads to whipsaw losses—needless reversals of positions. The best value for the change in the seven-day change for initiating positions is the one that picks tops and bottoms as soon as possible after the event and yet minimizes the number of false signals in between the tops and bottoms.

The optimization procedure just described is admittedly general, as it is dependent on (1) the choice by the individual trader as to what combination of late guesses on tops and bottoms and false signals he is most comfortable with (i.e., a risk–reward utility profile) and (2) the state of the science of optimization in commodity system parameter choice, which is still in its infancy.

Tewles [General, 15], for instance, suggests three-day for smooth, seven-day for oscillator change, and plus thirty-day for strong positive and minus thirty-day for sharp negative soybean oscillator values, for example. Refer to his book for more detailed discussions and examples.

CRITIQUE

This type of approach to timing is much more a mathematician's delight. The trader here is actually trying to represent the main elements of price relationship in a quantitative fashion; he's going scientific! In quantifying problems, one can ask meaningful questions and have a much better chance at viable, real solutions. When the problems on physical stress and strain on a bridge are put into mathematics and physics perspective, the solution almost begs itself. When one learns diction, grammar, and advanced vocabulary, he can most effectively communicate.

Second, this approach eliminates much subjective judgment, namely, that old boogey that scotches good, consistent trading records and leaves the trader paralyzed in his expectations for future trading results. Quantitative decisions give a higher, more consistent trading performance than does rule of thumb or witchcraft.

The oscillator method is particularly good with smooth, medium-range (e.g., 30¢ or 40¢ in beans, 3¢ or 4¢ in cattle) trends and sideways movements (which occur 75% of the time that commodities are open for business, according to Gold [General, 9]).

It also catches trends early. There is nothing so heartening to a commodity trader than to buy soybeans at the start of a significant move —a dollar or more—except perhaps to also *sell* them at the very top! This particular method has an uncanny knack for picking tops and bottoms in special churning and sideways moving markets. However, the method does have its vulnerable spots.

First, there are simply too many parameters to optimize: the number of days to smooth prices, the number of days to smooth differences of the smoothed prices, and the oscillator positive and negative ceiling and floor values, respectively. Many traders have applied this method to past data to determine which values optimize the trade results. The result of all this is a super curve fit, or hindsight supreme. The massaged values carefully fit sixty zillion cases from the turn of the century until now. But watch out—that's looking back, and having omniscience to see what would have been best for those particular cases. There is no reason the same conditions—and the carefully orchestrated results—will occur again like that. It is a general rule in quantitative circles that the less to optimize, the better. Three-parameter optimization is really pushing it. The arguments for markets repeating to identically duplicate the tripartite parameter optimization is not especially convincing.

Second, smoothing itself is very critical. As pointed out in Chapter 8, the trader is introducing more trendedness than may already be in the prices. This automatically creates whipsaw loss problems: longs when prices rise a little, shorts when they dip a bit—or longs when prices have already gone too far (caught price change too late). The problem could also be compounded in that a contrary approach is being used on top of the moving average. A long position is taken contrary to the trend (slope is down), even though prices seem to have stopped falling. The second smooth, on price differences, introduces even more danger of moving average problems.

Third, introducing moving-average and contrary-opinion elements of timing can improve performance at times, but can also degrade performance more than moving average or contrary opinion by themselves. Conceivably, a trader could lose when both moving-average and contrary-opinion techniques would have kept him out of a position. In a slightly volatile but steadily downward market, oscillators might be a lot more sensitive to the wiggles than either a moving average or contrary opinion method by itself.

Fourth, judgment unfortunately still enters in when using this approach. If the trader judges the market to be sideways or moderately trended (no great moves), then oscillators will work very well, and he probably will perform better than any other system (moving averages by themselves would get clobbered, contrary opinion perhaps wouldn't signal trades in either direction). But if some big trend markets come along (and they do, when you least expect it), then the trader using oscillators will probably get killed, just as with contrary approaches.

11 Congestion-phase Timing

There are a number of specialized methods that result from knowledge of particular or unusual market behavior. An observer may note a basic cyclical movement in hogs, a seasonal trend (e.g., "the voice from the grave," which foretells when to buy and sell wheat annually), or the tendency for a commodity to change price and react in a certain way (corn prices almost always bob and weave, whereas soybean prices tend to spurt or shoot straight one way).

The congestion-phase system of timing, as developed by Eugene Norfi, is aimed at trading for limited profit objectives with limited risk in trading, in sideways markets. It is also claimed to be an aid to other trend systems (e.g., moving averages) to refine entry points, again reducing risk. Norfi [Trading Methods, 20] has used it extensively as a floor trader on the Chicago Board of Trade for many years.

This particular method is difficult to classify, for it has elements of the contrary approach (prices are temporarily abnormal, and will return to a normal state, or "snap back"), and a little bit of pattern recognition. Because it is basically looking for a return to another (normal) state and advocates taking a position contrary to price movements at the moment, it must be ruled a part of the no-trend or random school of timing.

133

THEORY AND APPLICATION

Prices that go into trading ranges tend to act like ping-pong balls: relatively balanced buying and selling forces push and pull prices up and down with great regularity. If prices started drifting one way (e.g., close two or more days successively higher or lower), opposing market forces would batter or hit prices oppositely, back toward the center of the trading range. Norfi has observed it is highly probable that prices will retreat on the close following two days of successively higher closing prices (he feels 75% is accurate). Thus it is a good strategy to sell short or to sell existing long positions when this event occurs, in anticipation of lower prices on the following close.

Figure 39 demonstrates the theory. After closing higher for two days in a row (days 3 and 4), we can expect the close on day 5 to be lower than on day 4. One can sell on the close on the fourth day, when it is obvious prices have gone higher for two days; or sell on the open or during the day or as long as the selling price is the same or higher than the close on day 4.

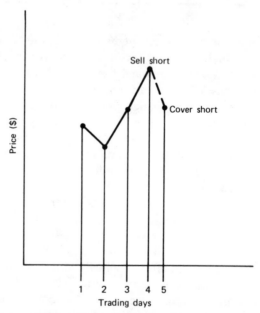

Figure 39. In congestion, probability is high that two successive up (down) days will produce a down (up) day next.

Of course, one should not sell on the fifth day or on the close of the fourth day if the fourth day's close prices have busted out of the congestion or trading range previously established. Likewise, if prices do bust out of a congestion after a position contrary to the busting direction has been established, the position should be closed out.

There are certain rules for telling the trader when he is in a congestion range to begin with. Initially, the trader must chart ten days' worth of closing prices prior to determining whether there is in fact a (current) congestion market. The rule for determining this (congestion) condition is to wait for a daily high and low price not exceeded by subsequent closing prices, and (the high and low) is followed by two consecutive closing prices in a direction opposite to the very first price change that ended with the high and low mentioned. As long as closes stay under the high and above the low, the market is in congestion.

Consecutive days' closings apart by a small amount ($0.5¢$ in grains) should be ignored and treated as one close. Finally, if a price breakout of the congestion range occurs, graphing should continue until a new congestion has formed, then apply the two-day up (down), one-day down (up) rule for again initiating trades.

Several additional strategies could be employed. More shorts could be added as more consecutive up days (more than two) continue to occur, with anticipation that prices are increasingly probable to reverse on the next close, for example.

ADVANTAGES AND PROBLEMS

Because of the relative balance of sellers and buyers in congestion periods, any price runups will be countered with selling pressure and a close or two down. This chain of events, ebb and flow of buying and reaction selling, gives the trader good leverage for trades using an oversold or overbought rule. As a result, a high percentage of trades will be successful (Norfi claims 75%), thereby limiting losses by limiting the *frequency* of their occurrence.

There is limited risk inherent in this type of strategy. A natural stop at just above the congestion ceiling tells the trader that he had better close out his short because the prices are no longer in a congestion, or trading, phase.

Many opportunities abound in congestion-phase timing. According to a number of marketers, prices in most major commodities spend an average of 70–75% of the time in congestion phases. Moreover, many two day up (down), one day down (up) sequences occur in each congestion market (typically, from several to several dozen over a couple of months).

The congestion-phase system is very much a quantitative trading technique, with little room for personal judgmental decisions. One can logically explore certain price consequences and opportunities and can follow automatic decisions.

However, risk is not completely limited. Whenever one takes an overnight (and sometimes day) trading position, the trader's position is open to price effects of overnight news and price movements within the day, if a strategy is based on entry and exiting of positions at closings only. Limits up could follow day after day just after our hapless trader initiated a short position the night before. Not even a buy stop or market order will close his position in the case of limit moves.

A more probable instance is the day-to-day inching of prices upward on the close against the trader's short position. If the closes change by 0.5¢ or less each day, he doesn't ever get out, since he is not supposed to count changes in closing prices that small. An arbitrary close stop above the congestion market could solve that problem, but there is a danger that his position might be needlessly closed by a fluke, adverse closing, after which prices fall in his favor.

Still there is subjective judgment entering in the trader's plans. Even though Norfi gives the ten-day charting rule prior to deducing any congestion phases, the definition of the phase is not completely precise and is left open to individual interpretation. The trader could have started his charting after prices had already entered a congestion phase and marked out a trading ceiling and floor. His congestion range could be but a narrow version of the real one, and he could be stopped out needlessly or not have many opportunities compared to the real situation using the broader definition prior to chart beginning. Also, ten days is a rather arbitrary number, used merely for convenience.

To make it worse, the definition is perhaps too rigid, at the same time. If prices move even just a bit out of the preestablished range, the congestion phase is considered broken, the position closed out or reversed. However, prices could easily fall back into the trading range again. There is no reason why price moves must stop *exactly* at a previous high. Rather, realistically prices might move some reasonable way below and above the high price (same thing for low), reflecting temporary buying and selling imbalance but keeping to a general trading *area* as a ceiling, but *not* a specific price (which occurred only once and perhaps with not much following or importance).

Also, there may be a number of "false" congestion ranges coming from and changing into trends quickly, which could mean (considerable) loss on each of several trades in a row. It is similar to going contrary short when one thinks one is in a trading range and prices have come up, only to find out prices are very much trending on the upside, and to repeat this several times, looking for the (principal) top to the trend.

Gains are also small, probably even smaller than losses on the average, so the trader needs many gains to offset some losses and to make any substantive profit headway. This could disillusion him when others are making big money in trended situations and he is on the sidelines with no position.

12 Breakout Methods

Perhaps one of the greatest speculators that lived was Jesse Livermore. According to Sarnoff [Trading Methods, 19], he made and lost four fortunes, *each* one in the millions of dollars! (In fairness, though, he lived in an era when stocks were as commodities are today—volatile in price and high leverage, so fortunes could be made and lost in a short amount of time, and with more probability than now.) His timing system, based on a "pivotal point," was essentially a breakout or breakaway technique. Once a pivotal price was surpassed, prices were thought to breakaway into new high ground, in the case of an uptrend, or breakout of a trading range to establish a new trend.

Many traders in the stock and commodity markets use this type of approach. In fact, there are probably as many users of this approach as with all other technical methods *combined!* Some use it plain—any price move that breaks trading range highs or lows indicates a trend starting in that direction. Others prefer it fancy—prices have to move in steps— so much up, so much down, then holding, and finally a breakaway—or prices must break highs or lows by so much for a new trend to be surmised. This technique is quite the opposite of the congestion-phase approach and the contrary-opinion method. The last two assume any breakout to be essentially a random event and that prices must ultimately return to the original state, whereas the breakout method postulates just

138

the opposite—that a new, counterdirection trend is getting underway. Along with the moving-average approach, it falls into the trend following school of timing.

THEORY AND APPLICATION

Figure 40 portrays the two basic breakout situations. Case 1 shows essentially a breathing spell for a bull trend, a minisideways (trading) area in which profits are being taken by bulls and new shorts are entering, in hopes that the last high proved to be a turning point, and the start of a bear occurs thereafter. But prices stabilize, a low is formed that is subsequently not violated, and prices edge up and break through to new high ground after point *a*. Case 2 shows a breakout from a trading range between a bottom, *a*, and top, *b*. Prices trade between the two boundaries for a long time, and then break through the ceiling established before at point *b*, past point *c*.

A number of strategies lend themselves to these situations. One that is used most frequently is to go long whenever current prices pierce the old high barrier (and perhaps by a minimum amount, x) (see Figure 41, situation 1). This strategy assumes prices are on their way to drifting higher and at sometime in the future, establishing a new trading range. In fact, the entire market could be looked at (especially by a random-walk theoretician) as a collection of trading ranges (relative price equilibriums) and drifts of prices, long in extent but short in time. That is, prices are generally in trading ranges (70% of the time) and in disequilibrium (trends) a short part of the time, reflecting a piece of news that changes (fairly immediately, for efficiency's sake) the equilibrium price from one level to another.

Another strategy that presents itself is a pattern strategy. Some traders hold that breaking away from a trading range by even a certain amount is not significant in itself—the move could simply be a random move in an essentially stable price area, and the last high and low prices were *not* good measures of the boundaries of the range of the price equilibrium. These traders would suggest some more sophisticated means of detecting an equilibrium price-level shift.

One possible criterion would be the amount of *time* spent outside of a current stable price range—the more time (especially compared to previous instances of prices spent outside of a well-defined stable price area) spent outside, the more probable a drift was in progress (see Figure 41, situation 2). The trader determines after prices have stayed

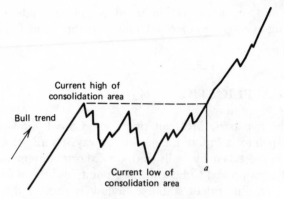

1. Breakaway at point *a* from consolidation area in a bull trend into new, higher territory

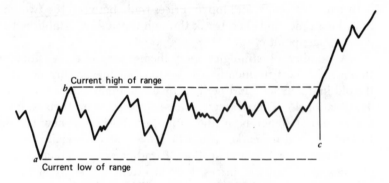

2. Breakout at point *c* from long, sideways trading market into new high ground and a bull trend

Figure 40. Breakaway situations.

above the trading range for *c* minus *b* days, that prices are drifting significantly out of the trading ranges, and a long position is now in order.

A second alternative is to test for significant *ways* prices can break out of trading ranges to lead to significant price drifts. For instance, in Figure 41, situation 3, prices have made four new tops outside of the current trading range. This may indicate persistent, constant, and thus significant buying pressure on the part of traders, indicating a long-term or long-extent price change, as opposed to a single buying surge that occurs briefly during a few days, makes a new top outside of the trading range, but soon falls back into the range after no follow through buying occurs. A one-time buying spree means nothing about prolonged, large buying pressure in the future.

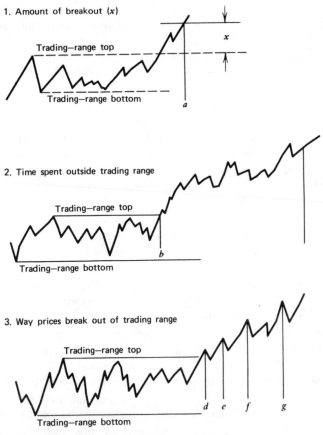

Figure 41. Three breakout strategies.

CRITIQUE

As with other quantitative methods, the breakaway approach allows little judgment and hence personal interpretation, bias, faults, and the choice for inconsistency (varying interpretations on different occasions). Once a means of identifying trading range is defined and the breakout spelled out, the trader simply records prices and waits. After that, it's automatic.

Also, breakaway methods are able to always identify major moves and catch them fairly early. Because of the nature of the method, any price movement beginning with or continuing after a period of tight price range will be almost always caught. It may take longer for some breakaway variations to catch particular types of trends (e.g., slowly developing or wandering ones), but if the move is persistent and extending, a signal will eventually be given to jump aboard.

Another point is that these methods generally do not jump at every minor move. All wiggles, pushes, and pulls in a trading range are ignored —only moves outside of it are examined. This saves the trader from losing often and dearly on whipsaw, meaningless trades.

Finally, breakaway techniques are one of the closest in compatibility to what academics generally regard financial market price movements as random walks. That is, many scientists feel traders cannot use just the past sequences of price changes to forecast *future* price changes, although some hold the opinion that price levels might be forecast using information including price changes and fundamentals, say. Still others hold that prices can drift significantly, but usually rather quickly and efficiently to a new price level (trading range) once a new piece of news has come out, and is thus quickly discounted or reflected in the price adjustment.

From this one can see that breakaway theory is designed to test for significant alterations or adjustments in the price level to another price level. The crux of the matter is whether the net gain after detection, on the average, is profitable. This then points to an analysis of whether enough sizable major price adjustments will occur in the future to warrant using the method. The analyst finally has to depend on some mixture of relying on past frequency of occurrences and future possibilities, given the structure and probabilities of events that conceivably could occur in the future. There are also some disadvantages, however.

First, the trading range is difficult to define. Initially, a chartist must determine what high and low price to choose for the first trading range. This is especially difficult, since the first few prices may be just a small part of a larger, truer trading range with different high and low, or a trend may have been unfolding up to that point, and the closer high and low at the beginning of charting or data collecting may truly be the start of a trading range.

The problem of identifying trading ranges even after trends and other trading ranges have been acknowledged initially is still difficult. Why a particular high or low? Very few transactions, and hence buying and selling interest, occurred at those extremes. Should closings be used, instead (much more volume of trades occur there)? The main problem of naming or identifying the trading range is identical to stating when a trend has ended. If prices in a given trend are showing a retreat, where does one classify the bottom of a consolidation of prices (trading range), after which prices are supposed to resume or reverse the current trend?

For instance, a retreat in a bull trend could stop at one low, go up one notch, and then make new lows. Which is the true range? The first? Then a whipsaw loss on the short side (a bottom really hasn't been realized yet) could result. Suppose prices kept retreating, never having an uptick (on a daily or whatever basis). Then not only is there no trading range (or it is monstrously huge), but all, or much, of the trader's profits on a long position may have washed away!

Second, losses can still occur often. The criteria for breakout for any of the three discussed and displayed in Figure 41 give room for false breakouts and subsequent losses when positions are initiated on the false premise. For instance, if prices break out on the upside by 0.5¢ in wheat and the breakout criterion is 1¢, prices could and have retreated soon after back into the trading range, with little care to break out thereafter. This happens because trading ranges are too rigidly defined and break-through criteria too small.

Even a delayed wait criterion (Figure 41, strategy 2) is vulnerable to false signals and losses. Prices could move aimlessly above the trading range for some time, trigger a buy signal, and then soon after retreat slowly back into the trading range. And these situations do happen.

Third, the conditions just alluded to (false breakouts and subsequent signals to take positions) could repeat successively. Prices could repeatedly break out of trading ranges, trigger signals, and then fall back into the former trading range. As with moving averages, this could (and often does) present the trader with strings of (whipsaw) losses, with no end in sight.

Fourth, there is no really dependable history or past experiences one can rely on to say, "there will at maximum be three false price breakouts in a row." Unfortunately, much of the future of price ranges and break-outs depend on the frequency, type, and influence of current events on the commodity studied. For instance, how often will Arab–Israel conflicts occur, and how much influence will they have on silver prices? Silver has been in many trading ranges, has some false breakouts and small price-level changes (not enough to profit from, after detecting the change), but is heavily dependent for long trends on inflation and international major events, both of which are hard to predict. The trader is indirectly, subconsciously betting on the heavy occurrences of Mid East conflicts and returning inflation when he plays with silver.

Finally, breakout methods must have big trends (price-level adjustments) to be lucrative. All strategies inherently wait for a goodly price move to have occurred, time to have passed, or even both. The "minimum time" variation (Figure 41, situation 2) waits for some time to have passed after penetration of the trading range. But the prices may have moved way away from the trading range by then, and most of the trend's profit may have occurred (similarly with situation 3). By the time three or four new tops and the buy signal have occurred, prices could have moved up, at each successive top, by a great amount.

13 Wave Theories

Probably the most fascinating concept in financial price analysis is the theory that prices move in basic rhythms. Just as much aquatic and even terrestrial life is ruled by lunar tides, humans also are affected: female menstruation is thought to be tied to the tides, and "lunatics" are named because of supposed sensitivity to moon times, to name a few. Life–death cycles in animal life is quite evident. Cycles in weather, politics, and yes, the stock and commodity markets have been cited.

Although cycle strategies are not heavily used by stock and commodity practitioners, there are a number of schools and users. Stock-market traders use Elliot wave theory, Dow theory, and cycles like sine waves to describe price movements. Commodity traders seem to stick to cycle theory and some to Elliot wave usage. Since these methods describe sequential relationships in price movements and do not place great emphasis on trendedness, they most properly belong to the pattern school of timing.

THEORY AND APPLICATIONS

Three basic theories of how markets work constitute the bulk of wave theory: the Dow theory, Elliot-type waves, and cycles (see Figure 42).

145

1. Dow theory

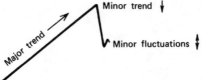

2. Elliot wave theory: total uptrend move is three moves up, two down (alternating ups and downs)

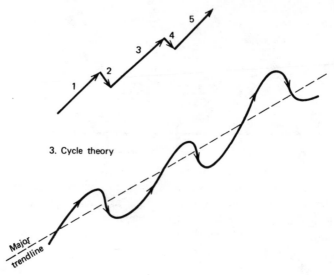

3. Cycle theory

Figure 42. Three basic wave theories.

Dow Theory

The Dow theory was first promulgated by Charles Dow around the turn of the century and later carried on and amplified by others. Dow felt there were a number of waves or movements occurring and recurring in stock prices (and by some traders, in commodities, by extension). Analogous to the waters of the great oceans, there are the great trend movements in stocks: secondary moves, like local storms or calms; and tertiary or minor waves, which continually lap up on beaches without fail. The three moves in the market place are depicted in Figure 42, situation 1. A major bull trend is in effect, whereas a secondary bear trend, or selling off, is the current price emphasis. Within these two trends are daily or within-day price fluctuations, reflecting the push and pull of buying and selling but signifying nothing of importance.

For example, the major trend for gold in Figure 42, situation 1, might be upward. At $250.00 per ounce, a temporary peak may have been met. A drop to $200.00 per ounce may constitute the secondary trend, whereas fluctuations of $2.00 to $7.00 per ounce about the secondary downtrend may be occurring daily.

Most strategies connected with Dow theory would tell the trader to maintain (in this situation) a bullish stance (positions) until the minor or secondary trend became a major bear trend, in which case the trader should sell existing longs and go short. Traders would examine daily fluctuations to see whether they made the secondary trend into a major one. Some use penetration criteria with long-term moving averages, and others wait for the minor trend to grow in size large enough to constitute a change from minor trend to major, as compared to minor and major trend measurements in the past. Rhea, one of Dow's followers, suggests major bull trends are reversing when succeeding bear moves are lower and the same for bull moves (e.g., lower tops, lower bottoms of moves).

Elliot Waves

Elliot wave-type methods are much more specialized. Their adherents believe that there are specific rhythms in nature and the markets that can be uniquely determined mathematically at every point in time. Unlike Dow proponents of waves—which move in harmony (minor fluctuations within minor trends, minor trends within major trends) but are not rigid and cannot be predicted in extent or time—Elliot wave theorists hold that there is a basic rhythm to the stock (and commodity) markets.

For instance, "a stone thrown in calm water sets up a basic wave pattern, i.e., the waves make a series of concentric circles. The waves are not bigger on the shore side and smaller on the opposite side; the distance between the waves is the same at any point in the circle, etc. In other words, the wave pattern set up by the stone has consistent and distinguishable characteristics. Elliot said that the (stock) market also has consistent and distinguishable wave patterns" (see note, page 148).

The basic rule of market behavior is the market moves upward in a series of three waves. An uptrend is depicted in Figure 42, situation 2. The uptrend consists of three moves up, two moves down, up and down moves alternating. A downtrend is composed of three moves, two down, one up, and again alternating. Several idiosyncrasies or modifications should be kept in mind, such as the fact that an upmove may be composed of three very short moves upward alternating with two small down moves (sort of like mini Elliot waves within Elliot waves). If the second wave up is smaller than the third, then it must be a mini Elliot wave, and the trader must perforce discount the third as part of the *real* first, extend the waves two more, and so on.

Surprisingly, the theory is based on some intriguing properties of a mathematical series of numbers, named after a thirteenth-century Italian mathematician, Fibonacci. Elliot wave theorists use only part of the series, but its characteristics are interesting enough to reproduce here (after Fraser[1]).

Fibonacci Series

This series is as follows:

$$1, 2, 3, 5, 8, 13, 21, 34, 55, 89, 144, \cdots$$

1. The sum of any two consecutive numbers is equal to the next number; that is, 3 plus 5 equals 8, 5 plus 8 equals 13, and so on.

2. Each number divided into the second above it goes twice and the left-over is the number below it, that is, 8 goes into 21 twice and the left-over is 5.

3. In music "octave" means 8, and each octave consists of eight white keys and five black for a total of thirteen. All of these are Fibonacci numbers.

4. Except for the very early numbers, the ratio of any number to the one above it is 61.8 : 100.

5. The ratio of any number to the one below it is 161.8 : 100.

6. Euclid's geometric problem as to dividing a line so that the smaller segment is to the larger is to the whole line is a Fibonacci division; that is, if the line is 21 inches long and then is divided at the 8-inch mark, then the smaller segment, 8 inches, will be to 13 as 13 is to 21.

7. In the Great Pyramid of Gizeh, the ratio between the elevation of the pyramid to its base is 61.8%, and the number of inches of its height is exactly 5,813—all of these are Fibonacci numbers.

This theory of market behavior lends itself to forecasting-type strategies. That is, if an Elliot wave is starting up, the trader can jump aboard with

[1] Fraser, James L., "The Neill Theory of Contrary Opinion," in *Encyclopedia of Stock Market Techniques,* Investors Intelligence Laboratory, Larchmont, N.Y., 1965.

the end of the wave (the fifth smaller wave) as the exit point. He may even wish to reverse positions at that point, in anticipation of a major, reversed wave starting up.

If the trader is right, the results can be quite incredulous. After all, if one gets aboard cattle long at 40¢ and each up wave has previously shown a 2¢ climb and down moves only 1¢ or less, then the net potential could be 4¢ gain or more, from start to finish. This, plus the knowledge (if the forecast is accurate) that the end (44¢) of the wave could reasonably be the start of a major downtrend, could make for even *greater* profits for the trader.

Also, additional positions and profits could be added during or at the end of waves 2 and 4, when further downside price slippage risk was minimal.

Cycle Theory

Cycle theory, represented as situation 3 in Figure 42, is a broader and more-followed market representation than are the other two wave theories.

In general, cycle adherents hold that prices vacillate in drifting markets about some general trend line in a predictable, rhythmic manner. In trading ranges or nontrended markets, prices move like a sine wave on an oscilloscope, going back and forth, up and down.

The rhythmic behavior is due to the constant imbalance of buying and selling forces, which creates surges one way or the other. The surges tend to alternate even in drifting markets, because bull moves tend to beget overbought conditions, and bear moves bring about oversold markets and ripe conditions for buying.

Representations of cycle movements run from simply drawn tangent lines under lower and higher prices of the trading range or trend, to second-order partial differential equations as sophisticated mathematical models of cyclic price behavior. In one mode of representation, frequency of ups and downs and amplitudes (magnitudes) of the ups and downs constitute the major variables to estimate. Sine-wave theory has wide applications in electrical engineering (household current—alternating current—is one simple example), but little has been done formally in investment applications.

Three trading strategies are generally employed with cycle theory. Speculators should buy (initiate a long position) when prices come close to the low end of a channel, near the predicted next bottom, and sell when prices come close to the top. In a way, this strategy is based on quality control—most prices should tend to occur near the trend line, with less and less occurring farther and farther away from the trendline. The trader should expect less price occurrence near the boundaries, and so should take an opposite stance (sell at the high boundary, buy at the low) in anticipation of prices returning closer to the middle of the chan- nel, or even toward the other boundary. Stops (close out of positions) are placed just outside the boundary.

A second trading method hypothesizes that if prices break out of the undulating channel's boundaries, then prices are headed higher (up- side breakout) or lower (downside breakout). This is based on the be- lief that the cycle model will represent the current price range or trend, and that any violation of the channel enveloped about the range or trend means a new state of being for prices—a new trend or drift is underway. The trader takes a position in this new direction when the channel has been violated and he holds the new position until a violation of the new trend envelope occurs in the opposite direction.

The third technique involves the use of predictions. Some analysts use sinusoidal functions to forecast the next set of tops and bottoms, whereas others use linearly drawn lines to do the same. The strategy used here is to buy if current prices are well below the next projected top, and sell if prices are considerably above the next predicted bottom price. The trader is essentially going for short-term profits, not holding on for long-term profits resulting from a sizable drift in prices.

CRITIQUE

This type of representation (especially cycle theory) is one of the most realistic ways to represent price behavior in financial markets. The idea of a mechanism that accurately models pulsating prices superimposed on a drifting or stationary price structure seems close to what is really happening—buying and selling forces are constantly pushing and shov- ing, creating wiggles in calm markets and sawtooths in drifting markets. The market can then be seen as having two components: (1) *major drifts* caused by sudden or cumulative events and stability occurring with the absence of major influences and (2) day-to-day *ripples* caused by local (temporary) imbalances of buying or selling forces. Commodity data seem to back these philosophies, too. Four-year hog cycles are well known, and seasonal tendencies of grains are established facts, although major events do distort the normal patterns abruptly and with heavy long-term impacts (e.g., Russian wheat deal).

Reasonably accurate forecasts for short-term behavior can be obtained. Usually predictions are made several days or weeks in the future. Errors of several percent on price are common, as opposed to 10% or 20% ones using fundamental data for long-term forecasts. Some traders trade within the day looking for cycle profit opportunities of only 1%, or 3–4¢ on grains.

Risks are more limited with cycle strategies. If prices break through on the downside from a tight channel of uptrend-bound prices, this is a warning to the trader with a long position to consider closing out and/or reverse the position. The major part of the risk involved is the height of the channel, or less if the trader got in favorably (in the lower part for a long position, higher part for a short). However, there still are major problems involved.

First, the representations are not always accurate or current. A trading range can quickly change to a seemingly trended market, and then proceed back into the trading range. Wave theorists would vouchsafe a change to trend from trading, jump aboard, and then be abruptly stopped out. Unfortunately, strategies used with wave theories have disadvantages of trend and contrary methods: (1) whipsaws resulting from trend to trading changes and (2) many or big losses from contrary sales of a large bull trend bursting out of a trading range.

The truth is, that prices don't follow cycles rigorously, uniformly, or even necessarily in majority. Prices spurt because of single or multiple events during currently stable trading ranges, which *do* resemble waves. Even more ruefully, prices don't act mostly trended or wave like—they are about evenly split in time consumed in each and bounce intermittently and randomly between traded and trending states.

Second, strings of losses can result—from much the same reasoning that showed whipsaw losses using moving average or contrary methods, for different reasons and different markets. Successive losses would result from taking trend positions with breakouts of trading range waves. Likewise for contrary positions (selling tops of waves), when trading range prices suddenly erupt in an upside volcano, producing sizable and frequent losses for shorts.

Third, theoretically good places for stops (which are acknowledgment of a wrong position and a return of prices to a former trended or trading range) are difficult to determine. Simply breaking a channel of one's own creation doesn't necessarily mean a trended situation has ended. Markets don't act as the trader wants them to. Even using mathematical statistics—*probabilities* of an event taking place—the trader doesn't know whether a break of 2¢ by wheat under its current uptrend channel constitutes a change in trend or just a fluke, a temporary selling off caused by one event, and after which prices could quickly readjust upward after panic selling had subsided.

Fourth, cycle traders often shoot for short-term profit objectives—usually small gains. They need a high degree of accuracy in prediction and batting percentage (success rate) to accumulate enough gains to offset periods when markets are turbulent.

14 Secondary Reaction Method

The question now arises as to whether there is a method to continually monitor trends to test for changes in trend direction, and which tests are not dependent on *how* the trend grows (cycle, linear, or whatever). The following describes a particular application of mine from mathematical statistics to test for trend beginnings. It fits comfortably into the trend following school of timing.

The other methods have had more to do with the primary trend itself. The trendline technique [see Trading Methods, 9] is used to determine when the current primary trend's latest prices have significantly deviated from a straight growth line. When this happens, a new, opposite trend is likely to come about, and the trader should take a position in the new, anticipated direction.

The moving average method is similar to the trendline method except that it determines when the current primary trend's latest prices are significantly different from the latest growth trend, and not necessarily a straight growth line since the start of the trend, as with the trendline method.

Contrary-opinion approaches essentially determine when the current primary trend has reached its zenith. One way is to test whether a bull trend has entered its third phase, one of speculation and rampant inflation, when prices suddenly grow at a great rate compared to previous

153

growth in the bull trend. The other approach is to determine when the trend extent is abnormally large, or larger than that experienced in the past. This too would indicate the nearing end of the current trend, if the past trend extents are a good guide. The contrarian then takes a position opposite in direction to the current trend, anticipating an early change.

Dow, and especially Rhea, however, put much emphasis on the use of secondary trends in determining primary trend changes. Rhea's technique was to view ascending tops and bottoms of successive secondary reactions as the beginning of a growth line for a new, oppositely directed primary trend. This start was thought to be a new trend, irrespective of the sizes of the two or more secondary trends.

One major disadvantage of this approach from a theoretical viewpoint is that these two or more secondary trends might be so small that they are more properly a part of the current trend rather than constituting a new major trend. In fact, one countersecondary reaction (return to the current trend) could negate all or more of the move of the two or more secondary reactions! After all, the idea of a trend is for it to be large in extent and (perhaps) time. Only if a trend is large in extent, at least, can a trader profit from it.

There is a simple but plausible way of utilizing the size information about secondary reactions to determine when the current trend might possibly be reversing to a new major trend.

The central idea is to determine what were normal and abnormal ranges of secondary reaction sizes in the past for bull and bear trends. The trader would take a position opposite in direction to that of the current trend when an abormal (unlikely) secondary reaction occurred in the current trend.

THE THEORY

The secondary trend size method, as introduced in the preceding paragraphs, indicates when a trader should take a position due to an abnormal secondary reaction.

Figure 43 is a snapshot of the theory's essence. The prices are currently in a bear trend. In the trend, of course, are secondary reactions carrying the prices upward and against the trend. Reactions 1, 2, and 3 are quite normal in size [secondary reaction (Sr)], judging from past history. Reaction number 4, however, is abnormally large. It would not normally have been expected to occur, as it had occurred very infre-

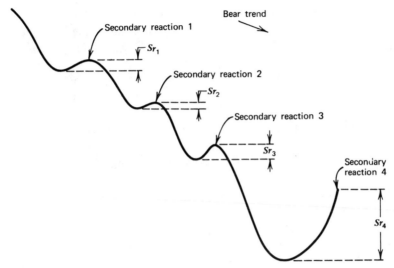

Figure 43. The secondary reaction-size method: studying secondary reactions to a bear trend.

quently in the past. In fact, in the past most occurrences of that size were part of new, oppositely directed trends. This is what would lead one to believe that reaction 4 is part of a new trend, and not part of the current trend. The trader would take a position in the direction of the newly anticipated trend at the point that the reaction became abnormally large for the current trend.

APPLICATION

How do we go about determining normal and abnormal secondary reactions?

The first step is to compile a history of secondary-reaction sizes. One does this by first choosing a basis for price measurement—every hour, daily, or weekly, for instance. Then, graph prices for every hour, day or week, whichever was chosen for the time period. Next, decide what size move constitutes a major (primary) trend—say, 50¢ in wheat, 4¢ in cattle, and so on. The criteria should be large enough for the trader to have made a decent return (e.g., at least 50%) on his capital after commissions and allowing for slippage in getting in and out (e.g., ½ cent for cattle, five cents for wheat).

Following that, successive highs (lows) in the identified trends and their companion price movements following the high (low) should be identified. The extent of reactions to the new highs (lows) should be recorded.

Next, graphs and statistical computations for these reactions should be made. Figure 44 portrays the numbers of occurrences, or frequencies, of reactions for each reaction size interval. Figure 44 pertains to wheat prices for bull and bear trends combined. For instance, in Figure 44 there were seventeen reactions in wheat that were 1¢ in size (magnitude: sign (+, −) not counted) for the period under study, thirteen reactions of 2¢ in size, and so on.

As explained in Chapter 9, we can obtain percentage cutoff points, theoretical and actual, for graphs as shown in Figures 36 and 44. The cutoff point, referred to by statisticians as *critical value,* describes the value below which most actual or anticipated values will occur. Those below this value we will call *normal secondary reactions* and those above the value, *abnormal reactions.*

This means if we specify the cutoff point or critical value separate

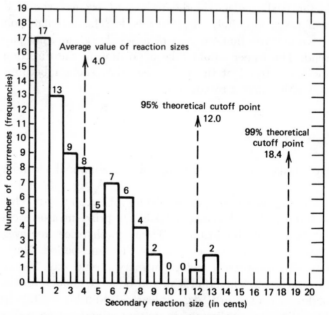

Figure 44. Frequencies of secondary reaction-sizes interval for theoretical wheat reactions (in cents), assuming 50¢ major trend size.

or cut off the largest 10% of the reaction sizes from the other 90% of the sizes, then we are specifying the 90% cutoff point, or critical value. That is, the 90% critical value is a certain reaction size value below which 90% of the values have occurred.

The critical value can be arrived at in one of two ways. Either we can manually count (starting with the lowest size reaction) in ascending order of size, the observed number of reactions, and stop when we have counted 90% of the reaction values and note the value of the next reaction as indicating the cutoff or critical value. Or we can use a theoretical curve or formula to approximate the shape and values of the reactions.

A theoretical curve (exponential distribution) was fitted to the data in Figure 44 and the critical values were calculated. These results are shown in the figure. The 95% critical value for Figure 44 is approximately 12¢ and the 99% value, around 18.4¢.

These values can be arrived at by the following formula:

Critical value	Critical reaction-size formula
90%	2.3 × average of reaction sizes (in cents)
95%	3.0 ” ” ” ” ” ” ”
99%	4.6 ” ” ” ” ” ” ”

For Figure 44 data, the average of reaction sizes is 4¢, so the 95% critical reaction size is $3 \times 4¢ = 12¢$.

The data can be raw price moves (e.g., cents) or price percentage moves (e.g., 4% drop).

CRITIQUE

This strategy has some attributes similar to but perhaps better than those of the "determining the trend" method. The two methods attempt to determine abnormal secondary reactions in a primary trend. When these do occur, a position in the direction of the newly anticipated trend is taken. The "determining the trend" method requires at least two successively higher (lower) secondary reactions, with no size criteria, whereas the secondary-reaction size method is only concerned with one secondary reaction and does require a size criterion for position inception. With respect to the size criteria requirement, the secondary reaction technique is better than the other method, as it stipulates that the abnormal secondary reaction represents in size a part of the new trend. If the secondary reaction is really a part of a new trend, then the entire extent of the new trend will be most satisfactory for trading.

The one secondary reaction, however, could be just a random, large, normal-though-infrequent move against the current trend, with a continuation of the current trend to follow. In that case the trader would be closing out a profitable position and instituting a future losing one. This is a form of "whipsaw," or the frequent reversing of unprofitable positions.

Likewise, as with many methods examined earlier, this technique does not relate events in a theoretical fashion. That is, the secondary reaction is not shown to be a specific consequence of some price and external events, a causal relationship. It is, like most methods, a statistical accounting and classification system that uses indices to measure or monitor the goings-on in the stock or commodity markets.

15 Marrying Trend and Contrary Opinion Methods

As can be guessed from the title, this particular method is a hybrid one, and straddles or belongs to both the contrary and trend schools of timing techniques.

King Arthur and his round-table friends spent a lot of time fighting for honor and high ideals; they made many a voyage in search of the Silver Chalice. Today, many still strive for perfection—in their work, sports, politics, and even (or should we say, especially) in the commodity-trading methods they use.

Have you found the perfect trading technique? One that makes good gains in trending markets and also dips and dives with sideways or undulating markets to make money in them, too? Such a find is worth more than a silver chalice—and probably equally impossible to achieve.

All traders are frustrated when their trading method works beautifully in certain markets and then turns around and bombs out in the following ones. Usually, a method that works well during trends loses in sideways markets, and vice versa. Usually.

TO FOLLOW OR NOT

From a technical point of view, there are two basic approaches to timing commodity trades. One, generally referred to as a "trend-following" technique, is predicated on the assumption that a breakout of prices from a current trading range signals a significant change in price equilibrium and an imminent move of some consequence. The trend-following trader goes with the breakout direction and stays with it until a new plateau or price equilibrium is established.

The others are often called *contrary* methods. These tell the trader to do just the opposite of what appears to be happening in the market. Contrary-opinion methods advocate taking a position opposite to the apparent consensus only when such thinking comprises a very large majority (90% or more) of current opinion. The contrary approach is based on the presumption that prices are in, and will tend to stay in, a broad trading range—price moves to the edges of this range are simply aberrations that will be corrected with a return of prices to the middle or opposite edge of the trading range. Thus it is opportune to take a position in opposition to the sudden price move, anticipating this "readjustment."

Both approaches have their good and bad points. The discussion here covers the construction, use, and relative advantages and disadvantages of the two approaches—and offer a possible "hybrid" trading plan that combines the best features of each.

FOLLOWING THE TREND

There are many ways to construct trend-following methods. All are predicated on detecting a trend change through price movement, out of either an equilibrium area or a sharp reversal from a drift in one direction to the opposite direction. Used as a basis for these methods are moving averages, forecasting formulas, filtering devices, statistical tests, and examination of price charts.

For simplicity, the moving average is used for this discussion. It represents well the bulk of trend traders' methods and is easy to construct and understand. Briefly, a moving average is constructed by first deciding on the number of days (or other time periods) you wish to average. This is denoted by N. A moving average is calculated by summing the closing prices over the past N days and dividing the total by N. When the daily closing price jumps above this value, that is a signal that prices are seeking a new plateau or equilibrium. So the trend follower buys.

Likewise, should current prices fall below this value, this signals a further drop in price, and the trend follower sells.

Referring to Figure 45, had a trader used a ten-day moving average of daily closes and the preceding simple rule, he would have made $3,800 per contract on April 1975 cattle while being short from April through June of 1974 and another $5,040 on the long side from late June to early August. However, had he started trading in mid-January of 1975, his losses would have amounted to a stinging $3,600 over 12 trades by February.

The reason for these dramatically different performances by the same method for the same commodity in different periods is the nature of the markets during these periods and how this method responded to them. In the first period there were two spectacular trends, one up and one down. The trend-following method did beautifully.

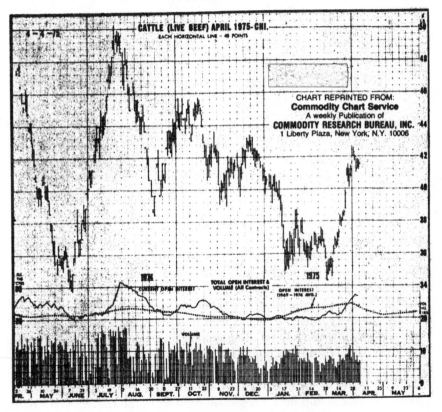

Figure 45. Price chart for April, 1975 Cattle Futures.

During the second period prices fluctuated in a broad trading range between 35¢ and 38¢ per pound. The trader got twelve lashes of whipsaw for his troubles, as prices bounced back and forth and gave "false" breakout signals on both the upside and downside.

The trend-following approach, not surprisingly, does well when there are trends to follow. It fails miserably in sideways markets. As long as there are long spells of trendless "drought" between bonafide trends, the patience and pocketbook of the trend-following trader will be strained.

ESCAPING THE WHIP

But what about those trading or sideways markets? Are there any methods that can excel in them? The categorical answer is "Yes . . . the contrary-opinion approach."

There are also many ways to fashion and use contrary-opinion methods. The one used here is relatively simple, yet is practiced by many traders. Like the trend-following method mentioned above, it has a moving average for a starting point. However, instead of taking a position in the direction of a breakout, the trader will act contrary to the obvious move.

If the daily price goes above the current moving average, the trader will institute a short sale in the belief that prices will return to the trading range from which they have just erupted. Likewise, when prices drop below the moving average, that is our signal to buy the commodity in the hope that prices will correct back up into the trading range shortly.

Using this simple strategy with a ten-day moving average of closing prices, a trader would have done well trading April 1975 cattle during the period from mid-January to late February of that year. Profits would have been $2,640 over twelve trades. The first trade would have been a short sale on January 24 (see Figure 46), reversed to go long on January 27, and then reversed again to go short on January 29.

This strategy obviously works well in trading markets. But the same method used in a strongly trending market, like that in April 1975 cattle from April through August of 1974, would have been a disaster. The initial trade would have been a long position at $4600 on April 22. A reversal in mid-May and again in early June would have netted small short-side profits; but that would have been small comfort to the trader, who would have suffered a net total loss of almost $9,200 during the period. So where is the silver chalice?

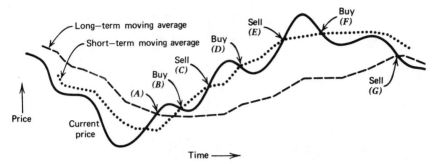

Figure 46. Composite-method trading strategy: using a short-term moving average to initiate positions under a contratrend method, but only in harmony with positions dictated by a longer-term moving-average method.

The truth is, each method is good for one kind of market and not good for the other. Is there no compromise? No "method for all seasons"? One that does at least moderately well in both trending and trendless markets?

A HYBRID METHOD

Ideally, one would like to combine the good points of both approaches, while casting out the bad. That is, the hybrid method should catch a trending market early, yet still provide some provision for selling rallies and buying dips in sideways markets. Neither method alone enables a trader to do both. But what about a combination of the two?

The strategy is as follows: Using a longer-term moving average (e.g., ten days) to represent and follow trends, and a shorter-term moving average (e.g., three days) to represent and identify momentary undulations in the market, take positions as dictated by a contrary method for the shorter-term moving average—but only when they are consonant with the longer-term trend-following method.

This strategy is depicted in Figure 46. The trader waits for the longer-term moving average to signal an uptrend (point A). He then looks for the shorter-term moving average to signal a buy, using the contrary approach. This first occurs at point B and is followed by a contrary sell at point C. At point D another contrary buy is signaled, with a contrary sell at point E. A third buy signal occurs at point F, but no subsequent sell signal appears. This is where the trader should close out his long position, however, as the longer-term moving average has flashed a sign that the current up move is ended.

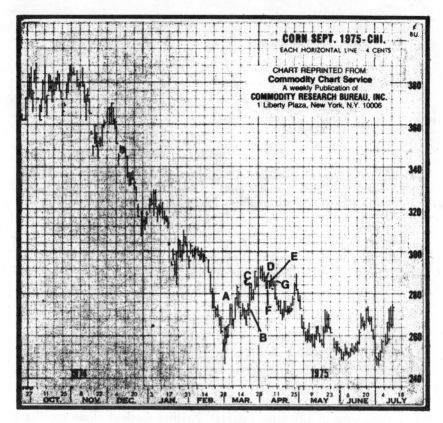

Figure 47. Chart for September 1975 corn prices.

Figure 47 is a chart for September 1975 corn. If we use a longer-term moving average of fifteen days and a shorter-term one of five days, we can see that the longer-term moving average indicates a bull market at point *A* on March 6. The shorter-term moving average signals a buy at *B* on March 21, and a closeout of our long position at point *C* on March 24. The profit is 8¢. Another contrary buy is signaled on April 2 at point *D*, with a closeout two days later at point *E*. Finally, a buy at point *F* is closed with a sell signal the next day at point *G*. A total of 10¢ profit, before commissions, was accumulated over the three trades.

During this period, corn prices seem to have exhibited partly trending and partly sideways action. This occurs often and illustrates the point of reducing losses but maintaining some moderate profits in different types of markets. A trend-following approach alone (as above) would have lost about 3¢. The contrary approach alone would have done about the same. Together, they earned 10¢.

JUNE SILVER

June silver on the Chicago Board of Trade offers another example during a more recent period when prices were particularly choppy, vacilating erratically between $4 and $4.60 per ounce (Figure 48).

An eighteen-day moving average of closing prices was set up to constitute the long-term trend; a five-day average was used for the short-term trend and for designating contrary trades when the long-term direction agreed with that of the contrary trade.

Table 9 lists the trend-contrary (blended) method trades for June silver for the period covered. These trades are also indicated on Figure 48.

The trades show a net profit after commissions of about $300 on a 5000-ounce contract. The profit sum is not particularly spectacular, but the success rate (number of successful trades divided by total number of trades) is high, almost 70%. However, gains are relatively small (10¢ the largest), and losses are as big or bigger than gains. One loss for almost $1,300 virtually takes away the advantage of a large success rate.

Two steps should probably be taken to improve the profit totals for silver (and probably for all other commodities). First, a tighter within-day stop loss should be instituted to reduce loss sizes to a tolerable level. Second, open gains should not be closed out until some temporary peak (for a bull position) has been made, and vice versa for a short position (looking for a temporary bottom).

The object of this composite of two methods is, of course, to reduce the risk of whipsaws during sideways markets but to pick up some profits in both trading and trending markets. This is done by applying a fine line of distinction between trending and trendless markets. One always assumes that there are no trends present at all, but to be on the safe side, should take contrary positions only in favor of a possible trend, as indicated by the longer-term moving average.

CRITIQUE

This assumption of no trend combined with a guard against the possibility of one has an interesting effect. During a trading market, the trader

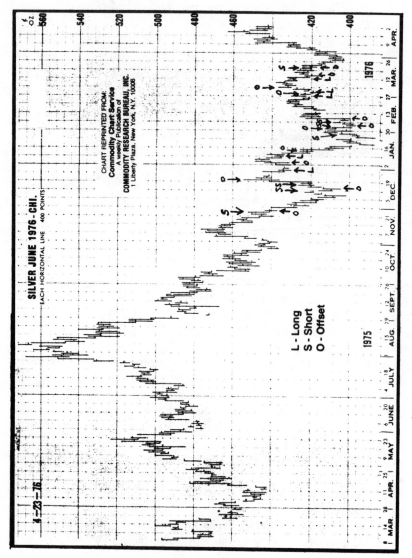

Figure 48. Chart for June 1976 silver prices.

166

TABLE 9   Profits/Losses For Trend-contrary System,
June 1976 Silver (CBT)—5000-ounce Contract

Position	Date in	Price in	Date out	Price out	Profit/loss ($)
Short	11/25/75	451.0	11/26	441.5	+435
Short	12/12	416.0	12/15	405.0	+360
Short	12/17	418.5	12/22	443.5	−1290
Long	12/30	433.5	1/05/76	435.5	+60
Long	1/09	438.5	1/13	435.0	−215
Short	1/29	407.5	2/02	410.0	−165
Short	2/03	409.5	2/04	401.0	+385
Short	2/06	408.0	2/10	400.0	+360
Long	2/27	423.0	3/01	425.0	+60
Long	3/02	420.5	3/05	431.0	+485
Long	3/12	428.5	3/16	422.5	−340
Short	3/22	425.0	3/23	421.0	+160
Totals					+295
Successes					8
Losses					4

will trade the contrary approach and make money but only about half as often as if he had traded both sides (long and short) with no longer-term moving average to act as a trend monitor. At worst, he will do about half as well as with the contrary method alone during the trading market. At best, he will do as well (or better) than the contrary method alone.

In any case, losses are small, and possible good profits abound. In a trending market, he will generally trade more often than with a pure trend-following approach and will make less profit. But there will be few or no losses.

The overall effect of this composite policy is to reduce losses considerably, but also to reduce gains to some extent. Its major virtue is the possibility of making some profit in almost all kinds of markets.

The major disadvantage with this hybrid approach to trading is that gains tend to be small (see cattle and silver examples discussed). The success rate tends to be high since trades are taken at advantageous prices (dips in uptrends, rises in downtrends) and *with* the trend. But losses can be occasionally large, and the trader needs a number of gains just to offset the loss.

16 Statistical Testing Methods

We live in a world of uncertainty, and events are only probable. A team winning a championship or just a game, a safe journey from home to office, New York City being able to pay bonds maturing next month, even the sun rising tomorrow—are all only probable to happen (some more than others, of course).

In the same vein, one should look at investment prices as highly variable and uncertain in direction or size of change (if any). That is, one can't draw lines on graphs or construct moving averages and expect that prices will certainly adhere to a charted course and will "dance to our tune." All the charts in the world and fundamental information ad infinitum won't tell us what will happen for sure tomorrow. The best one can hope for is to estimate the *probability* of something occurring.

For this reason it is beneficial to use methods for analyzing commodity and stock data and techniques that tell us something about how *likely* a fall or rise in prices is. Then strategies can be developed around this information.

Finally, the trader would like to have an objective means of determining probabilities, not a subjective personal interpretation and changing analysis. The following method tries to determine trend turning points, and so belongs to the trend following school of timing.

168

THEORY

Figure 49 depicts a string of consecutive daily closing differences for some general commodity. Differences were arrived at by simply subtracting yesterday's closing prices from today's. This gives us a direction (sign) and magnitude of net price movement overnight and through a day. In a way, it represents an indicator of present tendency for prices: heading up or down, and for how much. Traders could use weekly closings, which would smooth out or net five days' action, for a longer-term indication [but important price movement(s) could have gotten considerably underway by then]. Or use small time intervals, such as hour, half-hour, or quarter-hour price measurements (there is a danger here of having too many, meaningless changes in direction, though).

Academic treatises (random-walk studies, generally) tell us that analyzing consecutive price changes will produce little correlation between changes and hence hardly any predictability (over the long run) in price changes, using only previous price-change information (see the extensive grouping in the bibliography). Without heavily analyzing or qualifying this collection of articles, it can be seen that the results are somewhat limited; the studies generally pertain to the predictability of just one price change, given the previous change only, not all statistical methods are explored, and no examinations are made of nonrandom price-change events in an overall random market.

This last point is the launching pad for the general trend-testing methods discussed here. What if one looks for events in price changes that would rarely be found in a random market, but could signal the start of a new trend (*a drift in prices,* in random parlance)? Some of the events one spots will be random—nothing of lasting significance could result. But for the remainder, one might pick up trends (drifts of prices) that could last, on the average, well enough in the future to give goodly average profits.

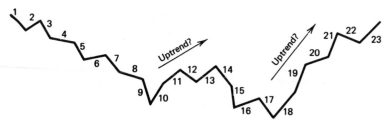

Figure 49. Dailing closing differences, hypothetical commodity.

In other words, one would look for nonrandom events in generally random markets and would expect to find more (but not much more) events that would be predicted by random happenings. Some will turn out to be just random blips, as predicted, but some will lead to sustained and substantial (in extent) drifts or total price moves.

Few would argue that there are no single set of events that strongly influence prices beyond the immediate time the event(s) become(s) known. For instance, the Russian wheat deal, both before and after the event, produced a long period of price upswing, from $1.50 per bushel to more than $6.00 over a two-year period. Inflation and drought also affected wheat prices. These events usually take a while to be completed, so the price effect is strung out over time.

In brief, we'd like to continually test prices to see whether some event(s) has (have) influenced prices significantly from a current state (trading range or trended). For instance, referring to Figure 49, prices for the commodity under study were "trending" or drifting down on balance from price-difference segments Nos. 1–9, with a few positive (upward) segments sprinkled in between (Nos. 2 and 6).

Now a string of upward (positive) price changes, with one downward (negative) price change (No. 12) occurs. Is this the start of an uptrend (a general, long drift resulting in a substantive move), or just a random collection of prices that just happened to be upward drifting momentarily? Of course, no one *can* know for sure at that point if they are or not, since we really don't know the future. Of the strings of upmoves or downmoves like this that do occur, some will turn out to be random blips, but others will turn into long drifts of prices.

The crucial question is, how many? Will there be enough of these drifts large in extent to counterbalance and show profit above the random blips, which result in no profit and mostly losses?

The natural analysis to perform is to test whether a given collection or group of price differences is suspected of being *different* from a prior collection that made up part of a downtrend (series of mostly negative price differences) or trading range (mixed set of positive and negative price differences). If the new group is statistically different (a set of price differences expected to occur infrequently, or not at all for practical purposes, in the current trend) from the prior group, which represents the old condition (trend or trading range), then we might have reason to believe a new trend is starting, with the new group comprising the first part of it.

STRATEGY

The strategy would be to continually test all sorts of price-difference groups that come along to see whether they differ from the bulk of those that constitute the current trend or trading range. When a significant change is found, a new trend is presumed to have started, and a trading position is taken in the direction of the new trend. This process is repeated until a change in the trend to an oppositely directed one is determined statistically; then the current position is reversed to an opposite one.

Literally dozens of statistical tests abound for analyzing data for statistical significance; see Owen [Testing Methods, 7] for one compendium. The tests differ mainly in computational characteristics and in assumptions about how the data relate to each other.

Two tests that are relatively simple in terms of computation but apply broadly to varying types of data are the runs of sign and G-test methods.

Runs of Sign

Refer to Owen for computations, and to Edgington [Testing Methods, 4] for theory (see Owen bibliography). Quoting, "a series of observations is ordered according to the time the observations were taken. The first differences of this series are calculated. The signs (plus or minus) of the differences are noted, and every time a sign differs from the preceding sign a run is counted." If a large number of runs is counted (like alternating plus and minus signs), then the data are rather choppy and random, for the magnitude (level) of each data is independent of that of the other data, and there is no (ascending or descending, or trended) order to the data.

If, on the other hand, the data show a string of negative signs on first differences followed by a string of positive signs (basically the data looks "U" shaped), then the occurrence of a run of 2 in a large amount of data would indicate an unusual, not expected pattern of data. This would prompt the trader to reject the hypothesis that the data were not ordered by magnitude (random price levels) and conclude that a drift upward was statistically probable. Hence a long position would be instituted.

Two qualifications should be made. First, a practical trader would probably insist on having at least two positive-sign price differences, to preclude jumping aboard a long position prematurely when only one price difference had shown positive. On the other hand, to have one positive difference preceded by six negative ones, for instance, would have only a 2.5% probability of occurring randomly and might give the trader a valid statistical signal that maybe prices were oversold and were due for a partial recovery.

Second, the trader may wish to average over several prices, to smooth out wrinkles in the data. This identifies more sharply net moves of considerable, significant magnitude that might be more likely found in a trend, but also introduces possible nonrandomness (trends) where there may not be any (see Granger, in Cootner's book [Price Models, 7]). Smoothing is often needed in data such as this, however, because of the constant tug of buying and selling that produces price changes, even in relative price equilibrium. Price changes of a 0.5¢ from one closing to another have absolutely no meaning, as it is well within the bounds of normal price behavior in an unchanged market (some trades in the day are 0.5¢ changes themselves). As an alternative or addition, the trader may wish to ignore or not count changes of less than a certain minimum move (e.g., 1¢ in the grains).

G-Test

Again, see Owen [Testing Methods, 4] for the tables and theory of applying the G-test.

This statistical technique is a bit more sophisticated in concept and computation. The trader again computes price differences. He may smooth (average) over several and/or not count minimal differences if he likes, but this method tends to handle craggy or small-change data well.

The next step is to compute the average magnitude of the differences (e.g., 2¢ for wheat). The positive value of this average magnitude (2¢) is then divided by the span (range) of magnitude between the largest and smallest difference. For example, if plus 4¢ were the largest difference and minus 3¢ the smallest, the range would be 7¢ (from minus 3 to plus 4, a span of 7). The trader would then check this value (dividend) in the statistical tables, for the number of observations (differences) made, to see what probability (1 less the "critical value" shown) it is of occurring randomly. If it is highly unlikely (e.g., .01), then he gambles that this collection of differences is not random and does constitute a new trend, different from the current one.

The philosophy of this method is that a series of like signs of price changes do not alone constitute a trend. A sequence of several small price changes of 1¢ or so in wheat would mean nothing, especially since the normal push and shove of buying and selling during a course of a day greatly exceeds that small change. However, a series of like signs of price changes of relatively large magnitude may very well constitute a non-random sequence of prices because of the rarity of sign and magnitude (like a double verification). This test also takes care of data that are widely dispersed—a large positive average of mainly positive price changes would be accepted as random if the range of differences was large (some large positive price changes, but also one or more large negative price change or one near zero and far away from the largest positive one).

In sum, the G-test checks for consistency in direction and magnitude of price changes. If a given set of price changes shows a streak of like signs and large and fairly uniform magnitudes, the method will conclude that these recent prices are significantly different from random by reason of persistence and consistency, and hence a new trend has started.

APPLICATION

Figure 50 is a graph of December 1974 wheat for the period January–June. The chart shows some very trended times when prices fell two dollars and rose over a dollar and some choppy markets when prices gave false signals to moving-average traders. Table 10 lists the closing prices of December 1974 wheat, starting on March 11, 1974, along with price differences, price differences smoothed (average over three differences), and a column for G-test calculations.

Run-test Application

If we were to use the run-of-sign test and assume that our trader had already detected a downtrend in prices prior to March 11 (downtrend started in the end of February at over $5.50 per bushel), then we would test each day's prices to look for possible reversal of the downward drift of prices, to an upward drift. First, the trader must choose a number for the (rare) probability of a sequence of price-difference signs being random, smaller than which he would reject the sequence as being random, and hence would conclude a new (reversed) trend is in effect at that moment. For this example and circumstances, he might pick 1% probability.

Next, should he work with the raw price differences or averaged

Figure 50. Chart for December 1974 wheat prices.

ones? There are advantages and disadvantages both ways. Let's see what happens with both sets of data, raw and smoothed.

Theoretically, every conceivable combination of runs—within practical limitations—should be tried each time new data (daily close) are recorded. For instance, on March 19 the raw price difference was −9½, −1½ for the day before, and so on. We should test not only the past day, day before, and so on, but back to perhaps ten or fifteen days prior, to see whether the numbers of runs in the signs of the raw differences are statistically significant, and not expected in a random set of plus and minus signs.

On this day, for instance, the minus sign recorded is the fourth minus in a row, preceded by two pluses. From Owen's tables [p. 391] this event has a probability of 8% or so, not high, but certainly not less than 1%, our critical value for rejecting the sequence as being random. In addition, the direction of the sequence at the March 19 close is down anyway, just confirming the current downward price trend.

Moving on, the next set of possible nonrandom movement in price-close differences occurs possibly on April 15, when five plus price differences in a row are noted. From the tables again, this is not quite significant, having a probability of 1.67% of occurring, not critical enough (1% is our critical value).

Again, looking for suspicious series of pluses only, there unfortunately is no next group that appears a likely candidate for starting an uptrend from that point on. This means the trader doesn't find an uptrend and must live through the rise from the $3.50 area to over $4.50, still being short.

On the other hand, if he were a little less stringent with the probability criteria, say 2% instead of 1%, then the April 15 test would show an uptrend breakout, he would go long at that point (at about $4.30), and then start testing for downtrends (test only groupings of minus signs). At no point past April 15 does the probability drop to 2% (8% is about the lowest), and so he holds onto the end of the data on June 20, when the closing price ended at 451½, showing a profit to the trader. But he had to hold his long position through an 80¢ drop, taxing his patience and pocketbook.

There were many combinations (strings of mixed pluses and minuses) with as many as thirty or so that could have been tested but would have exhausted even the fastest computer. We took a shortcut and examined only the past five to eight at every close.

If the trader instead examined smoothed data, his conclusions and positions would be different. Again, putting the critical probability number at 1% and examining the series initially for suspicious plus strings, the first one of importance the trader would come across would be four days past May 10, 1974, when the price closed at 383¼. Including that date, there were six pluses in a row, with a probability of occurring randomly of a fraction of 1%. Hence the trader reverses from a prior short position to long, at around $3.80. Almost immediately a setback occurs, with prices and differences diving. By the day before May 24, five minus price differences in a row had been recorded. This has a probability of 1.67% of happening randomly, not enough for us to reject the current drift or randomness to go short. (For purists, we could continue trying combinations of these five minuses and prior pluses and eventually get a significant probability below 1%, but practical considerations, such as overlapping and the beginning of trends, making this doubtful to pursue.) Thus the trader's position survives the dash downhill and he holds on through June 20 with a handsome profit of 70¢ or so.

TABLE 10 December 1974 Wheat (Chicago)

Date	Price close	Price difference	Three-average price difference	G-test $\|x-u_0\|/w$ (Raw differences)	G-test $\|x-u_0\|/w$ (Smoothed differences)
3/11/74	487	—	—		
	495½	+8½	—		
	496	+½	—		
	488	−8	+1		
	468	−20	−27½		
	466½	−1½	−29½		
3/19/74	457	−9½	−31		
	437	−20	−31		
	432	−5	−34½		
	444½	+12½	−12½		
	431½	−13	−5½		
	448½	+17	+16½		
	428½	−20	−16		
	414	−14½	−17½		
	409	−5	−39½		
4/01/74	399	−10	−29½		
	386	−13	−28		
	406	+20	−3		
	408	+2	+9		
	400½	−7½	+14½		
	404½	+4	−1½		
	405½	+1	−2½		
	409	+3½	+8½		
	414	+5	+9½	0.90	9.0
4/15/74	432½	+18½	+17	0.685	1.4
	420	−12½	+11		1.3 Long
	411½	−8½	−2½		
	407½	−4	−25		
	406	−1½	−14		
	409½	+3½	−2		0.4
	406½	−3	−1		0.4
	407	+1½	+1		
	427	+20	+17½		

TABLE 10—*Continued*

Date	Price close	Price difference	Three-average price difference	G-test $\|x-u_0\|/w$ (Raw differences)	G-test $\|x-u_0\|/w$ (Smoothed differences)
4/26/74	407	−20	+½		
	388¼	−18¾	−18¾		
	387	−1¼	−40		
	375	−8	−32		1.5
	375½	+½	−12¾		0.9
	367½	−8	−19½		0.9 Short
	347½	−20	−27½		
	354	+7½	−21½		
	366½	+12½	−1	2.0	
	353	−13½	+5½		
5/10/74	359½	+6½	+5½		Infinite–long
	372	+12½	+5½		Infinite
	367½	−4½	+14½		0.9
	382½	+15	+23		0.6
	383¼	+¾	+11¼		0.6
	368	−15¼	+½		
	357	−11	−25½		
	360½	+3½	−22¾		8.5
	354¾	−6¾	−13¼		1.7
	354½	−¼	−6		0.7
	354	−½	−6½		0.7 Short
5/24/74	361½	+7½	+6¾		
	376	+14½	+21½		
	371½	−4½	+17½		1.1
	366	−5½	+4½		0.7
	366½	+½	−9½		
	371½	+5	0		
	389½	+18	+23½		
	376	−13½	+9½		
	381	+5	+9½		Infinite–long
	375¾	−5¼	−13¾		
	394½	+18¾	+18½		
	401½	+7	+20½		
	400¼	−1¼	+24½		
	398½	−1¾	+4		
	418½	+20	+17		
	413½	−5	+13¼		
	433½	+20	+35		
6/20/74	451½	+18	+33	9.5	

G-Test Application

Refer to the data in Figure 50 again. Again assuming the trader looks only at possible uptrend (plus difference) events and stipulates a 1% critical probability, and looking at raw data (unsmoothed price differences), we find the first stiff test to be on the day before April 15, when a string of plus 4, plus 1, plus 3½, and plus 5 price differences occurred. The G-test statistic is computed as follows.

First, the average of the number (sum of the numbers divided by four), approximately plus 3, 4, is computed. Next, a theoretical average of zero is subtracted from this (we assume the net of price differences in a completely random sequence of pluses and minuses should be zero—for commodities, at least), and the result divided by the span of the least (plus 1) to largest (plus 5) number in the sequence, or 4.

This quotient, approximately 0.9, is checked against the G-test tables for the computation at the 99% critical-value number (the tables rearrange our probability to read 100% minus our value, 1%, or 99%) and for the number of data in the series under test (here, four). That critical value turns out to be 1.023, larger than the 0.9 we computed, so we continue to believe the numbers are random or belong to the current downtrend. No uptrend yet.

Even considering the next data, plus 18, with the series now having five pluses of varying magnitude, the G-test calculation turns out to be about 0.4, still lower than the equivalent critical value of 0.685.

The G-test for new data continues to reject any sign of an incipient bull trend, by continually accepting all other plus price difference combinations as within the possible range for random or continued downtrend markets, right down to June 20. It appears that the trader should apply the test to smoothed data, with direction.

Using Table 10 again, the first test of consequence the trader makes is the day before April 15. The G-test value for two smoothed price differences plus 8½ and plus 9½ turns out to be approximately 9, not enough to declare the recent price move a significant start on an uptrend (critical value is 15.91 for two data at 1% critical probability).

On April 15 a new computation is made for three price differences. The G-test value computes to 1.4, again not enough (2.11 is the magic number for three data). But a G-test value of 1.3, computed for four data including and preceding the day after April 15 when the smooth difference was plus 11, is larger than the 1.02 critical value in the tables, and hence the trader reverses from short to long position (at about $4.20).

A possible short is investigated three days prior to April 25, when a G-test value of 0.4 is computed for the second time. But the value is lower than the critical value of 0.685 for five data, and the long position is held.

Subsequently a short is taken after prices close at 367½, and a G-test value of 0.9 is calculated. This short is reversed on May 10 to a long position. The long is held until one day before May 24, when a value of 0.7 is computed for five preceding smoothed price difference data, higher than the critical value of 0.685 (very close, though).

Finally, the short is reversed to long when prices close at 381.

Although the trading record is not spectacular here (about break even from April 15 on), obviously improvements could be made to make it a profitable strategy. The critical probability could be tightened up (less than 1%), more smoothing could take place, and so on.

CRITIQUE

Both run-of-sign and G-test are extremely quantitative, reliable tests for nonrandomness. Only two parameter values are left to the judgment of the trader—the amount of smoothing and the critical probability for rejecting the assertion of randomness in a series of price differences. Given these two parameters, these two approaches to detecting trend changes (run-of-sign and G-test) are probably some of the most automatic, and reliable, as well.

Random blips (false trend signals) are avoided by testing how probable they would be in a random series. Only extremely improbable events in a random series would be taken as nonrandom, a signal for a drift in prices ahead. The error, as measured by the critical probability, would be small (on the order of 1% or so) for all sequences tested. Of course, false signals as a proportion of real signals that precede meaningful drifts, could be large. Indeed, my experience has shown almost equal numbers of false and real signals, with some edge even toward false ones.

The assumption on how prices act and the use of statistical tests to ferret out nonrandomness are quite close to how many people, especially academically inclined, think the stock and commodity markets act. We assume randomness until some very coincidental, highly unusual events tell us otherwise. This compels us to take a position in the direction of the unusual event's effect, with the proposition that prices will continue to drift that way, given the initial impetus and otherwise randomness in prices (i.e., prices will continue to drift one way, but not smoothly). Further tests are made to detect any major effects (trend reversal possibilities) from counterevents.

These tests do catch big moves when they occur. The 1972 Russian wheat deal affect on prices, the soybean carryover shortage the following year, the general bullish effects of inflation on cattle and silver—all were easily identified from the early and continual impinging of many bullish events during these years. One adage about investment strategies, however, is that each one has its Achilles' heel or heels. These are no exceptions.

First, the critical probability choice is subjective. Why pick 1% as opposed to 5% or 10%? As a rule, the more stringent the choice the less errors will be made in detecting events as nonrandom. If the trader makes a less critical choice (e.g., 5% or 10%), more events will be (erroneously) chosen as being nonrandom, producing more losses. Choosing tighter critical probabilities may cause the testing process to pass up significant, nonrandom events, however, and result not only in loss of a profitable true trend but *continued* loss in the current position.

Second, more smoothing differences introduces more nonrandomness and fake trends. This results in more losses and lesser profits in perfectly good trends that have continued, but the trader erroneously thought not.

Third, even if a trader has a computer to try all combinations of runs and G-test calculations from the current day back, how many should he limit himself to? Are there natural points he should stop at (such as the beginning of the current trend), and how far back do prices influence the current and following prices? The answers to these questions are subjective, too, and not easily solved.

Fourth, as for the G-test, the premium or emphasis in the test for *closeness* of data is not a good emphasis particularly. For instance, two successive price differences of plus 1 and plus 1 would have greater impact on a trader's decision to reverse to a long (uptrend) position than two successive price differences of plus 3 and plus 5, which are in anyone's lexicon more powerful beacons of upcoming bull moves than the first pair.

Fifth, a trader using a run-of-sign test could latch onto an insignificant dribble of prices upward, which showed significance on the run-of-sign test (e.g., plus ½, plus ½, plus ½, plus ½, plus ½, plus ½) but had a net magnitude change of small proportions (here plus 3), as opposed to the previous example that showed a net change of plus 8 in only two moves.

Finally, both methods are vulnerable to losing some good-sized trends. Both may show an 11% probability of the event(s) being random, not enough for rejecting randomness and taking a position because the trader had a tighter requirement (e.g., 1% or 5%). The trader's choice of reasonable critical probability really has nothing to do with this type of error—the trend is simply slow in developing, acting like random events all the way. The wheat example discussed earlier demonstrates this problem well. Some versions of both tests never even picked up the change from down drifting prices to sharply upward ones, whereas other versions caught the change rather late (after a 50¢ move from the bottom had begun).

17 Velocity and Acceleration Methods

Prior methods have dealt with patterns, forecasts, and trend testing in connection with price levels and occasionally with price changes, or direction. Not much has been written about the *way* prices move, especially with regard to the rate of movement (a strength measurement) and how that index (rate) is changing. This type of information may tell us more than just whether a price has changed and by how much, it hopefully will indicate something about the price structure as a whole, the undulating push and pull of prices. Even though prices may still be rising, is the diminishing rate of rise a clue to a top about to appear? Is a sudden price breakout from a trading area really a ground swell starting a new trend, or just a statistical fluke, a blockbuster that registers "important" on moving average, charting, breakout, and even G-test, but in reality is nothing more than a big commission house or two covering some positions?

Velocity and acceleration methods, strictly speaking, are neither trend-following nor random (no-trend) techniques. They essentially postulate the existence of groundswells and recedings of prices and are really only concerned with price behavior in the immediate future. Long-term price drifts are not assumed or predicted and hence are not trend-following approaches. On the other hand, a cause–effect relationship is assumed between a bottoming action in prices and the rise to a subsequent top. Prices do something special at bottoms and tops to indicate that a turn is about to occur, whereas random theory tells us nothing special happens at bottoms or tops, hence no predictions of where or how much prices will move from that point (bottom or top).

However, because these methods assume some causal effect and a minitrend movement (an immediate top and bottom), I would classify them as part of the second school of timing, trend methods.

About Velocity and Acceleration

Many of us probably think of a speedy aircraft when we think of velocity. The most common example, however, is the automobile. The speedometer measures the rate of movement of the vehicle, or miles driven each hour. Acceleration of the vehicle, is the measure of how fast the speed is changing (which we experience when we clomp our foot on the gas to pass another car). Similarly, physicists measure the velocity of a ball at each point it is falling down a plane, and the differences of these velocities at each point as the rate of change of velocity, or acceleration, to determine whether it is picking up speed or slowing down.

THEORY AND APPLICATION

Figure 51 capsules the problem faced by the trader in deciding as to whether a price move is meaningful and displays some underlying aspects of a price structure.

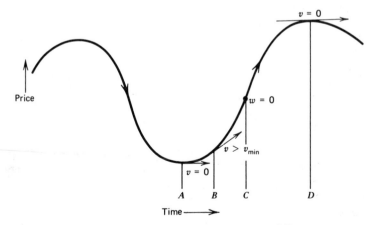

Figure 51. A continuous price model.

From mathematics, if the data are continuous (i.e., smooth), certain assertions can be made about how the data rise and fall, and at what rate. Velocity, or price differences here, slackens off at tops, firms up at bottoms, and becomes (nearly) zero at the actual tops and bottoms. Acceleration, the second difference of price, becomes positive before a bottom is reached, zero at about the midpoint of the price rise, and becomes less than zero before the top is reached.

Velocity tells us something about how strong prices are, and acceleration indicates when that strength is waning before it actually does. In other words, telltale signs in acceleration precede a leveling off of velocity at a price top.

A number of strategies present themselves here:

1. A trader can change (reverse) his position when velocity is within a small distance of zero just prior to point A or D in Figure 51. This approach assumes prices are about to round and turn (reverse direction), or at worst a plateau. Hence it is to the benefit of the trader to almost anticipate the price reversal and reverse his position before it actually happens.

2. A certain position can be taken when velocity (v) becomes large enough (greater than a preset amount, V_{min}) in a new direction, that occurs right after prices have bottomed or topped out (at point B in Figure 51). He waits for the topping or bottoming to have occurred to be sure the bottoming (topping) is at just another plateau, or rest period in the continuing trend.

3. The parameter of acceleration (w in Figure 51) can be used. The optimal strategy may be to be able to pick up a signal of prices topping or bottoming out just before they actually do. If prices are relatively smooth, this ideal situation can occur. The trader simply detects when acceleration is zero (point C in Figure 51), which detection usually occurs sometime *after* point C because of lag time (one can not act on today's close, usually, until tomorrow, or after the fact). This means his executed entry point for going short in Figure 51 would be between points C and D.

   This (acceleration near zero) usually occurs before even the first strategy can detect velocity tapering off to near zero. The trader, however, may have to sweat a bit in his short position before prices actually top out. This is similar to the contrary-opinion method of Chapter 9, except that here the trader is waiting for some real sign that prices are about to top or bottom out, according to mathematical continuity theory.

4. A fourth method involves using velocity and acceleration together, as confirmations of price topping or bottoming. The simplest tactic is to have acceleration pass through zero *and* velocity come close to zero or become greater than a minimum (V_{min}) in the opposite direction, before taking the new position.

5. Another, more sophisticated version is to wait for acceleration to pass through zero and for velocity to be at or greater than a maximum in the current direction. This latter tactic assumes that prices will reverse to down only when prices stop rising rapidly (acceleration goes through zero and becomes negative) *and* prices have been overbought (velocity is great, meaning panic or zealous buying), thus setting the stage for a plunge downward, like an oversized tomato falling from its plant.

6. Yet another spin-off of combining velocity and acceleration is to wait for sharp counterchanges in both velocity and acceleration. This means trading prices are breaking or coming to a halt fast (acceleration sharp change), or losing the stuffing in a trended direction, *and* aggressive countertrend selling or buying is coming in to *end* the trend (velocity sharp change). The combinations are endless.

For example, in the following little table car A is moving faster than car B at the tenth mile post but is experiencing less acceleration (rate of speed change) than car B. Even though it is traveling 101 miles per hour (mph) at that point as compared to 73 mph for car B, it will be overtaken by car B by about the fifteenth mile post, because it has less acceleration—a slower growth of velocity. Acceleration is calculated in this example by subtracting the speed at one mile post from the next one following, to find out how the speed is changing.

Mile Post		1	2	3	4	5	6	7	8	9	10
Car A speed	(mph)	10	15	22	31	42	55	70	83	94	101
acceleration	(mph)	—	5	7	9	11	13	15	13	11	7
Car B speed	(mph)	10	13	17	22	28	35	43	52	62	73
acceleration	(mph)	—	3	4	5	6	7	8	9	10	11

In a similar way, investors may be interested to know how rapidly prices are rising, to determine whether there is a real ground swell or demand behind the latest price action. Moreover, the prices may be rising strongly, but the trader might want to know whether the rate of rising is continuing to strengthen or is diminishing, which may indicate whether a price surge is for real (and has a long ways to go) or is soon to subside.

Velocity of prices is calculated at each measurement point (e.g., daily, hourly) by subtracting the price at the prior measurement point from the price at that point. Likewise, acceleration is calculated at a point as the difference of velocity at that point and velocity at the previous point. That is,

$$V_1 = P_2 - P_1$$
$$V_2 = P_3 - P_2$$

where

$P_1 =$ price at point 1,

$P_2 =$ price at point 2,

$V_1 =$ velocity at point 1,

$V_2 =$ velocity at point 2,

$A_2 =$ acceleration at point 2,
$\quad = V_2 - V_1.$

As a practical matter in using velocity and acceleration calculations for prices, it is often advisable to average velocity calculations heavily as the differencing of prices makes for volatile or more varied velocity calculations and is difficult to interpret. Even more smoothing is likewise needed for acceleration calculations.

CRITIQUE

The methods that use velocity and acceleration as explained earlier are simple and elegant in mathematical purity. First, prices act like continuous mathematical functions; in such cases the use of velocity and acceleration for buying and selling strategies is ideal. Second, tops and bottoms occur as predicted, and velocity and acceleration monitors can pick them up before or immediately after they happen.

Third, they have a good feeling for basic, underlying market behavior. There have been times (especially in the last two years) that grain and meat prices acted smoothly and turned almost always at every top (i.e., no plateaus or resting places on the way to continuing the current trend). Slowing up of acceleration does mean a slackening of adding power (more buying in an uptrend) to the trend, and a tapering off of velocity means countertrend forces are entering against the trend and perceive an end to the current trend.

Fourth, these methods (especially for ones using acceleration) are good for trading markets, when the grains trade in 20¢ or 30¢ ranges over a long period. Even if acceleration devices tell the trader to short an uptrend before the actual top, the actual top is not far in coming and the trader is never really out much money before the position becomes profitable.

However, the reverse can be said for acceleration-type methods in long, trended markets. Whipsaw losses result. A trader may short wheat at what seems to be a top, but turns out to be just a plateau in a long uptrend. He is thus forced to cover his short for a loss as prices burst upward out of the plateau. Also, this can happen often—many plateaus could occur in the long trend, as well as a number of errant, losing short sales taken at each of these opportunities.

Velocity methods will do better in long trend markets, but poorer in trading markets. By the time detection is made, the bottom has been made or a considerable start on the (short-lived) uptrend has taken place. The tighter the trading range (tops are close to bottoms), the more the trader will be buying nearer the tops and selling nearer the bottoms, much like moving-average methods do in this predicament.

Finally, prices are *not* smooth much of the time. Even in trading markets prices jump and make quick turns, making it tough even for acceleration methods to pick up a turn before it actually occurs. And heavy smoothing doesn't help that much: velocity and acceleration numbers flip back and forth between positive and negative values and often will tear up or down from a small plus or minus. When heavy smoothing does help, acceleration methods are no longer able to pick up signals before prices top out, but signals are pushed over (lag) in time and often reversals in position occur well after the turn.

18 Equilibrium Method

In the last chapter ideal techniques for smooth-priced markets were discussed. As experienced traders know, many markets are often times not smooth. Most of the time they resemble streaks, squiggles, and straight side moves. Methods borrowed from continuous mathematics won't work. Discrete mathematics (probabilities) better describe these markets.

The method discussed here is more an attempt to use simple detection methods with better modeling of actual price behavior than to apply more sophisticated mathematical detection and analysis techniques to poorly defined, descriptive models of market behavior. The actual method of timing used is close to a breakout-method approach, but the economic model of price behavior is different. Because the intent is still the same (to detect the start of a new trend), it belongs to the trend-following school of timing.

THEORY AND APPLICATION

The concept of an equilibrium price comes from observation of how prices tend to bounce back and forth in ping-pong fashion between upper and lower boundaries, and then move to new ground and eventually establish another game of ping-pong. This is especially noticeable in trading market conditions, but even in surging markets, where a price

burst is followed by what market practitioners call *consolidation* phases—
a retreat, advance, retreat, and so on of prices between two limits. In
mathematics, we would call this type of function a *step function,* which
acts much like staircases going up and down—straight ups or downs followed by platforms or plateaus.

Prices tend to stay in a plateau region, a price-trading area bounded
by a ceiling and floor. Significant breakouts from this equilibrium (relatively stable) area constitute a reaction to a piece of news or market
makers, and a (relatively immediate) price move to a new level will
take place, at which another price equilibrium will form. Hence, the interpretation of step-function mathematics, is of prices "stepping" from
one equilibrium to another, usually in a quick time.

Figure 52 depicts this interpretation. Prices P_1, P_2, and P_3 constitute
a series of steadily descending prices. We don't know what happens between these prices, so we assume the last two of a series of prices heading in one direction or another constitute the last known definition of a
price making area, and may soon define an area of congestion or price
stability.

For instance, P_2 and P_3 form the last known price ceiling and bottom of a price range slipping down. Sure enough, P_4 and P_5 later occur
within this range (P_2 top, P_3 bottom), giving it the authenticity of a real

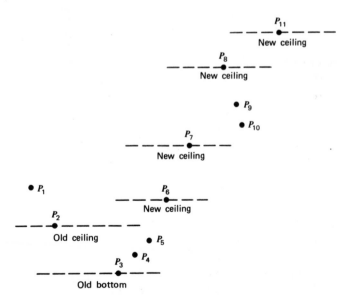

Figure 52. A discrete price model.

range. Finally P_6 breaks out on the upside of the P_2, P_3 equilibrium, forming a new (but moving) trading range of P_6 top, P_5 bottom. Then P_5 is used as the bottom of the new range because it is the latest definition of a price bottom.

The next price, P_7 forms another part of the step up and is a new ceiling for the current prices trading area, and P_6 now becomes the new bottom of the current trading area. Following that P_8 goes still higher, establishing a new ceiling to the current prices' trading range, with P_7 now the bottom. Prices P_9 and P_{10} retrace some of the price advance but trade well within the current trading area of P_8 top, P_7 bottom. This is now a new price equilibrium—prices seem to have found a new plateau between P_7 (bottom) and P_8 (top)—thus the first "step." A new trading area is established as prices head to P_{11} from P_{10}, now the top and bottom, respectively, of the new trading area.

One strategy would be to assume prices will drift far enough for an average profit in a breakout direction of a current price equilibrium (trading area). That is, when price P_6 broke out on the upside from trading area (price equilibrium) P_2 top, P_3 bottom, we believe prices will continue on the upside for quite a ways before reversing. The trader would establish a position in the direction of the breakout and hold it until prices broke out of a price equilibrium in a direction opposite to his position. In the diagram, he would hold his long established at P_6 until prices broke below the low end of the latest price equilibrium. If prices were to continue moving to higher and higher plateaus, he would hold and enjoy a good-sized profit.

An alternative would be to initiate a position when a breakout occurs as described in the preceding paragraph, but close it out once a trading plateau was established. This policy assumes prices break until finding a new plateau, at which point they could (randomly) break out in another direction from the plateau. Profits would be smaller on the average than for a holding policy (maintaining the position until a reverse signal occurred), but the success rate probably would be much higher.

AN EXAMPLE

Figure 53 is a chart of February 1975 silver, from June 3 to October 18. Table 11 lists daily closing prices for February 1975 silver, the equilibrium price range at each day's end, and an action column.

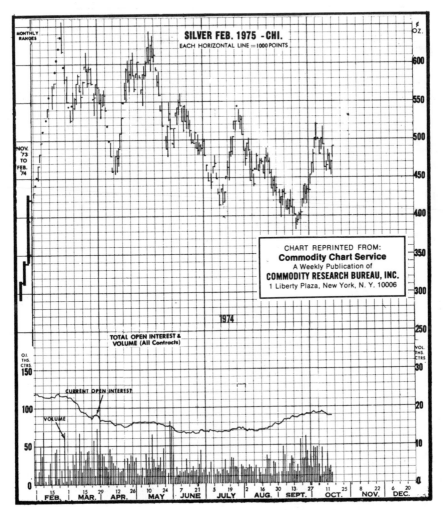

Figure 53. Chart for February 1975 silver prices.

    Three quantitative rules have to be constructed before both equilib-
rium ranges and buy–sell actions can be taken. A 5¢ penetration (approximately 1% of price level) of either boundary of the equilibrium will
be required to define or redefine an equilibrium range. Finally, a penetration of 5¢ is required for a significant breakout of either boundary of
the equilibrium, to consider for position reversal.

    Initially an equilibrium price range is defined at 495 (bottom) to

TABLE 11 Table for February 1975 Silver

Date	Closing price	Equilibrium range	Action	Date	Closing price	Equilibrium range	Action
6/3/74	495.0				461.5	″	
	515.0	495–515			478.7	461.5–478.7	Buy
	535.0	515–535	Buy		458.7	″a	
	542.0	535–542			472.5	″	
	549.0	542–549			470.7	″	
	544.5	″			455.5	455.5–470.7	Sell
	524.5	524.5–544.5	Sell		475.5	″	
	544.5	″			478.0	455.5–478	Buy
	524.5	″			471.0	″	
	530.5	″			456.5	″	
	520.5	520.5–530.5			436.5	436.5–456.5	Sell
	512.0	512–520.5			447.0	″	
	497.0	497–512			432.5	432.5–447	
	496.5	″a			437.2	″	
	509.0	″			417.2	417.2–437.2	
	489.0	489–509			424.5	″	
	486.5	″a			431.0	″	
	492.0	″			428.0	″	
	489.0	″			412.5	412.5–428	
	499.5	″			409.5	″a	
	479.5	479.5–499.5			419.7	″	
	466.0	466–479.5			411.5	″	
	446.0	446–466			420.2	″	
	445.0	″a			400.3	400.3–420.2	
	464.5	″			388.2	388.2–400.3	
	469.8	″			394.2	″	
	449.8	″			401.5	″	
	430.9	430.9–449.8			404.7	″	
	415.0	415–430.9			421.5	404.7–421.5	Buy
	435.0	″a			439.0	421.5–439	
	417.5	417.5–435			428.5	″	
	431.5	″			434.3	″	
	451.5	431.5–451.5	Buy		433.0	″	
	463.0	451.5–463			453.0	433–453	
	483.0	463–483			469.5	453–469.5	
	483.5	″			481.0	469.5–481	
	503.5	483.5–503.5			501.0	481–501	
	523.5	503.5–523.5			520.5	501–520.5	
	523.5	″			500.5	″	
	543.5	523.5–543.5			480.5	480.5–500.5	Sell
	523.5	″			500.5	″	
	526.8	″			483.0	″	
	506.8	506.8–526.8	Sell		463.5	463.5–483	
	486.8	486.8–506.8			466.0	″	
	475.0	475–486.8			479.5	″	
	495.0	475–495	Buy		461.0	″	
	486.2	″			471.3	″	
	466.2	466.2–486.2	Sell	10/18/74	491.3	471.3–491.3	Buy
	459.0	459–466.2					
	441.5	441.5–459					

a Too close to current boundary of equilibrium to redefine boundary.

515 (top). The next day an upside breakout of this occurs with a 535 closing. A buy is signaled here. The equilibrium price range now changes to 515 bottom, 535 top. New definitions occur until prices peak at 549. The last equilibrium at 542 to 549 is violated by a 524.5 closing, causing a sell signal and a new equilibrium definition of 524.5–544.5.

A long downhill slide occurs for over a month until prices temporarily bottom at 417.5–435. Two days later a buy is signaled at 451.5, a breakout on the upside and the start of a series of equilibrium redefinitions on the upside. A handsome profit of about 70¢ was realized on that first trade.

All in all, eleven trades are taken, five successful, six losing. Cumulative net profits amounted to about 65¢ after commissions, or about 5¢ per trade. There were five losing trades in a row, however, which occurred mostly in August (a period of relative congestion).

CRITIQUE

To academic pursuits, this type of model has many characteristics that conform to random-walk theory. Prices irregularly bouncing between bounds certainly are explainable by random perturbations of price about a "fair" price level. Even a "walk" or drift of prices to a new plateau is explainable by random-walk theory and is a believable consequence of major business news' immediate or prolonged influence on prices.

The strategy of leaving a position alone or staying out in times of relative trading ranges is a good one, which can cut down on individual, as well as strings of, losses. Furthermore, this method catches quick moves made to new plateaus and longer-term trends (many plateaus with no reversals), and the success rate, because of greater avoidance of trades in tight trading markets, does better than that of moving averages. Finally, stops (and reversals) are pretty close to entry prices, since they are placed at the opposite end of the equilibrium price range in which the breakout and position signal occurred.

However, this trading approach still suffers from whipsaw mania. If a trading range is sufficiently broad, and then alternating and displaced, up and down price equilibriums could result. This would mean alternate long and short positions are taken when breakouts outside of each equilibrium take place. For example, the February 1975 silver trades showed losses of 30¢, 13¢, and 24¢ in a broad trading range of August 1974.

Continuing on this point, losses can mount up as a trading range continues to stagnate. The total loss on five consecutive losses in the

August period was about 130¢, quite a lot for the ordinary trader to stomach at one time.

Choosing the breakout-size criteria can be a problem, and it is highly subjective. If the trader chooses a small magnitude, he will catch intermediate and large moves for handsome profits, but he leaves the door open to more miscues (false signals). If the breakout size is too large, he misses many whipsaws but the profitable trades diminish in size, and some will become losses, even replacing those whipsaws he just got rid of by enlarging the breakout criteria!

The best definitions for upper and lower bounds changes (5¢ change in the silver example) and the minimum spread of the range are open to question. One would like to keep the range as broad as possible to reduce chances for position reversal or closeout with minor price reactions, but must keep in mind that enlarging makes ultimate reversing of position lose money or have less profits for the last position.

19 Adaptive Forecast Method

Previous chapters have covered such diverse timing techniques as pattern recognition (charting), trend detection (moving averages, statistical testing methods), more sophisticated price models (continuous price, equilibrium price), marrying methods (contrary and trend), and even fundamental analysis. But there was a missing piece to fundamental approaches: the forecasting mechanism, given all available and pertinent data, was never really explored. They say "garbage in, garbage out" with computer applications that use inaccurate data, but what about "steak in, hamburger out"—good data with poor computer forecasts?

Most timing models assume either trends or randomness in prices and do not project in the main specific prices in the future. Prediction methods, on the other hand, do not assume trendedness or randomness in prices (it doesn't matter much to the forecaster), and *do* project specific prices to aim for entering and exiting positions.

Many forecast techniques, however, have been either too crude (e.g., drawing lines and projecting on charts) or too abstruse and not applicable (see bibliography section, "Forecasting Methods"). The most sophisticated one used by financial analysts in any number seems to be linear-regression projection. Occasionally one hears about "cyclical" forecasts, which means the analyst involved might use sine wave or related projections.

THEORY AND STRATEGY

An important school of prediction called *adaptive forecasting* came about in the early 1950s. The applications included industrial operations, space trajectories, and some business sales forecasting. See Brown for good coverage of the theory and application of the best-known adaptive forecasting method, exponential smoothing.

Essentially, adaptive forecasting is a sophisticated smoothing indicator, something akin to moving averages. In fact, in its most raw form (exponential smoothing) the adaptive forecaster is a finely tuned moving average. Whereas a moving average can smooth only over 1, 2, 3, 4, 5, or any integer number of days or whatever, the exponential smoothing index can smooth over 3.24 or 4.1765432 days, or any degree desired.

The mathematical representation takes the form of

$$S = \alpha X + (1 - \alpha) S_p$$

where

$\alpha =$ the weight placed on the latest data observation (<1), known as smooth factor

$X =$ the latest data observation,

$S_p =$ the previous forecast (smooth),

$S =$ the current forecast (smooth).

Like a moving average, the forecast tends to lag behind the data, although it bends and twists and responds to data changes much quicker. For instance, a user doesn't have to wait when he begins following prices for ten data to obtain a reasonable ten-day price smooth; he needs only two or three. Also, the exponential smoother can be used to forecast a number of data ahead, not just the next data, whereas moving averages are generally limited.

Many practitioners use the exponential predictor to indicate a *direction* of change, not necessarily a precise forecast for the next forecast. This is perhaps the most significant difference that separates the utility of adaptive forecasters from moving averages. Moving averages assume the trend of prices will continue, on the average, as either the unweighted average of the last N number of data or at least the direction indicated from first to last.

Adaptive forecasts, however, *learn* from previous mistakes. The formula for S allows that the new forecast will be influenced partly by the last observation plus a correction or addition of a part of previous forecasts.

The major problem with this represenation, however, is its inability to forecast *ahead* of the current observation. In cases where prices continue going up, albeit sometimes even at an accelerated pace, the forecast would never catch up. Ditto for plunging prices. The formula works best in moderately undulating markets moving persistently in one direction or the other.

One modification that can allow forecasts to jump ahead of current observations and yet respond accurately to undulations is to project the next data as being the current data plus a change due to the most recent pull or directional move.

Specifically, we can let a *new* price forecast be

$$F = X + (S - S_p)$$

where

F = a new price forecast for the following period,

$S - S_p$ = the change, or difference, of the current smooth price from the previous one.

Thus price forecasts will be equal to the current price plus the difference in the last two exponentially smoothed prices. As prices pull away from trading areas, future forecasts will adjust for the pull and place the next forecast an adjusted, smoothed amount ahead of the last for surging uptrends. If prices retract along the way, the next forecast will adjust for the (downwards) adjustment in smoothed differences. In trading markets, the next forecast will come closer and closer to prior prices as successive smoothed differences approach zero.

A trader can use these forecasts in several ways. The first, a standard one, is to buy when current prices are well below the next forecast by either a minimal profit amount or a small probability of prices continuing at current levels by the next time period and sell at or near the next forecast.

Second, he may wish to combine forecasts with other trend methods that indicate current drifts in progress. He would take positions in favor of the trend, with limited price objectives. Or random assuming methods may indicate to the trader that current prices relative to the next period's forecast are out of line, and should rebound, in a probability sense, closer to the next forecast.

Figure 54. Chart for February 1975 cattle prices.

Third, he may wish to apply trend-following, statistical testing, pattern recognition, or whatever, method on the forecasts themselves, as if to test for things *in the future,* before they actually occur and not after the fact. Figure 54 displays a chart of February 1975 cattle for the period April 1973 to October 1974.

Calculations for S, the smoothed average, and F, the new price forecast, for four different values of α (the smoothing factor) for cattle closing price data starting June 3, 1974 are listed in Table 12. The first value for α used in calculating S_1 and F_1 is .5, equivalent to about a three-day moving average. The next value, .333, is equal to roughly five-day moving average, and the rest, .2 and .1, to ten- and twenty-day moving averages, respectively.

As a rule, forecasts for larger values of α will move much quicker up and down and be very sensitive to data changes.

Traders who are in-and-out, primarily short-range profit hunters or day traders will wish to use larger values of α. Others who want to wait for longer term trends to develop and look for relative bargains and hold on until the trend (and forecasts) turn around, should use smaller values of α, either .2 or .1 or something close. Use of these small numbers means the investor is placing little emphasis or reliance on day-to-day price movements. We might test two simple strategies on these data.

First, for a short-term, in-and-out trader, we'll examine each day's forecast (for the following close), and if it is different from today's close, by at least 50 points we'll take a position in the forecast direction and close out the position when it reaches or betters the forecast, on following closes. A practical problem arises here in that one can not always buy or sell a commodity the next day for what it closed at the previous day. For purposes of illustration, however, we'll assume our redoubtable trader can either obtain it on today's close itself (he can obtain a list of forecasts ahead assuming various closings and place orders for the close contingent on certain prices occurring then), or on the open (he'll assume the next day's opening prices or the day's range will cross his price, which is the prior close).

Assuming he lets $\alpha = .5$, we'll then examine forecasts with $\alpha = .5$ (F_1), compared to the day's price close. Starting a day or two after June 3, 1974 (to allow smoothed prices and forecasts to dampen a bit), the first time the trader takes a position (short) is on the close (3472.5) of the fifth day. He looks for a close at 3407 or lower in succeeding days, to take a profit of 3472.5 less 3407 minus commissions.

The following day, however, prices close at 3520, well above the profit objective and even well above his entry price for the short sale position. Now, beforehand he should establish stops based on closings to protect against huge losses resulting from price rises (limit moves, even) continually against his position. We'll assume a 50-point stop, the same as his objective.

Of course, he could put a natural stop, equivalent to when he reverses position. That is, he'll hold on to a short until a buy signal (forecast 50 points or more above today's close) occurs, then reverse. For the sake of simplicity we'll still use a 50-point stop, closing basis, for the entry price.

The first trade is still held after the close (3520) on the sixth day, despite the price coming close to stopping out the position. Likewise, the objective (3407) is almost met on the seventh day, when prices close

TABLE 12   Adaptive Forecasts For February 1975 Cattle

Date	P	S_1	S_2	S_3	S_4	F_1 .5	F_2 .333	F_3 .2	F_4 .1
6/03/74	3610.0	3610.0	3610.0	3610.0	3610.0	3610.0	3610.0	3610.0	3610.0
	3630.0	3620.0	3616.6	3614.0	3612.0	3640.0	3636.6	3634.0	3632.0
	3662.5	3641.2	3631.9	3623.7	3617.0	3683.7	3677.7	3672.2	3667.5
	3565.0	3603.1	3609.6	3611.9	3611.8	3526.8	3542.7	3553.2	3559.7
	3472.5	3537.8	3563.9	3584.0	3597.9	3407.1	3426.8	3444.6	3458.5
	3520.0	3528.9	3549.3	3571.2	3590.1	3511.0	3505.3	3507.1	3512.2
	3420.0	3474.4	3506.2	3541.0	3573.1	3365.5	3376.9	3389.7	3402.9
	3520.0	3497.2	3510.8	3536.8	3567.7	3542.7	3524.5	3515.7	3514.6
	3620.0	3558.6	3547.1	3553.4	3573.0	3681.3	3656.3	3636.6	3625.2
	3720.0	3639.3	3604.7	3586.7	3587.7	3800.6	3777.5	3753.3	3734.6
	3820.0	3729.6	3676.4	3633.4	3610.9	3910.3	3891.6	3866.6	3843.2
	3732.5	3731.0	3695.0	3653.2	3623.0	3733.9	3751.1	3752.3	3744.6
	3632.5	3681.7	3674.2	3649.0	3624.0	3583.2	3611.6	3628.3	3633.4
	3727.5	3704.6	3691.9	3664.7	3634.3	3750.3	3745.2	3743.1	3737.8
	3780.0	3742.3	3721.2	3687.8	3648.9	3817.6	3809.3	3803.0	3794.5
	3880.0	3811.1	3774.1	3726.2	3672.0	3948.8	3932.8	3918.4	3903.1
	3855.0	3833.0	3801.0	3751.0	3690.3	3876.9	3881.9	3880.7	3873.2
	3955.0	3894.0	3852.3	3792.5	3716.8	4015.9	4006.2	3995.6	3981.4
	4055.0	3974.5	3919.8	3845.0	3750.6	4135.4	4122.4	4107.4	4088.8
	4070.0	4022.2	3969.8	3890.0	3782.5	4117.7	4120.0	4114.9	4101.9
	4170.0	4096.1	4036.4	3946.0	3821.3	4243.8	4236.6	4225.9	4208.7
	4070.0	4083.0	4047.6	3970.8	3846.1	4056.9	4081.1	4094.7	4094.8
	4170.0	4126.5	4088.3	4010.6	3878.5	4213.4	4210.7	4209.8	4202.3
	4270.0	4198.2	4148.8	4062.5	3917.7	4341.7	4330.4	4321.8	4309.1
	4365.0	4281.6	4220.8	4123.0	3962.4	4448.3	4436.9	4425.4	4409.7
	4415.0	4348.3	4285.4	4181.4	4007.6	4481.6	4479.6	4473.3	4460.2
	4315.0	4331.6	4295.3	4208.1	4038.4	4298.3	4324.8	4341.7	4345.7
	4415.0	4373.3	4335.1	4249.5	4076.0	4456.6	4454.8	4456.3	4452.6
	4392.5	4382.9	4354.2	4278.1	4107.7	4402.0	4411.5	4421.0	4424.1
	4475.0	4428.9	4394.4	4317.4	4144.4	4521.0	4515.2	4514.3	4511.7
	4397.5	4413.2	4395.4	4333.4	4169.7	4381.7	4398.5	4413.5	4422.8
	4497.5	4455.3	4429.4	4366.2	4202.5	4539.6	4531.4	4530.3	4530.2
	4597.5	4526.4	4485.4	4412.5	4242.0	4668.5	4653.4	4643.7	4636.9
	4697.5	4611.9	4556.0	4469.5	4287.5	4783.0	4768.1	4754.4	4743.0
	4735.0	4673.4	4615.6	4522.6	4332.3	4796.5	4794.5	4788.0	4779.7
	4725.0	4699.2	4652.0	4563.0	4371.5	4750.7	4761.4	4765.4	4764.2
	4825.0	4762.1	4709.6	4615.4	4416.9	4887.8	4882.5	4877.3	4870.3
	4922.5	4842.3	4780.5	4676.8	4467.4	5002.6	4993.3	4983.9	4973.0
	4845.0	4843.6	4801.9	4710.5	4505.2	4846.3	4866.4	4878.6	4882.7
	4945.0	4894.3	4849.6	4757.4	4549.2	4995.6	4992.6	4991.8	4988.9
	4897.5	4895.9	4865.5	4785.4	4584.0	4899.0	4913.4	4925.5	4932.3
	4967.5	4931.7	4899.5	4821.8	4622.3	5003.2	5001.4	5003.9	5005.8
	4867.5	4899.6	4888.8	4830.9	4646.8	4835.3	4856.8	4876.6	4892.0
	4767.5	4833.5	4848.4	4818.2	4658.9	4701.4	4727.0	4754.8	4779.5
	4667.5	4750.5	4788.1	4788.1	4659.8	4584.4	4607.2	4637.3	4668.3
	4767.5	4759.0	4781.2	4783.9	4670.5	4775.9	4760.6	4763.3	4778.2
	4795.0	4777.0	4785.8	4786.1	4683.0	4812.9	4799.5	4797.2	4807.4
	4695.0	4736.0	4755.6	4767.9	4684.2	4653.9	4664.7	4676.7	4696.1
	4595.0	4665.5	4702.1	4733.3	4675.2	4524.4	4541.5	4560.4	4586.0
	4495.0	4580.2	4633.1	4685.6	4657.2	4409.7	4426.0	4447.3	4476.9

TABLE 12—*Continued*

Date	P	S_1	S_2	S_3	S_4	F_1 .5	F_2 .333	F_3 .2	F_4 .1
	4595.0	4587.6	4620.4	4667.5	4651.0	4602.3	4582.2	4576.8	4588.7
	4695.0	4641.3	4645.2	4673.0	4655.4	4748.6	4719.8	4700.4	4699.3
	4595.0	4618.1	4628.5	4657.4	4649.3	4571.8	4578.2	4579.3	4588.9
	4495.0	4556.5	4584.0	4624.9	4633.9	4433.4	4450.5	4462.5	4479.5
	4395.0	4475.7	4521.1	4578.9	4610.0	4314.2	4332.0	4349.0	4371.1
	4432.5	4454.1	4491.6	4549.6	4592.3	4410.8	4402.9	4403.3	4414.7
	4332.5	4393.3	4438.6	4506.2	4566.3	4271.6	4279.5	4289.0	4306.5
	4237.5	4315.4	4371.6	4452.4	4533.4	4159.5	4170.5	4183.7	4204.6
	4337.5	4326.4	4360.2	4429.4	4513.8	4348.5	4326.1	4314.5	4317.9
	4375.0	4350.7	4365.1	4418.5	4499.9	4399.2	4379.9	4364.1	4361.1
	4275.0	4312.8	4335.1	4389.8	4477.4	4237.1	4244.9	4246.2	4252.5
	4175.0	4243.9	4281.8	4346.8	4447.2	4106.0	4121.6	4132.0	4144.7
	4080.0	4161.9	4214.6	4293.5	4410.4	3998.0	4012.7	4026.6	4043.2
	3987.5	4074.7	4138.9	4232.3	4368.1	3900.2	3911.8	3926.2	3945.2
	3887.5	3981.1	4055.2	4163.3	4320.1	3793.8	3803.7	3818.5	3839.4
	3787.5	3884.3	3966.0	4088.1	4266.8	3690.6	3698.3	3712.3	3734.2
	3887.5	3885.9	3939.9	4048.0	4228.9	3889.0	3861.3	3847.3	3849.5
	3987.5	3936.7	3955.7	4035.9	4204.7	4038.2	4003.3	3975.3	3963.3
	4087.5	4012.1	3999.6	4046.2	4193.0	4162.8	4131.3	4097.8	4075.7
	3987.5	3999.8	3995.5	4034.4	4172.5	3975.1	3983.4	3975.7	3966.9
	3887.5	3943.6	3959.5	4005.0	4144.0	3831.3	3851.5	3858.1	3858.9
	3987.5	3965.5	3968.8	4001.5	4128.3	4009.4	3996.7	3983.9	3971.8
	4087.5	4026.5	4008.3	4018.7	4124.2	4148.4	4126.9	4104.6	4083.4
	3987.5	4007.0	4001.4	4012.5	4110.5	3967.9	3980.5	3981.2	3973.8
	4087.5	4047.2	4030.0	4027.5	4108.2	4127.7	4116.1	4102.4	4085.1
	4187.5	4117.3	4082.5	4059.5	4116.2	4257.6	4239.9	4219.4	4195.4
	4270.0	4193.6	4144.9	4101.6	4131.5	4346.3	4332.4	4312.0	4285.3
	4230.0	4211.8	4173.2	4127.2	4141.4	4248.1	4258.3	4255.6	4239.8
	4207.5	4209.6	4184.6	4143.3	4148.0	4205.3	4218.8	4223.5	4214.1
	4307.5	4253.5	4225.5	4176.1	4163.9	4356.4	4348.4	4340.3	4323.4
	4380.0	4319.2	4276.9	4216.9	4185.5	4440.7	4431.4	4420.7	4401.6
	4315.0	4317.1	4289.6	4236.5	4198.5	4312.8	4327.6	4334.6	4327.9
	4380.0	4348.5	4319.7	4265.2	4216.6	4411.4	4410.0	4408.6	4398.1
	4480.0	4414.2	4373.1	4308.1	4243.0	4545.7	4533.3	4522.9	4506.3
	4440.0	4427.1	4395.3	4334.5	4262.7	4452.8	4462.2	4466.3	4459.6
	4445.0	4436.0	4411.9	4356.6	4280.9	4453.9	4461.5	4467.0	4463.2
	4535.0	4485.5	4452.8	4392.3	4306.3	4584.4	4575.9	4570.6	4560.4
	4562.5	4524.0	4489.3	4426.3	4331.9	4600.9	4598.9	4596.5	4588.1
	4462.5	4493.2	4480.4	4433.5	4345.0	4431.7	4453.5	4469.7	4475.5
	4375.0	4434.1	4445.3	4421.8	4348.0	4315.8	4339.8	4363.2	4377.9
	4475.0	4454.5	4455.2	4432.4	4360.7	4495.4	4484.8	4485.6	4487.6
	4485.0	4469.7	4465.1	4442.9	4373.1	4500.2	4494.9	4495.5	4497.4
	4390.0	4429.8	4440.1	4432.3	4374.8	4350.1	4364.9	4379.4	4391.6
	4290.0	4359.9	4390.1	4403.9	4366.3	4220.0	4240.0	4261.5	4281.5
	4390.0	4374.9	4390.0	4401.1	4368.7	4405.0	4389.9	4387.2	4392.3
	4435.0	4404.9	4405.0	4407.9	4375.3	4465.0	4449.9	4441.7	4441.6
	4497.5	4451.2	4435.8	4425.8	4387.5	4543.7	4528.2	4515.4	4509.7
	4470.0	4460.6	4447.2	4434.6	4395.7	4479.3	4481.3	4478.8	4478.2
	4537.5	4499.0	4477.2	4455.2	4409.9	4575.9	4567.5	4558.0	4551.6
10/22/74	4555.0	4527.0	4503.1	4475.1	4424.4	4582.9	4580.8	4574.9	4569.5

at 3420. His short position is stopped out on day 9, however, and also a buy signal occurs at that time (an objective at 3681 or better). This time the long trade (initiated at 3620) is closed out profitably the following day's close, 3720. Of course, we should raise the practical problem of whether he indeed could have entered the trade at 3620, which was limit up.

The third trade might have occurred that day if he had strictly followed the rules (a buy at 3720 because of a forecast of 3800), but perhaps he might have held his original long position that was to have been closed out that day, saving himself some commissions. He then would hold until the latest (and highest) forecast was met *and* no additional buy signal occurred at the same time. Pursuing that policy would have let him hold his original long at 3620 until prices closed the second time at 4170, on day 23.

All in all, there are many strategy variations using forecasts. Interesting time could be spent by the reader in going over the data of Table 12 and coming up with viable alternatives.

The second strategy, using trend-following methods on the forecasts instead of on closing price data, gives some interesting results. If we use a simple version of the run-of-signs test [see Chapter 16; namely, that three like signs of forecast differences in a row will (probably) constitute a nonrandom event], we will take a position in the direction of the forecast change. Since this is a long-range, trend-testing and following approach, we should heavily smooth to eliminate meaningless wiggles and thus unnecessary forecast changes. So we shall choose $\alpha = .1$, equivalent to a twenty-day moving average (refer to forecasts F_4). We will only initiate and reverse positions. No stops.

Applying this strategy, two like signs (+) appear after the first three forecasts, but not enough for us to go long. Starting on the eighth day a run of three plus signs in succeeding forecast changes occurs, which induces us to go long on the close of the tenth day, at 3720. Thereafter prices and forecasts move up steadily, with only a few minus sign interruptions, with the longest string being two days.

Finally, on day 45 or so (closing of 4667.5), three minus signs in a row appear, signaling a reversal of position to short. Net profit is about 950 points less commissions, about four times capital committed (margin). The short is held until day 69, when a string of three plus signs results in a buy signal at the day's close of 4087.5, a profit on the short side of nearly 600 points. The long initiated on that day is held to the end of the data on October 22, 1974, despite a few instances of runs of two minus signs in a row. The open profit is nearly 500 points in this final trade.

CRITIQUE

Forecasting methods offer good advantages to commodity trading:

1. The approaches by themselves don't assume trended or random (trading) markets and thus have greater instances for application: they can be used no matter what is happening to prices.

2. Predictors are good at catching and projecting long-trended, soaring markets. As was shown in the cattle example, either going for price objectives or longer term trends can yield goodly profits.

3. The approach is flexible. Many strategies can be used with forecasts. The trader can stipulate waiting for bargain prices, use trended tests, contrary positions, or whatever.

4. It is a totally mechanical method, removing individual interpretation and strengthening investment discipline.

5. Specific price objectives can be arrived at, and with some degree of precision or knowledge of probable occurrence.

6. Perhaps most important, this particular forecasting technique (adaptive) and my addition to it (the new forecast F as opposed to the smoothed prices S) is extremely responsive to market changes and basic, underlying movements.

On the minus side, any method that smooths and/or differences tend to distort price projections (although the proper combination of smoothing and differences would leave prices unchanged). Moreover, the trader has a problem of choosing between too much smoothing, which creates a lag in forecasts behind actual data; or too little smoothing, which makes forecasts react too violently and randomly to current, even moderate actual price changes. Finally, forecasts can often get caught in following a market past its peak, showing continued market movement in the last trended direction while current prices are rapidly changing direction. This happens no matter how current or responsive are the smooth and forecast. If markets keep alternating quickly between sharp ups and sharp downs over just a few days or weeks, the trader could experience a string of small profits and moderate to large losses.

CAPITAL MANAGEMENT

Like winning a battle but losing the war, commodity traders can experience winning trades and winning months but lose over a longer period of time, even lose most or all of it. And many are losing. But quite a few do enjoy winning moments, especially when trends abound (as in 1972, 1973, 1974), but if they had continued into 1975 and 1976, most would have lost, and substantially.

Is it the nature of the market system, the way commodities are traded (second-hand by speculators, first-hand by floor brokers), the costs involved (commission cut into about 4% of each trader's committed capital on the average), or the long-run random nature of it (prices do not seem to inflate upward over the years like the stock market, but usually bounce between fairly stable bounds)? Yes, a little of each enters in. Floor brokers do get better executions on the price of a commodity, costs are high relative to money actually invested, and random-walk theory may well describe much of general price movements over the long term.

If, indeed, the speculator on balance has no special skills for projecting trend-following prices and hence does not accumulate profits before commission, he will be killed by the cost of doing business. Each trade will lose him 4% of committed capital on the average, hence all within twenty-five trades, on the average. If he commits about a third of his capital to each trade and trades a few times a week (not at all unusual in commodities, because of quick decisions required when the investment shows a gain of 50% or 100% or an equivalent loss, on committed capital within a few days), the losses to his account could surpass 20% in a month's time—even though he basically had no losing trades! This loss figure could jump to 40% or 50% if he traded more frequently or committed more capital on each trade.

204

Nor is a highly successful timing method an assurance by itself of cumulative profits in the account. One trader's account grew from $3,000 to $52,000 in less than a month because he invested heavily and caught sharply moving and extended trends. But he lost most of it within three or four days in locked limit markets subsequent to that.

One also cannot evaluate a trading system and say that it will surely fail because it started off on a losing foot or experienced prolonged periods of losses. Many an account has come back from periods of doldrums to reach new highs. These periods of growth and decay are sporadic and highly unpredictable as to length or extent.

It takes some analysis and introspection to manage and review an account. The following three chapters address the problem of how to efficiently start, manage, and evaluate an account's performance.

Chapter 20 deals with initial and reinvestment tactics open to the commodity trader. Chapter 21 describes the theoretical and practical ways of measuring and analyzing an account's growth at any time, to tell whether it is "on schedule." Chapter 22 discusses practical aspects of simulating the account's growth with computers and reassuring examples of growth realism.

20 Initial and Reinvestment Strategies

Many traders often wonder how much capital they should start with when initiating a commodity-trading program. Naturally, with a good timing technique the account will grow upward. Just as naturally, there are bound to be periods of one or more losing trades, which will erode the account's value. Because there are no trading systems with extremely high gain : loss ratios of trades (or if so, they don't have good gain : loss *profit* ratios), significant losing periods and their effects on the trading portfolio must be taken into account.

What about these periods of losses, either of strings of losses, or combinations of losing and gaining trades that slowly erode the trading capital? How badly could these losses eat into capital? How far down, in dollar and percentage terms, could these bad spells carry the account value? Are there ways of telling how probable they could be?

And finally, are there ways of minimizing the frequency and size of these drops, by somehow dividing the capital in some efficient way amongst the various trades? Even more wishful, can these erosions be minimized and upward capital growth maximized, at the same time?

This chapter presents formulas, tables, and examples to determine how much capital a commodity trader should start with and how to allo-

206

cate his money to trades for minimizing capital erosions and maximizing capital growth.

STRATEGIES

Every commodity trader, novice or pro, has his favorite trading strategy. If he is a novice and a bit on the cautious side, he has traded "on paper" and evolved an overall trading success-percentage (3 out of 10, etc.). He has probably also computed his average gain–loss percentages per winning and losing trade.

The novice, or "paper" trader, might bask in his own sunlight secure with the feeling that his success percentage and average gain–loss percentage per winning and losing trade will compound monotonously upward. That is, until he wets his feet. Then he may learn, as has the experienced trader, that the road to riches is paved with many a setback.

The experienced trader will no doubt recall events of many consecutive, or almost consecutive, losses, even though his success percentage, or whatever, had proved out well in practice. He has learned, though, that these "flukes" go hand in hand with success: they can't be dismissed as improbable, but must be guarded against. Many traders have planned for such occurrences by investing only a portion (e.g., ⅓) of their capital at any one time. In this manner a succession of losses will not wipe them out.

Most of these capital-protection methods are rules of thumb, however, and no precise formulas have been devised to measure the amount of risk entailed with varying amounts of capital portions invested. This chapter addresses that question and presents formulas and tables for computing initial capital requirements, which will ensure with a specific probability that the initial amount will not fall below a specified amount of capital at any subsequent time. The formulas could be just as well interpreted to compute the capital requirement at some time other than the beginning of the investment, too.

For example, if the trader does not want to have his capital fall below $5,000, the tables developed here will tell him, based on his expected success rate and average loss per losing trade and his probability of capital falling to the $5,000, how much initial capital to start with. It might tell him to start with $10,000 if his success rate is 50% and average loss only $500 and he wanted only 5% chance of going down to $5,000. However, if his success rate is only 30% and average loss still $500, he might have to start with $20,000.

A further explanation is in order about the probability, or chance, that the initial capital will fall below a specified, or predetermined, amount. This is virtually the same as the weatherman saying that the "chance of rain today is 10%, so go on outside and have a picnic, there is little chance of being rained on." If he said the chance of rain was 50%, the picnicker might not wish to risk getting rained out. Some people may even wish to be more sure and require that the chance of rain only be 5% or even 1%, if they have put much work or money into the picnic activity or don't trust the state of the forecasting art of the weatherman.

The tables and formulas presented in this chapter apply to strategies of single investments (all the money is invested in each of succeeding trades) or to different mixed investments (varying amounts of money to different trades). The best strategy for allocating capital to trades for maximizing the portfolio's growth is derived as follows.

Initial Requirements

Suppose a trader would not like his investing capital to fall below a critical dollar level, C_R. This probably means the lowest acceptable margin requirements (under \$1,000 for most commodities, at present).

In either case, the trader will be investing C_0 capital at the outset, in hopes that at no point in the future will a combination of gains and losses diminish the initial capital to C_R (e.g., \$1,000) or below.

Single Investments

Suppose the speculator trades in only one commodity or plays only one trade at a time, perhaps even keeping a great deal of capital in reserve. During the investment process the initial capital committed to the trade (C_0) will be subjected to gain fractions $(1 + g_j)$ and loss fractions $(1 - L_j)$, where g_j is the fraction gain for commodity j, and L_j is the loss fraction. Both fractions are in relation to the commodity margin requirement, and both may be considered deterministic or stochastic (random) in nature. That is, the trader may have a gaining trade of 50% in which case $g_j = .50$; a losing trade of 40% would mean $L_j = .40$.

Without going into the mathematical derivation, the following formula can be used to calculate initial capital (C_0) required for sequential trading (all the money is placed in one trade, then it plus the gain or loss is put into the next trade, etc.):

$$C_0 = \frac{C_R}{(1 - L_j)^a} \tag{1}$$

where

$$a = \ln \alpha / \ln(P_j).$$

The trader need only specify the probability of the occurrence of his capital falling to or below C_R, which is α; compute or assume his probability of losing on any given trade (P) for commodity j; and calculate the fraction loss per losing trade (L_j).

Tables 13–19 give values of C_0 for varying values of α, P_j and L_j. These tables assume L_j is relatively constant; that is, all losing trades are (approximately) of the same value. For example, suppose our trader does not want his capital to fall below $1,000 ($C_R$), wants the possibility of this happening to be only 1% (α), estimates the probability of his trading system losing on any given trade (P_j) as 60%; and the loss per

TABLE 13 $C_R = \$1,000, L = .1$

	C_0			
P_i	$\alpha = .10$	.05	.01	.001
.2	$1,160	$1,215	$1,350	$1,550
.3	1,220	1,300	1,500	1,670
.4	1,300	1,410	1,700	2,200
.5	1,420	1,580	2,000	2,850
.6	1,600	1,860	2,570	4,050
.7	1,960	2,400	3,820	7,610
.8	2,800	3,850	7,875	22,075

$L =$ fractional capital loss per trade,
$a =$ probability that the critical level of capital will be reached,
$P_i =$ probability of losing on any given trade,
$C_0 =$ initial capital required,
$C_R =$ critical level of capital, below which the initial capital must not fall.

TABLE 14 $C_R = \$1,000, L = .2$

	C_0			
P_i	$\alpha = .10$	.05	.01	.001
.2	$1,370	$1,515	$1,900	$2,530
.3	1,530	1,745	2,350	3,605
.4	1,745	2,070	3,550	5,330
.5	2,100	2,640	4,420	9,300
.6	2,730	3,530	7,440	20,280
.7	4,160	6,410	17,240	71,930
.8	10,275	20,745	105,745	1,111,000

TABLE 15 $C_R = \$1,000, L = .3$

P_i	$\alpha = .10$	.05	.01	.001
		C_0		
.2	$1,650	$1,950	$2,800	$4,470
.3	2,000	2,460	3,970	7,930
.4	2,460	3,230	6,050	14,980
.5	3,320	4,770	11,025	36,630
.6	3,050	8,310	25,510	129,870
.7	10,010	20,040	99,010	1,000,000
.8	43,100	135,100	2,000,000	Indefinite

TABLE 16 $C_R = \$1,000, L = .4$

P_i	$\alpha = .10$	.05	.01	.001
		C_0		
.2	$2,040	$2,530	$4,300	$8,350
.3	2,660	3,580	7,050	16,760
.4	3,580	5,270	12,800	45,670
.5	5,475	9,150	29,940	163,930
.6	9,930	20,040	96,040	1,000,000
.7	26,180	70,000	666,700	Indefinite
.8	208,300	1,000,000	Indefinite	Indefinite

TABLE 17 $C_R = \$1,000, L = .5$

P_i	$\alpha = .10$	.05	.01	.001
		C_0		
.2	$2,625	$3,510	$7,190	$17,635
.3	3,760	5,610	14,040	52,910
.4	5,610	9,480	31,445	175,440
.5	9,970	20,000	100,000	1,000,000
.6	22,320	57,800	500,000	Indefinite
.7	62,640	312,500	10,000,000	Indefinite
.8	1,429,000	Indefinite	Indefinite	Indefinite

losing trade (L_j) of 20% (or .20 fractional loss). Then he would refer to Table 14, which pertains to loss fraction L_j of .20, under the appropriate headings, and find the initial capital required to be $7,440.

Similarly, for $C_R = \$1,000$, $P_j = .5$, $L_j = .30$, and $\alpha = .05$, we would use Table 15, and find C_0 equal to $4,770. This means the trader would not like his initial capital to fall below $1,000 with a probability of oc-

TABLE 18 $C_R = \$1,000, L = .6$

P_i	C_0			
	$\alpha = .10$	.05	.01	.001
.2	$3,625	$5,425	$13,890	$45,870
.3	5,650	9,960	33,900	200,000
.4	9,960	20,080	100,000	1,000,000
.5	21,550	49,020	454,500	Indefinite
.6	62,890	222,200	3,333,000	Indefinite
.7	357,100	2,000,000	Indefinite	Indefinite
.8	Indefinite	Indefinite	Indefinite	Indefinite

TABLE 19 $C_R = \$1,000, L = .7$

P_i	C_0			
	$\alpha = .10$	.05	.01	.001
.2	$5,370	$9,320	$30,960	$147,100
.3	10,020	20,080	99,010	1,000,000
.4	20,080	50,000	400,000	10,000,000
.5	54,350	181,820	3,333,000	Indefinite
.6	222,200	909,090	Indefinite	Indefinite
.7	2,000,000	Indefinite	Indefinite	Indefinite
.8	Indefinite	Indefinite	Indefinite	Indefinite

curring of 5%. His probability of losing on any given trade for the commodity in question is 50%, and these losses average out to 30% per trade, including commissions, figured on the margin.

If the trader doesn't want his initial capital to fall below some different critical capital amount, he simply multiplies the answer for $1,000 by the ratio of his desired critical capital to $1,000. In the last example, if he wanted C_R to be $2,000 instead of $1,000, he would double the tabled amount by 2, to $9,540.

The tables only approximate reality, as they assume losses of a constant size, which is not true with most system results. It would be more realistic to consider the case where losses were of random sizes. After constructing the appropriate mathematical expressions for the random case, and inserting data from some representative timing system's losses, these tables pretty well approximate the stochastic, or random situation.

If the trader's average loss divided by the standard deviation of these losses is less than 3 to 2, then he cannot use these tables. That is, if the losses vary greatly (e.g., 10–100%) and frequently, the tables will not hold. Needless to say, a system that has small or large average losses and the losses do not vary much, can easily be described by the tables. That is, systems that have fixed stops to keep losses on trades approximately the same or must rely on market conditions (e.g., trends to turn) to get out and have relatively small losses can use the tables and obtain accurate dollar entries.

Independent Investments

If the trader divides his capital into separate piles for each of a number of commodities but does not pool gains and losses between piles, the following equation describes how much initial capital he'll require:

$$C_0 = C_R \bigg/ \sum_{i=1}^{I} \frac{(1 - L_i)^{N_i}}{M_i} \tag{2}$$

where

$1/M_i$ = fraction of capital allocated initially to the commodity i (stipulated by the trader),

L_i = average percentage loss per losing trade, for commodity i,

C_R = desired minimum capital level (stipulated by the trader),

I = number of commodities traded.

and the N_i are solved in equations of the form

$$N_i = \frac{\ln \alpha}{\ln (1 - P_i)} \tag{3}$$

where

α = the probability that the initial capital C_0 will not fall below the stipulated minimum capital level C_R,

P_i = the probability that a trade in commodity i will be a losing one (the loss rate).

If the trader were to have equal proportions (*not* contracts) of capital in each commodity, equation (2) would reduce to

$$C_0 = IC_R \sum_{i=1}^{I} (1 - L_i)^{N_i} \qquad (4)$$

Equation (4) is just an arithmetic average of the losing fractions $(1 - L_i)$. If the trader were to use the strategy inherent in this equation (equal investment proportions per commodity), the effect would be to average his losses over all commodities. This offers some advantages, especially when there are no biases in losses between the particular investments, so that losing trades are randomly distributed among the various investments.

How does the trader use these equations? If he has equal amounts of capital invested in each commodity he would use equation (4); otherwise, he would use equation (2). He would first solve for each N_i by plugging in the specified probability level (α) that the initial capital C_0 will not fall below the stipulated minimum capital level C_R. The probability α usually ranges between .1 and .01 and is, of course, arbitrarily set by the trader to suit his purposes: .1 would mean he is rather speculative and is willing to risk the 10% possibility that the initial capital will reduce to C_R; .01 is a conservative value and means the trader wants only a 1% possibility that his initial capital will fall below C_R.

Next, he would compute the probabilities, for each commodity separately, that a trade in that commodity will be a losing one (P_i). For those traders who have systems, they will usually extract these figures from computer or other simulated runs on past data. For others, it means estimating or postulating their loss probabilities from their experience in trading.

These values, P_i and α, are used in equation (3) to compute each N_i. The calculations for N_i are then plugged into (4) or (5), depending on whether equal proportions of capital are invested in each commodity [use (4)], or unequal amounts are invested [use (2)].

For example, suppose the trader invests in three commodities with $\alpha = .05$; $P_1 = .30$, $P_2 = .50$, $P_3 = .40$; equal capital proportions in each of the three commodities; critical capital level $C_R = \$1,500$; and average losses for each commodity, respectively, of $L_1 = .30$, $L_2 = .20$, $L_3 = .35$. Then

$$\begin{aligned} N_1 &= \ln(\alpha)/\ln(1 - P_i) \\ &= \ln(.05)/\ln(1 - .80) \\ &= 8.4 \end{aligned}$$

Similarly,

$$N_2 = \ln(.05)/\ln(1-.50)$$
$$= 4.3$$
$$N_3 = \ln(.05)/\ln(1-.40)$$
$$= 5.9$$

Using equation (4) since he has equal proportions invested in each commodity $I = 3$ (commodities),

$$C_0 = 3 \times 1500$$

$$= \frac{4500}{i - .30)^{8.4} + (1 - .20)^{4.3} + (1 - .35)^{5.9}} \qquad (5)$$
$$= \$8,750$$

Pooling Gains and Losses

Many traders, especially computer oriented ones, use more sophisticated capital allocation schemes than putting all their capital (or some, with a reserve) into one trade, or splitting the money into separate piles for trading particular commodities. The more sophisticated speculator will not only split the initial capital amongst different commodities, but will also commingle funds. That is, gains and losses will be distributed amongst all the "piles."

If we further assume that the trader starts with equal-sized piles and *evenly* distributes gains and losses (he is, in effect, showing no bias toward any one or more commodities in his trading), the equation analogous to equation (4), the case of separating funds but not commingling gains and losses, becomes

$$C_0 = C_R \bigg/ \left(\prod_{i=1}^{I} (1 - L_i)^x \right)^y \qquad (6)$$

where $x = I/\ln P_i$
$\qquad y = \ln \alpha/I$

For the same data that we used in calculating initial capital requirements for the separate investment, case, equation (5) becomes

$$C_0 = \frac{\$1,500}{[(1 - .30)^{1/\ln.3} (1 - .20)^{1/\ln.5} (1 - .35)^{1/\ln.4}]^{\ln.05/3}}$$
$$= \$4,470$$

Portfolio Loss and Growth

I would most likely argue with anyone who could claim to both minimize portfolio risk and maximize return, at the same time. This is true (you can't do it) when several independent variables, like capital allocation, timing, and commodity-selection subsystems are all considered together. Usually one might pick one or more commodities that have the most potential at the time and accurately pick trend turning points. But the portfolio will most likely perform erratically, since at most only a few commodities will be traded, and this increases the variability of growth or decay on the portfolio. Likewise, a well-diversified portfolio, with a good timing system again, will get most or all of the major trend turns but will suffer from having only a small portion of funds in the big moves.

I am not considering timing systems or commodity selection [which commodity(ies) to generally trade in] systems in this chapter. Naturally, for a complete trading system, these are very important parts.

For capital allocation systems alone, however, one can use one strategy that will give the least risk (portfolio value degradation) and the most growth. From the three considered in this chapter (and they generally represent the only possible ones), the last one, pooling of gains and losses among the various commodities traded, is the best.

From an initial capital viewpoint, the separate-investments strategy (many independent, equal-sized piles are traded) needs $8,750 initially, and the pooling gains and losses method requires $4,470, the lower of the two.

Only when the average loss per trade is the same for all investments are the separate and pooling strategies equivalent in risk; otherwise the pooling method is always better. This means the pooling method is the least risky one, since it requires the least capital initially.

The reason for this is that the pooling method yields an inverted geometric return as opposed to an (inverted) arithmetic return for the separate-investments strategy. This results in a lower rate of degradation in capital when losses are incurred for the pooling method than for the separate-investments strategy.

Highest Growth Method

But this (inverted) geometric return also means greater growth when gains occur for the pooling of gains and losses method over the other two strategies. The geometric compounding of the pooling method now works to the advantage of the trader in a growing situation, by compounding faster than the arithmetic (average) compounding of the separate-investments technique.

Best Method

The best method for allocating capital to commodity trades, not considering timing or selection systems, is the pooling of gains and losses system, for reasons explained earlier. It minimizes the degradation of the portfolio due to losses, but maximizes the growth of the account in times of gains.

The practical strategy for using this method, is as follows:

1. Use formula (6) to estimate starting or initial capital.

2. Initially, split up the starting capital into N equal piles, one for each of the N commodities to be traded.

3. Keep a running account of the value of the average pile. Of course, the average pile will initially be equal to the original start capital divided by N.

4. For each gain (G_i) made in commodity trade i, add G_i/N to the running account value of the average pile.[1] Make sure commissions are included.

5. For each loss (L_i) made in commodity i, substract L_i/N from the running account value of the average pile. Again, make sure commissions have been included.

6. When a new signal occurs, trade only if there are piles available. That may sound silly, but some (including myself) follow more commodities than the piles or capital they have available.

Commit (generally) no more than the average pile's account value to the new trade. Because margins are of all different sizes for different commodities, it won't be possible to commit exactly the average pile's value to the new trade. Some discretion must be used here.

For instance, if the average pile's value is $500 and the new trade is in cattle, only one contract should be opened, since the margin may be $400. Two contracts would be too much, by totaling $800 and far outstripping the $500 average pile account value. This would give too much bias to a cattle trade: a big gain would add nicely to the account, but a big (disproportionate) loss would sour things considerably.

In some cases, good judgment must be exercised: if the new trade is in potatoes, whose margin may be $300 per contract and the average pile's value is again $500, two potato contracts should be opened rather

---

[1] Some traders may want to keep track of their average pile account value daily by figuring the equity value. Others may want to be more conservative and figure the average pile's account value based on realized gains and losses only. This latter course would not enable the trader to enlarge his account value (and initiate new trades) when equity on open trades, or paper profits, increased. But it would also tend to reduce margin calls, which calls might occur more frequently if he based his trades on open equity instead.

than one. This is because the $600 margin total for two contracts is much closer to the $500 average pile value than one contract trading for $300 margin. If the speculator traded only one contract, he would be under-biasing the trade, in which case all the other trades would have greater monetary emphasis (and probably gain or loss values).

The two trades, cattle and potatoes, now total $400 + $600 = $1000 in commitments, exactly twice the average pile's value. This is what the trader should aim for: minimize the difference between pile commitments at the same point in time, while also keeping the total committed in these new trades close to (or under) the average pile's current value.

SUMMARY

Two related topics were pursued in this chapter: (1) the way to determine initial capital needs for various types of capital allocation strategies for trading in commodity futures and (2) which of these strategies minimizes capital degradation and which maximizes growth. Formulas, examples, and tables for the three capital allocation methods were presented.

The pooling of gains and losses method was found to minimize the possible capital degradation, thus requiring the least initial capital for trading. Moreover, because of its geometric compounding characteristics, this technique also was found to maximize portfolio growth. Practical instructions about how to use it on a day-by-day and trade-by-trade basis were given.

21 Evaluating Trading Performance

The problem of evaluating the portfolio's growth when using a mechanical trading system is addressed in this chapter. We need to know beforehand the expected results for the method in question over an appropriate period of history and for a representative number of commodities. This chapter develops rules and numbers for determining when the method is performing well or badly. Other requirements for making the system perform well are also discussed. The evaluation approaches were put to the test in a particularly brutal market.

Many traders have tested mechanical systems for trading commodities over past periods in a number of commodities. Most will want to examine ten or fifteen active ones over a five-year period. And some will insist that at least 200 (independent) trades be recorded, so that average profit results are not highly biased because of one or two big gainers or losers.

DEFINING THE PROBLEM

But what about the range, or variation, of gains and losses around their averages? In practice, the trader will have varying sizes and strings of gains and losses adding and taking away from his capital. In other words, his portfolio will grow erratically (hopefully, upward). Chapter 20 addressed the question of how much capital a trader should start trading with and how best to trade after that, once gains and losses occur. But it really didn't aid the trader in analyzing the portfolio's growth.

Frankly, the trader who does not use a methodical, mechanical approach cannot really evaluate his approach and say it is doing well or badly. Many, perhaps the majority of traders, belong to this school of training—they look at a broker's recommendation, examine a news item, and draw a line or two on a chart—and then, if they haven't had a fight with their wife and the sun is shining, they will jump in and take a position.

This is not to say that a good number of these people will not be successful commodity traders. Quite the contrary, there are probably some who have an intuitive knack for picking the right trade at the right time. But there are very few of them, so most traders have to use more disciplined approaches with rational expectations.

This chapter tries to give the trader a set of rules to apply to the actual portfolio growth now, to let him know if the method is working according to his past expectations, or whether conditions are changing and his past evaluation was wrong.

The following steps outline a program for testing a method in history, developing growth numbers, and examining the method's result in practice.

CHOOSING A TEST PERIOD

Step 1. Choose a representative time period and representative commodities for testing the method in history.

As we all know the cost of living can be shown to have radically or modestly gone up, depending on the choice of a base year for comparison. Likewise, we can run into the same "relative" thinking by testing our methods on particularly volatile or calm periods of history, and on commodities that have shown 400% trend moves or little at all.

The trick, or more likely the art, here is to choose a period that not only will encompass all likely periods of volatility and stillness, and for commodities showing great, moderate, and little price swings, but in the proper proportion to future expectations. Knowing these future variables would put us a great distance on the path to total predictability. But it is possible to narrow the possibilities a bit.

For instance, frozen pork bellies and eggs will be quite volatile (pricewise) for years to come, due to the great variability of belly stocks and demand, seasonality of hogs, and, similar factors, for eggs.

We won't see light trading in wheat and soybeans in the immediate future because of the almost permanent effect of the Nixon administration in opening the doors of American produce to expanded European trade and initiation of significant and probably lasting barter with the communist bloc countries. In fact, a strong case can be made for great variability (and most likely higher prices) for all basic raw materials.

For this reason, we should choose past years for wheat and soybeans that yielded moderate to great variability, because those should better represent conditions the method would face in future practice.

In the absence of any really definitive knowledge or mild expectations about specific future markets, we should choose a past period that has a balance of calm and volatile periods, bull and bear markets, and stick to the mainstay commodities, such as the grains, animals, and produce (eggs); and international foodstuffs and basic material, such as cocoa, sugar, and silver. Some markets, such as coffee, flaxseed, wool, palladium, and hides, come and go in public favor or are too thin markets to trade in anyway. The small speculator, at least, should stay away from these smoking cauldrons.

Unless the trader will be biasing his trades consistently in one or another commodity, he should have an equal number of completed contract histories from the past for each commodity, so as not to heavily weigh the profit–loss results toward one or another commodity.

He should ensure that each commodity has at least one contract (e.g., February pork bellies) over the entire test period (e.g., 1966–71, five years). This is needed for simulating the portfolio growth, given that signals might occur in every commodity in the span of time covered by the test.

Finally, he should choose a long enough period to ensure that enough trades will be produced to give a statistically large enough sample and long enough (representative) time period for all sorts of bull–bear, mild–volatile markets. As a quick rule of thumb, five years seems to ensure both qualifications—unless the trader's method completes a trade only every six months or so on the average; then there's trouble. He is already open to a wide chasm of chance about the outcome anyway.

Step 2. **Test the method on each commodity contract selected from past history.**

For each of the commodities chosen in Step 1, determine the profits and losses (as a percent of margin) for completed trades the method would have yielded for each of the contracts of each commodity. For instance, the method may have recorded gains and losses of −26%, +15%, +70%, −62%, and +30% in 1966 July pork bellies. Be sure to record both the beginning and ending dates for each trade.

But make sure the calculations are correct. Don't fool yourself into dreaming fantastic gains. This can only hurt you when you put real money to the test, having spent a lot of time calculating the results.

Step 3. **Determine a capital allocation plan for the trades.**

Most of the time traders don't pay much attention to this part of a system. They generally commit to whatever they feel like (a hot, sure thing will command two or three times the commitment of another average trade), or in proportion to the margin required.

Unfortunately, this is a disastrous approach. Not only is the risk of loss greatly increased this way, but good gains could be inundated by small percentage losses in other commodities in which the trader has committed a larger stake of capital.

A growing number of researchers have developed approaches to capital allocations in portfolio analysis, especially and nearly exclusively related to stocks. The most famous is the Markowitz portfolio approach, which tries to minimize risk given a specified level of return desired, among various stock possibilities. However, this type of allocation approach really doesn't fit with commodities (because of holding period, risk, and return estimate requirements), and in any case is too sophisticated to pursue here (see Markowitz [Portfolio Selection, 18]).

A more suitable approach for allocating capital to new trades was outlined and examined in Chapter 20. The trader can reduce the size of overall loss to the portfolio by distributing the initial capital equally (in dollar terms) among new trades. Further, subsequent portfolio erosion was minimized and return maximized at the same time, when subsequent gains and losses were evenly distributed among new trades. For example, making available about 10% of the current equity or cash value of the account for each new trade is one plan I use for my own account.

In any case, a rational, good capital allocation system should be devised to simulate what happens to the portfolio for the gains and losses calculated for the method, for each past-history commodity tested.

Step 4. Allocate (paper) capital to trades as they arise.

Keep track of the cumulative value of the simulated account, adding dollar gains and losses to it as trades are completed in time. The beginning amount should be about equal to what you would start with in practice (e.g., $5,000 or $10,000 for small traders).

For example, starting with $5,000 and making available 10% of cash value of the account for new trades; gains and losses of +$300, −$220, +$450, +$75, −$152.50; and so on might be added in succession to the $5,000 as those trades are closed out. Most likely these trades will come from different commodities.

Thus, applying the capital allocation plan chosen in Step 2, as trades as they arise from Step 1, we might have the following sequence, from the gains and losses (mentioned earlier) of cumulative cash values of the account: $5,300, $5,080, $5,530, $5,605, $5,452.50.

The cumulative account values should now be graphed or tabled, and if graphed, preferably on semilogarithmic paper.

Step 5. Measure account growth or erosion.

There are at least two ways to measure the performance of an account. One is the standard approach: measure the growth (positive or negative; i.e., upward or downward) during subsequent fixed intervals of time—(e.g., month to month, quarter to quarter). The other is to measure the extent of erosion from the latest peak growth point. The application and limitations of each method are discussed in the paragraphs that follow.

As the growth-over-time approach is more traditional, it aims at determining the expected growth and variance about that expectation over fixed time intervals. It gives the trader an average growth that should occur, with upper and lower limits. For instance, the method might be expected to result in 8% compound growth per month, and only 2% of the time will a growth of −18% or +34% be expected to occur. Should the −18% or less monthly growth figure occur more than once in a row, or frequently over a number of months (e.g., over 5, 10, or 25 months) then the trading method should be suspect. Refer to Figure 55, part (1), for a synopsis and diagram of the approach.

The expected or average growth and the growth limits are arrived at in the following way:

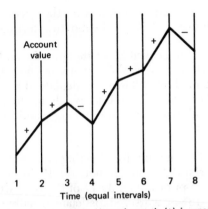

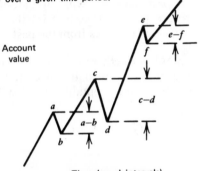

1. Growth—over—time approach. Upward growth (+) is measured over time intervals 1–2, 2–3, 4–5, 5–6, and 6–7. Downward growth (−) or erosion of the account value occurs in time frames 3–4 and 7–8. Objective is to determine expected (average) and variable growth (percent) over a given time period.

2. Erosion of the account approach. Downward growth of the account from latest peaks a, c, and e amount to loss fractions of $(a-b)/a$, $(c-d)/c$, $(e-f)/e$, respectively. Objective is to give the trader an idea of what size drops are expected and how often they will occur, and to judge whether his method is good enough, a priori or in practice.

Figure 55. Two approaches to evaluation of growth of a portfolio.

a. Choose a time period over which to measure the percentage growth of the portfolio. Usually a month or quarter is an appropriate period for commodities, as too much growth variation occurs over a span of a week, and a year is too long to wait to make a decision about the method's performance. The value could easily be at zero long before a year (even a quarter) had ended.

b. Measure the percentage growths (+) or decays (−) in the account's value, from the beginning to the end of the time period. For example, last month (if this is the time interval) the account grew (+) 30%, and this month it lost (−) 20% of the month's starting value.

c. Calculate the average (call it $\bar{x}$) of the growths and decays together. Hopefully the net average is plus; otherwise you might as well abandon the trading method. Likewise, calculate the standard deviation (call it s) for these growths and decays. Refer to a businessman's or student's statistical handbook for average and standard deviation calculations.

d. Choose a probability number for rejecting unacceptable account value growths. From prior data you will note the 1%, 5%, or 10% worst growth rates. That is, from prior data only 1% of the time would you expect a growth rate of −18% or worse. Statisticians usually choose the probability level first (1%, 5% or 10%, commonly), reflecting the chances you would expect a poor growth rate, and then calculate (as we will do), the border line growth rate for which to look. We are saying that whatever the range of past data, we will stipulate as unacceptable, growth rates in the future (in practice, that is) that are equal to or worse than 1%, 5% or 10% of worst cases from the past.

e. Calculate the unacceptable growth rate. Using the probability level chosen in (d) and the growth rate data calculated in (c), we can arrive at a growth rate that is unacceptable (G_{un}) with the following little formula:

$$G_{un} = \bar{x} - sy$$

where

$\bar{x}$ = average of growth rates (− and +) calculated in (c),

s = standard deviation of the growth rates calculated in (c),

y = constant, from the following table (we are assuming growth rates are normally distributed):

Probability level	y
1%	2.33
2%	2.05
5%	1.64
10%	1.28

f. As an example, $\bar{x}$ might be +8% per month, s could be 5.2%, and the probability level chosen might be 2%. Then

$$G_{un} = +8 - 5.2y$$
$$= +8 - 10.66$$
$$= -2.66$$

The trader would then reject the trading method if a growth rate of less than or equal to -2.66% occurred. Of course, a growth rate of -2.66% or so could occur and still mean the methods works in the future; all the probability level means is that there is only a 2% chance that you would expect a growth rate of -2.66% or worse, if the method were indeed working well, and would result in the $+8\%$ average growth rate in the long run. Perhaps if this happened too frequently (e.g., twice in a row or several times in a stretch of a year), it would seem that the account were not growing at that 8% per month, but indeed averaging much less (perhaps negative) because the -2.66% occurred so frequently and it or other low growth rates appeared to be more and more probable in the future.

EROSION DETECTION TECHNIQUE

The erosion of the account approach is a new technique in determining adequate stop losses for stocks and commodities. Once previous trends can be identified, the calculation of a stop loss to be set a distance from a trendline reference point (like closings) proceeds smoothly. Price reactions to the trend can be described accurately with an exponential distribution: many small ones, only a few big ones, and a smooth gradation in between.

And so it might be expected of an account's growth: if the method made the account grow upward in the long run, then there could and would be times of losses, a lot of little streaks of losses, and a few large streaks, with a smooth gradation in between. For example, one might expect one 30% drop from the last high growth point for every ten 5% drops and one 20% drop for every five 5% drops, and so forth.

Figure 55, part (2), depicts the gist of measuring erosions in an account's growth. Drop a–b occurs after the account's value has reached a high at point a. Further, drop c–d occurs after new top c occurs, and likewise for drop e to f after high point e has been reached.

The objective is to give the trader an idea of what drop sizes are expected from past history of his method and how often the different-sized drops will occur. This enables him to determine whether his trading method is acceptable (as far as drop sizes are concerned) on past history, and in practice.

The added information will help him sleep at night (his account is not dropping as severely as expected), or tear his hair out (his account has fallen through the floor, and it's time to dispose of the trading method in the ashcan).

The following instructions capsule the way to determine critical erosion percentages, larger than which in practice means the trading method is highly suspect:

a. Measure the percentage erosion from the cumulative account value graph tops, as depicted in Figure 55, part (2). Erosion percentages in that diagram are $(a-b)/a \times 100$, $(c-d)/c \times 100$, $(e-f)e \times 100$, respectively. These percentages will be positive. Record the series of erosion percentages.

b. Calculate the average (call it x) erosion value.

c. Choose a probability number for rejecting unacceptable account value erosion sizes. Refer to (d) for the growth over time approach, for interpretation and examples.

d. Calculate the unacceptable erosion percentage. Using the probability level chosen in (c) and the erosion percentage average obtained in (b), we can arrive at an erosion percentage value that is unacceptable (E_{un}) with the following formula:

$$E_{un} = y\bar{x}$$

where

$\bar{x} =$ the average erosion percentage,

$y =$ constant, from the following table (we are assuming erosion percentages are exponentially distributed):

Probability level	y
1%	4.6
2%	3.9
5%	3.0
10%	2.3

e. For example, suppose the average erosion percentage (x) were 10% and the probability level chosen were 5%. Then, from the preceding table, $y = 3$, and

$$E_{un} = y\bar{x}$$
$$= 3 \times 10\%$$
$$= 30\%$$

The trader would then reject the trading method if an erosion from a recent top of 30% or more occurred. Even though 5% of the time that an erosion occurred he would expect a drop of 30% or more, he is making this (30%) an unacceptable percentage because it rarely would happen if the trading method were indeed working well. It is more likely that the occurrence of an erosion of that size ($\geq$30%) means larger erosions can be expected, with probably less upward growth.

Thus it would appear likely that little or erratic upward growth could be expected, and the trading method should be tossed out. Of course, there is always the possibility that the (single) $\geq$30% drop is an isolated, though normal, occurrence with the trading method. For this reason it might be better to hang on to the trading method until several large drops around $\geq$30% occur, in a relatively small number of erosions.

A TEST CASE

Step 6. **Evaluate an actual trading system.**

There comes a time when all good theories must be put to the test. I've developed over the years a number of timing methods and fairly recently more broadened approaches, which include how much to start with, how to allocate capital to trades, and now, how to evaluate the whole system's account growth performance.

I did not start trading in earnest until I had what I felt was an adequate stake. I believed just normal loss strings for any method could severely cripple the trader's account to the point of not being able to trade the account if he started with just enough (e.g., $1,000 or $2,000 at present margins) for a couple of trades. So I started with $5,000.

I used a trend-following method for timing trades. Latest price moves were examined and tested statistically to determine whether they (as a group) constituted a significant new trend, counter to the present one. The prediction system I developed later on was aimed at predicting price ranges, going short when current prices were near the top of the channel and taking longs when current prices were near the bottom of the range.

For both of these approaches I wrote an IBM 360 simulation program, which took as input the profit and loss distributions, trade rate of success (number right out of total), time distributions for gains and for losses, and the percentage of capital allocated to each trade (I allowed compounding, or reinvesting of gains and losses). Figures 56 and 57 are the graphs of the tabled output of the program. The time unit (line) shown is one month for the trend-following method and one week for the prediction system.

The total time covered was roughly five years for the trend-following approach and one year for the prediction one. The cash value of the account, in dollars, is graphed vertically.

The graphs depict the expected growth of an account using the

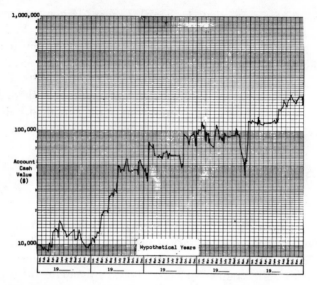

Figure 56. Computer simulation of account cash value for a trend-following timing system.

trend following method (Figure 56) and the prediction approach (Figure 57).

Note that the graphs are semilogarithmic. This makes it easy to read the percentage changes from time-to-time or point-to-point. All equal-sized upward differences measure the same percentage moves, the same for equal downward moves.

I allowed a maximum of 10% of the account's value at any given time to be invested in any one trade, for the simulation and in practice. From my own experience and studies, I knew risk (big losses) had to be guarded against. Heavy diversification in commodities really pays off, unlike the stock market, where all stocks will head down or up together (in varying degrees), depending on the general market direction at the time. Because soybeans bear no resemblance and are independent in fundamentals of silver and cocoa, really independent trades in each can work to offset losses (gains, too, unfortunately).

I then used the two methods for measuring and evaluating growth and erosion in the account to judge whether the variation in growth was acceptable before even starting to trade, and if so, to test whether the account in practice was living up to the growth standards on the upside and erosion or loss on the downside. Too big a loss in the account would force me to reevaluate whether the trading method was working at all

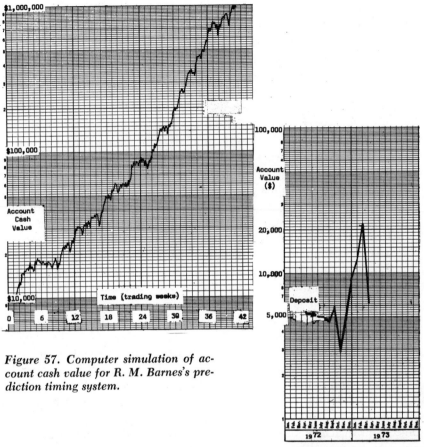

Figure 57. Computer simulation of account cash value for R. M. Barnes's prediction timing system.

Figure 58. Approximate account value—R. M. Barnes's account with Greene & Collins, Inc. (end of month).

well in the current environment and generally was living up to expectations.

For evaluation method No. 1 (the growth-over-time approach), the average growth of the account (from the simulation) per month for the trend-following method from a five-year test on ten major commodities was 6.3%, with a standard deviation of 22.6%. Assuming a 1% probability level for rejecting the trading method, the critical growth comes to

−46.4%. The growth data were read from Figure 56; the method's profits–losses from individual trades were based on Dunn and Hargitt's five-year computerized commodity price data. Refer to instruction 5 for the calculation method for growth numbers.

The same procedure was followed for the prediction timing system. The profit–loss data spanned only a year, however (and only about one hundred trades). The data base was *Wall Street Journal* daily commodity data. The average growth per week of the account for the prediction method (we use Figure 57 now) was 12.0%, with a standard deviation of 12.7%. Again assuming a 1% probability level, the critical growth figure is −17.6%. The growths were read from Figure 57.

For the second evaluation method, I computed the average erosion percentages for the two timing methods from the computer-output tables. The average erosion for the trend-following method came to 16.8%, and 6.5% for the prediction approach. Again assuming a 1% probability level for rejecting the trading method in question, I came up with unacceptable erosion percentages of $4.6 \times 6.5 = 77.3\%$ and $4.6 \times 6.5 = 29.9\%$ for the trend following and prediction timing approaches, respectively. Refer to instruction 5 for calculation instructions and examples.

The account was opened for $5,000 in late June 1972. I started trading early in July, using the trend-following method, and by September, after two listless months, the account had grown to $7,000, a 40% gain. The market seemed to sag after then, and after a series of losing trades and open trades losses, the account's cash value hit bottom around $1,500 in mid-November. Should the trend-following method have been scrapped at that point? The loss was 78% of the last top value at that time. The unacceptable erosion value was 73%, so I (marginally) decided to keep trading the method, using that evaluation. If I had used the growth-over-time approach, the unacceptable monthly rate would be −46.4%. But in no week did the account grow that poorly (the closest was around −30%), so again I decided to keep the trend-following method. Refer to Figure 58, July through November 1972, for the graphed results of the trend-following method.

By that time, however, the search was on for a better method. I felt there was too much growth variation in the account for the reward (40% growth at the highest point to that time). I came across and fell in love with a prediction system, and after briefly testing it on contemporary data (past six months), I started trading. The graphed account values from December 1972 through March 1973 represent the results of the prediction timing system on my account.

The results were spectacular and in accordance with the simulation's projection (see Figure 58). In December the account grew from $6,000 to $9,000, or 50% growth. In January it pushed up to $12,000, a 33% increase, and in February the account nearly doubled, from $12,000 to $22,000. In March it grew from $22,000 to $27,000 in cash value in the first week alone. Then there was a sudden lull before the storm.

And what a holocaust. I had bought eight contracts of May flaxseed on a dip from its high at about $5.90 per bushel, and had bought two contracts of May coffee, off two daily limits from its high of 83¢ per pound. Then an awful nightmare occurred. Prior to this time, world sugar back in 1964–1965 had set a record of seven daily limits in one direction, in a row. Coffee broke this older record with eight in a row, with virtually no trading (big sell pools). It had broken a record that stood for decades, perhaps a century.

But that was only the beginning. Flaxseed contracts promptly broke that new record a day or so later and went on to post thirteen daily limit trading days, with virtually zero sales each day. Each limit move, on coffee and flax, represents about 50% of a trader's margin committed to that position. If I had placed all my money into those two trades, I would owe the broker, in addition to losing my entire $27,000, a round sum of $60,000.

That is a lesson in diversification. Fortunately, I had only 20% total in the two trades and managed to come out of the blackness with $7,000 or so intact.

You can imagine having two record setters and wreckers simultaneously: the coincidence is something like one in fifty years times one in fifty years, or like finding the planet earth with a telescope if you happen to be lost in space a hundred or so light years away! Had I experienced just one of those record setters alone, I would still have $15,000–$16,000, a respectable tripling of the account in a little over three months.

However, even though it was extremely rare, it did happen. I can't dismiss it by rationalization. Using the erosion-evaluation approach, the loss (75%) certainly was greater than the unacceptable erosion percentage (30%) for the prediction-timing-method system of trading.

Should the approach be tossed out? I had about 100 trades during the three months or so, and two of those were the coffee and flax trades. The success rate (number of gains out of 100) was 60.2%, precisely that achieved in a paper test on the prior six months, which period had no losses equal to even a fraction of these two.

Some dilemma.

Without trying to rationalize further, it is safe to say the coincidence of these two events is very unlikely to happen again, even using the identical prediction system again (but often times are very turbulent, and several limit day strings can happen easily). As a further check, I should probably avoid thin or volatile (high frequency of limit move days) markets entirely, or if I must invest in these, commit only half or less of what I would normally commit to a position. I also have a way of keeping out of a prospective long position, until prices "bottom out."

These methods should help, but the damage to my trading pysche was great, and I was extremely timid in reentering the market in great force. And this is just as important as a fantastic timing system; if the trader cannot adhere to it (especially in bad times), then the method is no good. In this business, one must have iron nerves.

SUMMARY

Two sets of procedures for evaluating a commodity portfolio's growth were detailed and examples given.

The first approach, the growth-over-time method, was concerned with measuring and evaluating periodic (e.g., monthly) growth percentages of the account. If the growth for one or more periods was found to be below a preset amount, the continued usefulness of the trading system employed was suspect.

The second method, the erosion of the account-value approach, was aimed at measuring and evaluating the drop in value that occurs between new peaks in the account-value's growth. If the drop were larger than a preset (precalculated) value, then the trading system again might be suspect.

The calculation of the preset drop value or growth value in these two approaches is arrived at by using the simulated profits and losses over representative commodities and periods in the past and a capital allocation plan to simulate a hypothetical account's growth and decay over an appropriate stretch of time.

22 Account Growth Simulation

Once you've started investing (whether in stocks, commodities, currencies, or whatever), what do you expect your account's equity to do? Should it grow straight up? Bounce around and stay just at or under the starting amount for a long period? Or lose steadily and never get above the starting line but get worse and worse each month?

A computer simulation of account growth can answer these questions. The real answer depends on what historical data is put into a growth simulation. A computer-simulation program takes an input historical data on trade success rate, gain and loss sizes, amounts of capital to be committed to each trade, reinvestment percentages for growing accounts, and so on. It then "randomly" generates successful or unsuccessful trades and adds or subtracts the gain or loss to the current account size to arrive at the new one. The investor can then follow the process of the account as it gains and loses on trades.

COIN-FLIP EXAMPLE

For instance, if you flipped a coin, what results would you expect? A head followed by a tail, followed by a head, then a tail, and so on (or vice versa)? No. The fact is, you would probably have more likely the following: a head, tail, tail, head, head, tail, head, head, head, tail, head, tail, tail, tail—a series of *streaks* of heads and tails. Overall, the average number of tails and heads should be equal after a large number of tosses. This does *not* mean the cumulative amounts will stay equal or very nearly so—only that the net number of heads over tails or vice versa will wander up and down, frequently being equal.

Confusing? Let's look at Table 20 output for a coin flip. Let's also pretend it's a trading account, that each head means a gain of $5, each tail a loss of $5, 50% of gain over $50 are reinvested, and away we go. Trade No. 1 shows a gain after the computer randomly picks between a gain and loss. So the investor now has $100 (starting money) plus $5 first gain. Refer to column 5 for the account's size after each trade's results. Trade No. 2 is another gain, so the investor now has $110 in his account. And so on. Trade No. 4 shows a loss (−1, col. 2), making the account $110. By trade No. 18, he has amassed an account value of $150, an amazing streak of gains. The account continues to flip-flop up and down thereafter (mostly down) until it hits a peak on trade No. 66 at $175. Sounds like a lot of stocks you know?

From there on, everything is downhill. The account reads $62.50 after 150 trades! Quite a reversal for the unfortunate investor. Refer to Figure 59 for a graphical representation of the coin-flip simulation.

But he should have *expected* results like this (not so drastic, perhaps). Because a coin flip is an equal head–tail probability, no one should reasonably expect a steady uphill march of heads. An onslaught of tails is *bound* to bring the account back down to the starting point, and below it, too. On the other hand, our hapless investor should not expect all downhill, either, as the reverse reasoning applies equally (account must come back up to starting line, and above).

MORALS OF THE COIN-FLIP TALE

What are the morals of the tale? First, you should *not* infer from short-term results what will happen later on (in the beginning, that heads—profits—would continue upward). Second, don't be unreasonable and expect narrow results—that heads and tails will strictly alternate (hence the account stays almost exactly on the starting line, forever).

In the first case, you *will* have streaks of heads and tails—but don't think profits or losses will continue in one direction. As for the second, please *do* expect streaks of gains and losses—these are meaningless, as the account (not heads and tails) will wander away from the starting

TABLE 20 Coin-flip Simulation

ACCOUNT (CASH) GROWTH SIMULATION

GAIN FRACTION, NO. CELLS, TOTAL TRADES: .5, 10, 150
INVESTMENT COMMITTED FRACTION, EQUITY STEP SIZE FRACTION, EQUITY STEP
COMMITTED FRACTION: 1, .5, .5

GAIN CELL AVERAGE SIZES: .5, .5, .5, .5, .5, .5, .5, .5, .5, .5

LOSS CELL AVERAGE SIZES: .5, .5, .5, .5, .5, .5, .5, .5, .5, .5

NO. TRADES, GAIN (LOSS), GAIN SIZE, INVESTMENT COMMITTED, EQUITY, NEXT GOAL, NEXT BASE, RANDOM NO.

NO. TRADES	GAIN (LOSS)	GAIN SIZE	INVESTMENT COMMITTED	EQUITY	NEXT GOAL	NEXT BASE	RANDOM NO.
1	1	.500	10	105.0	150.0	100.0	.663
2	1	.500	10	110.0	150.0	100.0	.197
3	1	.500	10	115.0	150.0	100.0	.258
4	−1	.500	10	110.0	150.0	100.0	.478
5	−1	.500	10	105.0	150.0	100.0	.298
6	1	.500	10	110.0	150.0	100.0	.046
7	1	.500	10	115.0	150.0	100.0	.306
8	1	.500	10	120.0	150.0	100.0	.105
9	−1	.500	10	115.0	150.0	100.0	.375
10	−1	.500	10	110.0	150.0	100.0	.611
11	1	.500	10	115.0	150.0	100.0	.722
12	1	.500	10	120.0	150.0	100.0	.082
13	1	.500	10	125.0	150.0	100.0	.618
14	1	.500	10	130.0	150.0	100.0	.828
15	1	.500	10	135.0	150.0	100.0	.204
16	1	.500	10	140.0	150.0	100.0	.620
17	1	.500	10	145.0	150.0	100.0	.030
18	1	.500	10	150.0	225.0	125.0	.176
19	−1	.500	12	143.7	225.0	125.0	.394
20	−1	.500	12	137.5	225.0	125.0	.246
21	1	.500	12	143.7	225.0	125.0	.798
22	−1	.500	12	137.5	225.0	125.0	.420
23	−1	.500	12	131.2	225.0	125.0	.517
24	−1	.500	12	125.0	225.0	125.0	.035
25	−1	.500	12	118.7	225.0	125.0	.593
26	1	.500	12	125.0	225.0	125.0	.541
27	1	.500	12	131.2	225.0	125.0	.241
28	1	.500	12	137.5	225.0	125.0	.999
29	1	.500	12	143.7	225.0	125.0	.116
30	−1	.500	12	137.5	225.0	125.0	.410
31	1	.500	12	143.7	225.0	125.0	.113
32	−1	.500	12	137.5	225.0	125.0	.435
33	−1	.500	12	131.2	225.0	125.0	.016
34	1	.500	12	137.5	225.0	125.0	.337
35	1	.500	12	143.7	225.0	125.0	.903
36	1	.500	12	150.0	225.0	125.0	.217

TABLE 20 *(Continued)*

37	−1	.500	12	143.7	225.0	125.0	.096
38	−1	.500	12	137.5	225.0	125.0	.578
39	−1	.500	12	131.2	225.0	125.0	.751
40	1	.500	12	137.5	225.0	125.0	.838
41	1	.500	12	143.7	225.0	125.0	.560
42	1	.500	12	150.0	225.0	125.0	.851
43	−1	.500	12	143.7	225.0	125.0	.846
44	−1	.500	12	137.5	225.0	125.0	.220
45	1	.500	12	143.7	225.0	125.0	.593
46	1	.500	12	150.0	225.0	125.0	.846
47	−1	.500	12	143.7	225.0	125.0	.022
48	1	.500	12	150.0	225.0	125.0	.163
49	1	.500	12	156.2	225.0	125.0	.421
50	−1	.500	12	150.0	225.0	125.0	.633
51	−1	.500	12	143.7	225.0	125.0	.874
52	−1	.500	12	137.5	225.0	125.0	.335
53	1	.500	12	143.7	225.0	125.0	.404
54	1	.500	12	150.0	225.0	125.0	.535
55	1	.500	12	156.2	225.0	125.0	.749
56	1	.500	12	162.5	225.0	125.0	.058
57	−1	.500	12	156.2	225.0	125.0	.499
58	1	.500	12	162.5	225.0	125.0	.732
59	1	.500	12	168.7	225.0	125.0	.631
60	−1	.500	12	162.5	225.0	125.0	.392
61	−1	.500	12	156.2	225.0	125.0	.607
62	1	.500	12	162.5	225.0	125.0	.749
63	1	.500	12	168.7	225.0	125.0	.470
64	−1	.500	12	162.5	225.0	125.0	.591
65	1	.500	12	168.7	225.0	125.0	.375
68	−1	.500	12	162.5	225.0	125.0	.447
69	1	.500	12	168.7	225.0	125.0	.047
70	−1	.500	12	162.5	225.0	125.0	.094
71	−1	.500	12	156.2	225.0	125.0	.460
72	1	.500	12	150.0	225.0	125.0	.252
73	1	.500	12	156.2	225.0	125.0	.842
74	−1	.500	12	150.0	225.0	125.0	.940
75	−1	.500	12	143.7	225.0	125.0	.765
76	1	.500	12	137.5	225.0	125.0	.528
77	−1	.500	12	131.2	225.0	125.0	.714
78	−1	.500	12	125.0	225.0	125.0	.719
79	−1	.500	12	118.7	225.0	125.0	.818
80	1	.500	12	125.0	225.0	125.0	.264
81	−1	.500	12	118.7	225.0	125.0	.737
82	1	.500	12	125.0	225.0	125.0	.986
83	1	.500	12	131.2	225.0	125.0	.323
84	−1	.500	12	125.0	225.0	125.0	.133
85	1	.500	12	131.2	225.0	125.0	.807
86	1	.500	12	137.5	225.0	125.0	.345
87	−1	.500	12	131.2	225.0	125.0	.855
88	−1	.500	12	125.0	225.0	125.0	.635
89	−1	.500	12	118.7	225.0	125.0	.920
90	1	.500	12	125.0	225.0	125.0	.322
91	−1	.500	12	118.7	225.0	125.0	.973
92	−1	.500	12	112.5	225.0	125.0	.376
93	1	.500	12	118.7	225.0	125.0	.396
94	−1	.500	12	112.5	225.0	125.0	.225
95	1	.500	12	118.7	225.0	125.0	.587
96	−1	.500	12	112.5	225.0	125.0	.545

Index						
66	1	.500	12	175.0	225.0	125.0	.791
67	−1	.500	12	168.7	225.0	125.0	.389
99	1	.500	12	131.2	225.0	125.0	.198
100	1	.500	12	137.5	225.0	125.0	.356
101	−1	.500	12	131.2	225.0	125.0	.515
102	−1	.500	12	125.0	225.0	125.0	.539
103	1	.500	12	131.2	225.0	125.0	.019
104	−1	.500	12	125.0	225.0	125.0	.631
105	−1	.500	12	118.7	225.0	125.0	.318
106	−1	.500	12	112.5	225.0	125.0	.135
107	1	.500	12	118.7	225.0	125.0	.582
108	−1	.500	12	112.5	225.0	125.0	.385
109	−1	.500	12	106.2	225.0	125.0	.166
110	1	.500	12	112.5	225.0	125.0	.552
111	−1	.500	12	118.7	225.0	125.0	.477
112	−1	.500	12	112.5	225.0	125.0	.703
113	1	.500	12	106.2	225.0	125.0	.822
114	1	.500	12	112.5	225.0	125.0	.191
115	−1	.500	12	106.2	225.0	125.0	.347
116	−1	.500	12	100.0	225.0	125.0	.806
117	1	.500	12	106.2	225.0	125.0	.361
118	1	.500	12	112.5	225.0	125.0	.264
119	−1	.500	12	106.2	225.0	125.0	.368
120	1	.500	12	112.5	225.0	125.0	.790
121	−1	.500	12	106.2	225.0	125.0	.849
122	−1	.500	12	100.0	225.0	125.0	.257
123	−1	.500	12	93.7	225.0	125.0	.983
124	1	.500	12	100.0	225.0	125.0	.397

Index						
97	1	.500	12	118.7	225.0	125.0	.327
98	1	.500	12	125.0	225.0	125.0	.741
125	1	.500	12	106.2	225.0	125.0	.310
126	−1	.500	12	100.0	225.0	125.0	.245
127	1	.500	12	106.2	225.0	125.0	.470
128	−1	.500	12	100.0	225.0	125.0	.556
129	1	.500	12	106.2	225.0	125.0	.812
130	1	.500	12	112.5	225.0	125.0	.389
131	−1	.500	12	106.2	225.0	125.0	.715
132	−1	.500	12	100.0	225.0	125.0	.754
133	1	.500	12	106.2	225.0	125.0	.353
134	−1	.500	12	100.0	225.0	125.0	.011
135	−1	.500	12	93.7	225.0	125.0	.046
136	1	.500	12	87.5	225.0	125.0	.284
137	−1	.500	12	81.2	225.0	125.0	.957
138	−1	.500	12	75.0	225.0	125.0	.686
139	1	.500	12	81.2	225.0	125.0	.343
140	−1	.500	12	75.0	225.0	125.0	.813
141	1	.500	12	81.2	225.0	125.0	.953
142	−1	.500	12	75.0	225.0	125.0	.853
143	−1	.500	12	68.7	225.0	125.0	.099
144	1	.500	12	75.0	225.0	125.0	.879
145	−1	.500	12	68.7	225.0	125.0	.856
146	−1	.500	12	62.5	225.0	125.0	.250
147	1	.500	12	68.7	225.0	125.0	.000
148	−1	.500	12	62.5	225.0	125.0	.957
149	−1	.500	12	56.2	225.0	125.0	.670
150	1	.500	12	62.5	225.0	125.0	.422

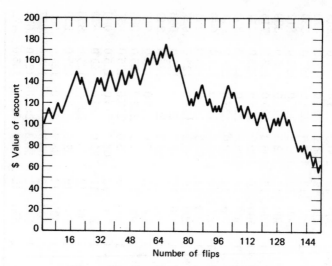

Figure 59. Graph of coin-flip simulation.

line, even considerably, as in the computer example, but will always come back to and cross the starting line, if run long enough.

A REAL TRADING SYSTEM'S SIMULATED RESULTS

What should you expect from a real system's trading?

In general, it will resemble the coin-flip results just referred to, except instead of vacillating about the starting line forever, a real system's results should vacillate about a line sloping upward, that is, upward growth over the long run, with periods of losses and gains below and above the growth line (assuming past conditions will generally continue in the future).

No one knows what conditions (and hence profits–losses) will be present in the future, so we assume from many historical trades (hundreds) that roughly similar conditions will occur in the future. Next, we assume on the average roughly 12% of a base amount is committed to each trade. We know each trade is not independent (cattle, hogs, and bellies act the same very often; likewise the grains), so we have to assume a larger amount, say double the original, actually 12%, is actually gaining or losing on each trade (like hogs and bellies acting together at 12% each for an effective result of 25% invested).

Further, we assume that after each 50% increase in account equity we increase subsequent investment commitments by 50% of the gain in account equity from the last time we changed our commitment size (i.e., for each $1 gained on last $2 account size, 50% or $.50 is reinvested).

Account Simulation No. 1

We assume the account starts at $100.

Looking at simulation run No. 1 in Table 21 and the graph in Figure 60, we see the first trade (1 in column 1) is a loss (−1, column 2) of 56.4% (column 3) on $25 (column 4) invested, bringing the account down from $100 to $85.90 (column 5). The next point of reinvestment of profits is $150 (column 6), the current investment base is $100 (column 7), and the random number to tell us which cell average size to use is 0.094 (column 8).

The next trade is a gain of 14.3%, bringing the account back up slightly to $89.40. A streak of fifteen subsequent gains makes the account soar to $134 (trade No. 17). A little series of losses occurs right after, and then the account continues to march up to $185.90 (trade No. 35). Pretty good gains for thirty-five trades.

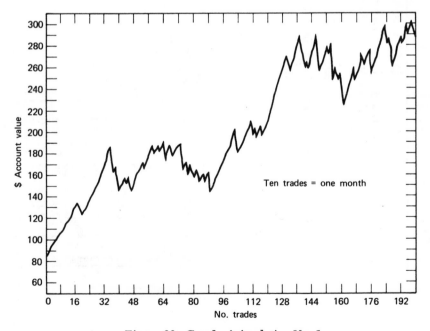

Figure 60. Graph of simulation No. 1.

TABLE 21 Trading System Simulation No. 1

ACCOUNT (CASH) GROWTH SIMULATION

GAIN FRACTION, NO. CELLS, TOTAL TRADES: .77, 10, 200
INVESTMENT COMMITTED FRACTION, EQUITY STEP SIZE FRACTION, EQUITY STEP
COMMITTED FRACTION: .25, .5, .5

GAIN CELL AVERAGE SIZES: .301, .204, .177, .155, .143, .126, .112, .097, .086, .072

LOSS CELL AVERAGE SIZES: .564, .398, .35, .312, .262, .235, .196, .156, .132, .124

NO. TRADES, GAIN (LOSS), GAIN SIZE, INVESTMENT COMMITTED, EQUITY, NEXT GOAL, NEXT BASE, RANDOM NO.

NO. TRADES	GAIN (LOSS)	GAIN SIZE	INVESTMENT COMMITTED	EQUITY	NEXT GOAL	NEXT BASE	RANDOM NO.
1	−1	0.564	25	85.9	150.0	100.0	.094
2	1	0.143	25	89.4	150.0	100.0	.460
3	1	0.177	25	93.9	150.0	100.0	.252
4	1	0.086	25	96.0	150.0	100.0	.842
5	1	0.072	25	97.8	150.0	100.0	.940
6	1	0.097	25	100.2	150.0	100.0	.765
7	1	0.126	25	103.4	150.0	100.0	.528
8	1	0.097	25	105.8	150.0	100.0	.714
9	1	0.097	25	108.2	150.0	100.0	.719
10	1	0.086	25	110.4	150.0	100.0	.818
11	1	0.177	25	114.8	150.0	100.0	.264
12	1	0.097	25	117.2	150.0	100.0	.737
13	1	0.072	25	119.0	150.0	100.0	.986
14	1	0.155	25	122.9	150.0	100.0	.323
15	1	0.204	25	128.0	150.0	100.0	.133
16	1	0.086	25	130.2	150.0	100.0	.807
17	1	0.155	25	134.0	150.0	100.0	.345
18	−1	0.132	25	130.7	150.0	100.0	.855
19	−1	0.196	25	125.8	150.0	100.0	.635
20	−1	0.124	25	122.7	150.0	100.0	.920
21	1	0.155	25	126.6	150.0	100.0	.322
22	1	0.072	25	128.4	150.0	100.0	.973
23	1	0.155	25	132.3	150.0	100.0	.376
24	1	0.155	25	136.2	150.0	100.0	.396
25	1	0.177	25	140.6	150.0	100.0	.225
26	1	0.126	25	143.7	150.0	100.0	.587
27	1	0.126	25	146.9	150.0	100.0	.545
28	1	0.155	25	150.8	226.2	125.4	.327
29	1	0.097	31	153.8	226.2	125.4	.741
30	1	0.204	31	160.2	226.2	125.4	.198
31	1	0.155	31	165.0	226.2	125.4	.356
32	1	0.126	31	169.0	226.2	125.4	.515
33	1	0.126	31	172.9	226.2	125.4	.539
34	1	0.301	31	182.4	226.2	125.4	.019
35	1	0.112	31	185.9	226.2	125.4	.631
36	−1	0.312	31	176.1	226.2	125.4	.318

37	−1	0.398	31	163.6	226.2	125.4	.135
38	1	0.126	31	167.6	226.2	125.4	.582
39	−1	0.312	31	157.8	226.2	125.4	.385
40	−1	0.398	31	145.3	226.2	125.4	.166
41	1	0.126	31	149.3	226.2	125.4	.552
42	1	0.143	31	153.8	226.2	125.4	.477
43	1	0.097	31	156.8	226.2	125.4	.703
44	−1	0.132	31	152.7	226.2	125.4	.822
45	−1	0.204	31	159.1	226.2	125.4	.191
46	1	0.312	31	149.3	226.2	125.4	.347
47	−1	0.132	31	145.1	226.2	125.4	.806
48	1	0.155	31	150.0	226.2	125.4	.361
49	1	0.177	31	155.5	226.2	125.4	.264
50	1	0.155	31	160.4	226.2	125.4	.368
51	1	0.097	31	163.4	226.2	125.4	.790
52	1	0.086	31	166.1	226.2	125.4	.849
53	1	0.177	31	171.7	226.2	125.4	.257
54	−1	0.124	31	167.8	226.2	125.4	.983
55	1	0.155	31	172.7	226.2	125.4	.397
56	1	0.155	31	177.5	226.2	125.4	.310
57	1	0.177	31	183.1	226.2	125.4	.245
58	1	0.143	31	187.6	226.2	125.4	.470
59	−1	0.235	31	180.2	226.2	125.4	.556
60	1	0.086	31	182.9	226.2	125.4	.812
61	1	0.155	31	187.7	226.2	125.4	.389
62	−1	0.156	31	182.9	226.2	125.4	.715
63	1	0.097	31	185.9	226.2	125.4	.754
64	1	0.155	31	190.8	226.2	125.4	.353
65	−1	0.564	31	173.1	226.2	125.4	.011
66	1	0.301	31	182.5	226.2	125.4	.046
67	1	0.177	31	188.1	226.2	125.4	.284
68	−1	0.124	31	184.2	226.2	125.4	.957
69	−1	0.196	31	178.0	226.2	125.4	.686
70	1	0.155	31	182.9	226.2	125.4	.343
71	1	0.086	31	185.6	226.2	125.4	.813
72	1	0.072	31	187.8	226.2	125.4	.953
73	−1	0.132	31	183.7	226.2	125.4	.853
74	−1	0.564	31	166.0	226.2	125.4	.099
75	1	0.086	31	168.7	226.2	125.4	.879
76	1	0.086	31	171.4	226.2	125.4	.856
77	−1	0.350	31	160.4	226.2	125.4	.250
78	1	0.301	31	169.9	226.2	125.4	.000
79	−1	0.124	31	166.0	226.2	125.4	.957
80	−1	0.196	31	159.8	226.2	125.4	.670
81	1	0.143	31	164.3	226.2	125.4	.422
82	−1	0.124	31	160.4	226.2	125.4	.958
83	−1	0.196	31	154.3	226.2	125.4	.676
84	1	0.112	31	157.8	226.2	125.4	.669
85	1	0.086	31	160.5	226.2	125.4	.862
86	−1	0.196	31	154.4	226.2	125.4	.629
87	1	0.204	31	160.8	226.2	125.4	.107
88	1	0.072	31	163.0	226.2	125.4	.942
89	−1	0.564	31	145.3	226.2	125.4	.056
90	1	0.086	31	148.0	226.2	125.4	.803
91	1	0.143	31	152.5	226.2	125.4	.459
92	1	0.177	31	158.1	226.2	125.4	.218
93	1	0.112	31	161.6	226.2	125.4	.657
94	1	0.177	31	167.1	226.2	125.4	.292
95	1	0.097	31	170.2	226.2	125.4	.755
96	−1	0.126	31	174.1	226.2	125.4	.512
97	1	0.126	31	178.1	226.2	125.4	.551
98	1	0.143	31	182.5	226.2	125.4	.450

TABLE 21 (Continued)

99	1	0.086	31	185.2	226.2	125.4	.827	128	1	0.143	41	261.2	345.8	165.2	.402
100	1	0.086	31	187.9	226.2	125.4	.877	129	1	0.143	41	267.1	345.8	165.2	.442
101	1	0.301	31	197.4	226.2	125.4	.081	130	1	0.097	41	271.1	345.8	165.2	.709
102	1	0.177	31	202.9	226.2	125.4	.234	131	−1	0.196	41	263.0	345.8	165.2	.696
103	−1	0.564	31	185.2	226.2	125.4	.087	132	−1	0.132	41	257.5	345.8	165.2	.836
104	−1	0.124	31	181.3	226.2	125.4	.900	133	1	0.112	41	262.2	345.8	165.2	.620
105	1	0.072	31	183.6	226.2	125.4	.996	134	1	0.126	41	267.4	345.8	165.2	.500
106	1	0.126	31	187.6	226.2	125.4	.592	135	1	0.155	41	273.8	345.8	165.2	.325
107	1	0.143	31	192.0	226.2	125.4	.452	136	1	0.204	41	282.2	345.8	165.2	.145
108	1	0.155	31	196.9	226.2	125.4	.341	137	1	0.177	41	289.5	345.8	165.2	.288
109	1	0.126	31	200.8	226.2	125.4	.544	138	−1	0.312	41	276.6	345.8	165.2	.320
110	1	0.097	31	203.9	226.2	125.4	.727	139	−1	0.132	41	271.2	345.8	165.2	.852
111	1	0.204	31	210.3	226.2	125.4	.128	140	−1	0.262	41	260.3	345.8	165.2	.462
112	−1	0.398	31	197.8	226.2	125.4	.164	141	1	0.112	41	265.0	345.8	165.2	.636
113	1	0.177	31	203.4	226.2	125.4	.258	142	1	0.124	41	259.8	345.8	165.2	.983
114	−1	0.235	31	196.0	226.2	125.4	.512	143	1	0.301	41	272.3	345.8	165.2	.010
115	1	0.177	31	201.5	226.2	125.4	.255	144	1	0.086	41	275.8	345.8	165.2	.845
116	1	0.126	31	205.5	226.2	125.4	.521	145	1	0.143	41	281.7	345.8	165.2	.499
117	−1	0.262	31	197.3	226.2	125.4	.496	146	1	0.204	41	290.2	345.8	165.2	.142
118	1	0.126	31	201.2	226.2	125.4	.547	147	−1	0.398	41	273.7	345.8	165.2	.158
119	1	0.143	31	205.7	226.2	125.4	.401	148	−1	0.398	41	257.3	345.8	165.2	.186
120	1	0.143	31	210.2	226.2	125.4	.421	149	1	0.143	41	263.2	345.8	165.2	.484
121	1	0.204	31	216.6	226.2	125.4	.167	150	1	0.072	41	266.2	345.8	165.2	.970
122	1	0.143	31	221.1	226.2	125.4	.409	151	1	0.177	41	273.5	345.8	165.2	.268
123	1	0.301	31	230.5	226.2	165.2	.074	152	1	0.155	41	279.9	345.8	165.2	.346
124	1	0.143	41	236.4	345.8	165.2	.435	153	−1	0.398	41	263.4	345.8	165.2	.153
125	1	0.204	41	244.8	345.8	165.2	.196	154	1	0.204	41	271.9	345.8	165.2	.175
126	1	0.126	41	250.0	345.8	165.2	.505	155	−1	0.564	41	248.6	345.8	165.2	.089
127	1	0.126	41	255.3	345.8	165.2	.501	156	1	0.301	41	261.0	345.8	165.2	.031

157	−1	0.156	41	254.6	345.8	165.2	.783	179	1	0.126	41	273.1	345.8	165.2	.561
158	−1	0.132	41	249.1	345.8	165.2	.840	180	1	0.204	41	281.5	345.8	165.2	.123
159	1	0.126	41	254.3	345.8	165.2	.519	181	1	0.072	41	284.5	345.8	165.2	.935
160	−1	0.350	41	239.8	345.8	165.2	.261	182	1	0.204	41	292.9	345.8	165.2	.147
161	−1	0.350	41	225.4	345.8	165.2	.282	183	−1	0.155	41	299.3	345.8	165.2	.348
162	1	0.155	41	231.8	345.8	165.2	.331	184	1	0.398	41	282.9	345.8	165.2	.135
163	1	0.204	41	240.2	345.8	165.2	.186	185	−1	0.097	41	286.9	345.8	165.2	.700
164	1	0.177	41	247.5	345.8	165.2	.224	186	−1	0.235	41	277.2	345.8	165.2	.577
165	1	0.204	41	256.0	345.8	165.2	.197	187	1	0.398	41	260.7	345.8	165.2	.126
166	1	0.126	41	261.2	345.8	165.2	.582	188	1	0.143	41	266.6	345.8	164.2	.450
167	−1	0.312	41	248.3	345.8	165.2	.377	189	1	0.301	41	279.1	345.8	165.2	.058
168	1	0.126	41	253.5	345.8	165.2	.552	190	1	0.126	41	284.3	345.8	165.2	.531
169	1	0.177	41	260.8	345.8	165.2	.275	191	1	0.097	41	288.3	345.8	165.2	.773
170	1	0.301	41	273.2	345.8	165.2	.064	192	−1	0.124	41	283.1	345.8	165.2	.934
171	−1	0.124	41	268.1	345.8	165.2	.953	193	1	0.086	41	286.7	345.8	165.2	.846
172	−1	0.132	41	262.7	345.8	165.2	.840	194	1	0.301	41	299.1	345.8	165.2	.070
173	1	0.086	41	266.2	345.8	165.2	.811	195	−1	0.196	41	291.0	345.8	165.2	.606
174	1	0.177	41	273.5	345.8	165.2	.263	196	1	0.112	41	295.7	345.8	165.2	.673
175	1	0.097	41	277.5	345.8	165.2	.778	197	1	0.155	41	302.1	345.8	165.2	.347
176	−1	0.564	41	254.2	345.8	165.2	.039	198	−1	0.132	41	296.6	345.8	165.2	.851
177	1	0.204	41	262.7	345.8	165.2	.132	199	−1	0.124	41	291.5	345.8	165.2	.961
178	1	0.126	41	267.9	345.8	165.2	.557	200	1	0.196	41	283.4	345.8	165.2	.610

But wait. The market is not all uphill. A series of losses thereafter brings the account back down to $145.10 by trade 40, roughly a 25% loss from that peak. Okay, the investor still has a 45% gain from the start, so this may not bother him. But what if another investor had just started at trade 35? Would he get jittery, not stand a loss of 25%, and disbelieve the (prior) performances because *he* had not experienced the gains, and had a 25% *loss*, not a 45% *gain?*

Even the lucky investor who started at the very beginning has some roller-coaster days ahead. After bottoming at $145.10, he makes new highs by trade No. 64 ($190.80), *but* thereafter falls back down to $145.30 by trade No. 89, no better than trade No. 40. Very disillusioning to the investor, but *very, very* realistic, unfortunately. For the timid investor the story might end there (he quits in agony), but for the sturdy, pioneer-type investor, survival and perseverance means climbing to new peaks thereafter, to $302.10 by trade No. 197, despite hills and valleys. A graphical portrayal is found in Figure 60 for simulation No. 1 account growth results.

Account Simulation No. 2

Scores of computer-simulation runs were made to test the effects of thousands of simulated gains and losses on the account, assuming past trade results for success rates and gain–loss sizes. One is interested in seeing how accounts started off (either at the beginning of our run or somewhere in the run), how big the ups and downs became. From this one could find out what to expect in growth and losses, on a probability basis.

The second example, simulation No. 2, (Table 22), shows basically the same events as Table No. 21—good growth over the account's life, but interrupted by important retreats, both sizable in time and extent of drops. The graph for Table 22 is shown in Figure 61.

The account starts off with a little gain but drops almost immediately to a low of $66.80 after trade No. 10, a loss of 33%, and doesn't make new highs until trade No. 65 ($106). From there the uphill climb is good, in fact almost uninterrupted, until trade No. 154, a new high (a good one), at $282.60, a gain of roughly 183%. But then the old devil in the market takes the gain back (partially) until trade No. 201, with what looks like a breakout to new high ground at $283.60. Unfortunately for the weaker, more timid investor, the account cracks back down to a low of $181.80, a loss of almost 40% (a real one for the poor soul who started at trade No. 201). However, for the patient investor who realizes

TABLE 22 Trading System Simulation No. 2

ACCOUNT (CASH) GROWTH SIMULATION

GAIN FRACTION, NO. CELLS, TOTAL TRADES: .77, 10, 400
INVESTMENT COMMITTED FRACTION, EQUITY STEP SIZE FRACTION, EQUITY STEP
COMMITTED FRACTION: .25, .5, .5

GAIN CELL AVERAGE SIZES: .301, .204, .177, .155, .143, .126, .112, .097, .086, .072

LOSS CELL AVERAGE SIZES: .564, .398, .35, .312, .262, .235, .196, .156, .132, .124

NO. TRADES, GAIN (LOSS), GAIN SIZE, INVESTMENT COMMITTED, EQUITY, NEXT GOAL,
NEXT BASE, RANDOM NO.

NO. TRADES	GAIN (LOSS)	GAIN SIZE	INVESTMENT COMMITTED	EQUITY	NEXT GOAL	NEXT BASE	RANDOM NO.
1	1	0.155	25	103.8	150.0	100.0	.316
2	−1	0.262	25	97.3	150.0	100.0	.423
3	−1	0.262	25	90.7	150.0	100.0	.490
4	1	0.155	25	94.6	150.0	100.0	.381
5	1	0.072	25	96.4	150.0	100.0	.955
6	−1	0.564	25	82.3	150.0	100.0	.034
7	−1	0.350	25	73.6	150.0	100.0	.256
8	−1	0.235	25	67.7	150.0	100.0	.597
9	1	0.097	25	70.1	150.0	100.0	.784
10	−1	0.132	25	66.8	150.0	100.0	.889
11	1	0.204	25	71.9	150.0	100.0	.189
12	1	0.155	25	75.8	150.0	100.0	.313
13	−1	0.196	25	70.9	150.0	100.0	.609
14	1	0.072	25	72.7	150.0	100.0	.918
15	1	0.143	25	76.3	150.0	100.0	.455
16	1	0.204	25	81.4	150.0	100.0	.110
17	1	0.086	25	83.5	150.0	100.0	.831
18	1	0.177	25	87.9	150.0	100.0	.213
19	−1	0.398	25	78.0	150.0	100.0	.113
20	1	0.143	25	81.6	150.0	100.0	.454
21	1	0.112	25	84.4	150.0	100.0	.676
22	1	0.072	25	86.2	150.0	100.0	.966
23	1	0.126	25	89.3	150.0	100.0	.597
24	1	0.126	25	92.5	150.0	100.0	.554
25	1	0.112	25	95.3	150.0	100.0	.696
26	1	0.143	25	98.8	150.0	100.0	.436
27	1	0.143	25	102.4	150.0	100.0	.424
28	−1	0.196	25	97.5	150.0	100.0	.637
29	−1	0.398	25	87.6	150.0	100.0	.121
30	1	0.143	25	91.1	150.0	100.0	.462
31	1	0.155	25	95.0	150.0	100.0	.393
32	1	0.086	25	97.2	150.0	100.0	.865
33	−1	0.350	25	88.4	150.0	100.0	.212
34	−1	0.196	25	83.5	150.0	100.0	.621
35	1	0.155	25	87.4	150.0	100.0	.390
36	−1	0.156	25	83.5	150.0	100.0	.781

TABLE 22 *(Continued)*

37	−1	0.156	25	79.6	150.0	100.0	.780
38	−1	0.156	25	75.7	150.0	100.0	.781
39	−1	0.235	25	69.8	150.0	100.0	.597
40	1	0.086	25	72.0	150.0	100.0	.817
41	1	0.072	25	73.8	150.0	100.0	.969
42	1	0.126	25	76.9	150.0	100.0	.594
43	1	0.112	25	79.7	150.0	100.0	.695
44	1	0.143	25	83.3	150.0	100.0	.425
45	−1	0.235	25	77.4	150.0	100.0	.559
46	1	0.126	25	80.6	150.0	100.0	.587
47	1	0.126	25	83.7	150.0	100.0	.563
48	1	0.112	25	86.5	150.0	100.0	.622
49	1	0.112	25	89.3	150.0	100.0	.684
50	1	0.097	25	91.7	150.0	100.0	.798
51	1	0.204	25	96.8	150.0	100.0	.140
52	−1	0.235	25	91.0	150.0	100.0	.552
53	1	0.301	25	98.5	150.0	100.0	.038
54	−1	0.350	25	89.7	150.0	100.0	.227
55	1	0.112	25	92.5	150.0	100.0	.635
56	−1	0.132	25	89.2	150.0	100.0	.818
57	1	0.301	25	96.8	150.0	100.0	.009
58	1	0.177	25	101.2	150.0	100.0	.259
59	−1	0.398	25	91.2	150.0	100.0	.169
60	1	0.126	25	94.4	150.0	100.0	.549
61	1	0.177	25	98.8	150.0	100.0	.205
62	1	0.143	25	102.4	150.0	100.0	.468
63	−1	0.262	25	95.8	150.0	100.0	.456
64	1	0.204	25	100.9	150.0	100.0	.170
65	1	0.204	25	106.0	150.0	100.0	.119
68	1	0.204	25	119.1	150.0	100.0	.149
69	1	0.097	25	121.6	150.0	100.0	.710
70	−1	0.312	25	113.8	150.0	100.0	.391
71	1	0.204	25	118.9	150.0	100.0	.138
72	1	0.204	25	124.0	150.0	100.0	.191
73	−1	0.196	25	119.1	150.0	100.0	.695
74	1	0.204	25	124.2	150.0	100.0	.194
75	1	0.155	25	128.0	150.0	100.0	.382
76	1	0.156	25	124.1	150.0	100.0	.751
77	1	0.112	25	126.9	150.0	100.0	.668
78	1	0.097	25	129.4	150.0	100.0	.780
79	−1	0.156	25	125.5	150.0	100.0	.741
80	1	0.177	25	129.9	150.0	100.0	.267
81	1	0.112	25	132.7	150.0	100.0	.686
82	1	0.112	25	135.5	150.0	100.0	.610
83	1	0.301	25	143.0	150.0	100.0	.074
84	1	0.301	25	150.5	225.8	125.2	.052
85	−1	0.398	31	138.1	225.8	125.2	.187
86	1	0.177	31	143.6	225.8	125.2	.229
87	1	0.112	31	147.1	225.8	125.2	.660
88	1	0.301	31	156.5	225.8	125.2	.008
89	1	0.086	31	159.2	225.8	125.2	.834
90	1	0.072	31	161.5	225.8	125.2	.973
91	1	0.177	31	167.0	225.8	125.2	.210
92	−1	0.398	31	154.6	225.8	125.2	.108
93	1	0.301	31	164.0	225.8	125.2	.028
94	−1	0.235	31	156.6	225.8	125.2	.545
95	1	0.177	31	162.2	225.8	125.2	.269
96	1	0.112	31	165.7	225.8	125.2	.618

66	1	0.143	25	109.6	150.0	100.0	.499
67	1	0.177	25	114.0	150.0	100.0	.269
99	−1	0.235	31	163.6	225.8	125.2	.580
100	−1	0.132	31	159.5	225.8	125.2	.815
101	1	0.204	31	165.9	225.8	125.2	.198
102	1	0.155	31	170.7	225.8	125.2	.319
103	−1	0.235	31	163.4	225.8	125.2	.529
104	1	0.086	31	166.1	225.8	125.2	.855
105	−1	0.156	31	161.2	225.8	125.2	.774
106	−1	0.350	31	150.2	225.8	125.2	.271
107	1	0.301	31	159.6	225.8	125.2	.025
108	1	0.097	31	162.7	225.8	125.2	.726
109	1	0.086	31	165.4	225.8	125.2	.809
110	1	0.301	31	174.8	225.8	125.2	.060
111	1	0.072	31	177.1	225.8	125.2	.915
112	1	0.204	31	183.4	225.8	125.2	.149
113	1	0.097	31	186.5	225.8	125.2	.731
114	1	0.086	31	189.2	225.8	125.2	.891
115	1	0.112	31	192.7	225.8	125.2	.677
116	1	0.204	31	199.1	225.8	125.2	.166
117	1	0.177	31	204.6	225.8	125.2	.244
118	1	0.177	31	210.2	225.8	125.2	.257
119	−1	0.156	31	205.3	225.8	125.2	.759
120	1	0.155	31	210.1	225.8	125.2	.349
121	−1	0.196	31	204.0	225.8	125.2	.607
122	1	0.177	31	209.5	225.8	125.2	.223
123	1	0.097	31	212.6	225.8	125.2	.752
124	1	0.143	31	217.1	225.8	125.2	.458
125	1	0.112	31	220.6	225.8	125.2	.633
126	−1	0.235	31	213.2	225.8	125.2	.511
127	1	0.301	31	222.6	225.8	125.2	.067

97	1	0.072	31	167.9	225.8	125.2	.995
98	1	0.097	31	171.0	225.8	125.2	.770
128	1	0.086	31	225.3	225.8	125.2	.822
129	1	0.112	31	228.8	343.3	164.4	.620
130	1	0.086	41	232.4	343.3	164.4	.883
131	1	0.072	41	235.3	343.3	164.4	.993
132	1	0.155	41	241.7	343.3	164.4	.365
133	1	0.126	41	246.9	343.3	164.4	.580
134	−1	0.235	41	237.2	343.3	164.4	.542
135	1	0.301	41	249.6	343.3	164.4	.077
136	−1	0.196	41	241.5	343.3	164.4	.604
137	1	0.155	41	247.9	343.3	164.4	.339
138	1	0.143	41	253.8	343.3	164.4	.463
139	1	0.072	41	256.7	343.3	164.4	.941
140	−1	0.262	41	246.0	343.3	164.4	.452
141	1	0.204	41	254.4	343.3	164.4	.158
142	−1	0.132	41	248.9	343.3	164.4	.886
143	1	0.177	41	256.2	343.3	164.4	.246
144	1	0.086	41	259.7	343.3	164.4	.827
145	1	0.301	41	272.1	343.3	164.4	.006
146	1	0.097	41	276.1	343.3	164.4	.755
147	1	0.097	41	280.1	343.3	164.4	.782
148	−1	0.350	41	265.7	343.3	164.4	.200
149	1	0.126	41	270.9	343.3	164.4	.503
150	1	0.143	41	276.8	343.3	164.4	.441
151	1	0.112	41	281.4	343.3	164.4	.632
152	−1	0.350	41	267.0	343.3	164.4	.254
153	1	0.177	41	274.3	343.3	164.4	.207
154	1	0.204	41	282.6	343.3	164.4	.141
155	−1	0.564	41	259.5	343.3	164.4	.007
156	−1	0.398	41	243.1	343.3	164.4	.152

TABLE 22 (Continued)

157	1	0.126	41	248.3	343.3	164.4	.531	186	1	0.112	41	248.1	343.3	164.4	.627
158	1	0.097	41	252.3	343.3	164.4	.712	187	1	0.097	41	252.1	343.3	164.4	.713
159	−1	0.132	41	246.8	343.3	164.4	.848	188	1	0.177	41	259.3	343.3	164.4	.285
160	1	0.143	41	252.7	343.3	164.4	.470	189	−1	0.350	41	244.9	343.3	164.4	.276
161	−1	0.398	41	236.4	343.3	164.4	.121	190	1	0.097	41	248.9	343.3	164.4	.725
162	1	0.086	41	239.9	343.3	164.4	.821	191	1	0.155	41	255.3	343.3	164.4	.396
163	1	0.143	41	245.8	343.3	164.4	.468	192	1	0.204	41	263.7	343.3	164.4	.193
164	−1	0.132	41	240.3	343.3	164.4	.872	193	−1	0.156	41	257.3	343.3	164.4	.723
165	1	0.143	41	246.2	343.3	164.4	.413	194	1	0.143	41	263.2	343.3	164.4	.432
166	1	0.072	41	249.2	343.3	164.4	.958	195	−1	0.132	41	257.7	343.3	164.4	.851
167	−1	0.132	41	243.8	343.3	164.4	.855	196	1	0.156	41	251.3	343.3	164.4	.716
168	−1	0.235	41	234.1	343.3	164.4	.597	197	1	0.301	41	263.7	343.3	164.4	.037
169	1	0.112	41	238.7	343.3	164.4	.659	198	1	0.126	41	268.9	343.3	164.4	.540
170	1	0.204	41	247.1	343.3	164.4	.153	199	1	0.072	41	271.8	343.3	164.4	.994
171	1	0.143	41	253.0	343.3	164.4	.469	200	1	0.143	41	277.7	343.3	164.4	.441
172	−1	0.124	41	247.9	343.3	164.4	.915	201	1	0.143	41	283.6	343.3	164.4	.427
173	1	0.086	41	251.4	343.3	164.4	.896	202	−1	0.235	41	273.9	343.3	164.4	.507
174	1	0.112	41	256.0	343.3	164.4	.697	203	1	0.072	41	276.9	343.3	164.4	.954
175	−1	0.350	41	241.6	343.3	164.4	.292	204	−1	0.156	41	270.5	343.3	164.4	.770
176	1	0.177	41	248.9	343.3	164.4	.202	205	1	0.124	41	265.4	343.3	164.4	.976
177	1	0.301	41	261.3	343.3	164.4	.098	206	1	0.086	41	268.9	343.3	164.4	.856
178	1	0.112	41	265.9	343.3	164.4	.683	207	−1	0.564	41	245.7	343.3	164.4	.032
179	1	0.143	41	271.7	343.3	164.4	.431	208	1	0.086	41	249.3	343.3	164.4	.887
180	−1	0.262	41	261.0	343.3	164.4	.430	209	1	0.097	41	253.2	343.3	164.4	.774
181	−1	0.262	41	250.2	353.3	164.4	.415	210	−1	0.312	41	240.4	343.3	164.4	.310
182	1	0.177	41	257.5	343.3	164.4	.225	211	1	0.143	41	246.3	343.3	164.4	.467
183	1	0.097	41	261.5	343.3	164.4	.720	212	−1	0.196	41	238.2	343.3	164.4	.647
184	1	0.126	41	266.7	343.3	164.4	.526	213	1	0.126	41	243.4	343.3	164.4	.594
185	−1	0.564	41	243.5	343.3	164.4	.080	214	1	0.072	41	246.4	343.3	164.4	.972

215	1	0.177	41	253.7	343.3	164.4	.257
216	−1	0.398	41	237.3	343.3	164.4	.129
217	−1	0.124	41	232.2	343.3	164.4	.950
218	−1	0.312	41	219.4	343.3	164.4	.381
219	1	0.155	41	225.7	343.3	164.4	.327
220	1	0.097	41	229.7	343.3	164.4	.787
221	−1	.124	41	224.6	343.3	164.4	.988
222	1	0.097	41	228.6	343.3	164.4	.717
223	1	.086	41	232.2	343.3	164.4	.842
224	1	0.126	41	237.3	343.3	164.4	.577
225	−1	0.196	41	229.3	343.3	164.4	.649
226	1	0.072	41	232.2	343.3	164.4	.949
227	−1	0.156	41	225.8	343.3	164.4	.739
228	1	0.301	41	238.2	343.3	164.4	.099
229	1	0.112	41	242.8	343.3	164.4	.644
230	−1	0.124	41	237.7	343.3	164.4	.933
231	1	0.177	41	245.0	343.3	164.4	.266
232	1	0.072	41	247.9	343.3	164.4	.976
233	1	0.086	41	251.5	343.3	164.4	.864
234	−1	0.398	41	235.1	343.3	164.4	.156
235	−1	0.196	41	227.1	343.3	164.4	.689
236	1	0.097	41	231.0	343.3	164.4	.704
237	−1	0.398	41	214.7	343.3	164.4	.196
238	1	0.143	41	220.6	343.3	164.4	.439
239	1	0.143	41	226.4	343.3	164.4	.416
240	1	0.177	41	233.7	343.3	164.4	.292
241	1	0.072	41	236.7	343.3	164.4	.947
242	−1	0.312	41	223.9	343.3	164.4	.382
243	−1	0.235	41	214.2	343.3	164.4	.522
244	−1	0.350	41	199.8	343.3	164.4	.250
245	1	0.126	41	205.0	343.3	164.4	.522

246	−1	0.564	41	181.8	343.3	164.4	.076
247	1	0.126	41	187.0	343.3	164.4	.569
248	1	0.204	41	195.4	343.3	164.4	.155
249	−1	0.124	41	190.3	343.3	164.4	.989
250	1	0.204	41	198.7	343.3	164.4	.111
251	1	0.155	41	205.0	343.3	164.4	.342
252	1	0.126	41	210.2	343.3	164.4	.550
253	1	0.126	41	215.4	343.3	164.4	.587
254	1	0.072	41	218.3	343.3	164.4	.980
255	1	0.143	41	224.2	343.3	164.4	.409
256	1	0.126	41	229.4	343.3	164.4	.550
257	1	0.204	41	237.8	343.3	164.4	.124
258	1	0.072	41	240.8	343.3	164.4	.966
259	1	0.143	41	246.6	343.3	164.4	.449
260	1	0.112	41	251.2	343.3	164.4	.638
261	−1	0.156	41	244.8	343.3	164.4	.756
262	1	0.072	41	247.8	343.3	164.4	.903
263	1	0.155	41	254.2	343.3	164.4	.358
264	1	0.204	41	262.5	343.3	164.4	.195
265	1	0.204	41	270.9	343.3	164.4	.180
266	1	0.086	41	274.5	343.3	164.4	.867
267	−1	0.262	41	263.7	343.3	164.4	.469
268	−1	0.156	41	257.3	343.3	164.4	.744
269	1	0.086	41	260.8	343.3	164.4	.861
270	−1	0.312	41	248.0	343.3	164.4	.327
271	1	0.072	41	250.9	343.3	164.4	.994
272	1	0.112	41	255.6	343.3	164.4	.688
273	1	0.177	41	262.8	343.3	164.4	.270
274	1	0.301	41	275.2	343.3	164.4	.063
275	−1	0.262	41	264.4	343.3	164.4	.409
276	1	0.204	41	272.8	343.3	164.4	.104

TABLE 22 *(Continued)*

277	−1	0.124	41	267.7	343.3	164.4	.919	308	1	0.097	56	370.1	530.7	226.9	.758
278	1	0.097	41	271.7	343.3	164.4	.756	309	1	0.086	56	375.0	530.7	226.9	.819
279	1	0.177	41	279.0	343.3	164.4	.263	310	1	0.155	56	383.8	530.7	226.9	.329
280	1	0.126	41	284.2	343.3	164.4	.582	311	1	0.155	56	392.6	530.7	226.9	.368
281	−1	0.312	41	271.3	343.3	164.4	.361	312	1	0.072	56	396.6	530.7	226.9	.973
282	1	0.204	41	279.7	343.3	164.4	.175	313	1	0.155	56	405.4	530.7	226.9	.346
283	−1	0.564	41	256.5	343.3	164.4	.045	314	−1	0.156	56	396.6	530.7	226.9	.706
284	1	0.204	41	264.9	343.3	164.4	.108	315	−1	0.156	56	387.7	530.7	226.9	.722
285	1	0.072	41	267.9	343.3	164.4	.900	316	1	0.301	56	404.8	530.7	226.9	.055
286	1	0.086	41	271.4	343.3	164.4	.817	317	1	0.086	56	409.7	530.7	226.9	.885
287	1	0.177	41	278.7	343.3	164.4	.205	318	1	0.072	56	413.8	530.7	226.9	.993
288	−1	0.097	41	282.7	343.3	164.4	.707	319	1	0.204	56	425.4	530.7	226.9	.120
289	1	0.912	41	269.9	343.3	164.4	.335	320	1	0.112	56	431.7	530.7	226.9	.690
290	1	0.155	41	276.2	343.3	164.4	.369	321	1	0.155	56	440.5	530.7	226.9	.395
291	1	0.112	41	280.8	343.3	164.4	.646	322	1	0.155	56	449.3	530.7	226.9	.354
292	1	0.086	41	284.4	343.3	164.4	.871	323	1	0.155	56	458.1	530.7	226.9	.309
293	1	0.143	41	290.2	343.3	164.4	.443	324	1	0.155	56	466.9	530.7	226.9	.382
294	1	0.155	41	296.6	343.3	164.4	.338	325	−1	0.196	56	455.8	530.7	226.9	.650
295	1	0.086	41	300.2	343.3	164.4	.896	326	1	0.155	56	464.5	530.7	226.9	.347
296	1	0.112	41	304.8	343.3	164.4	.620	327	−1	0.196	56	453.4	530.7	226.9	.627
297	1	0.143	41	310.6	343.3	164.4	.448	328	1	0.204	56	465.0	530.7	226.9	.146
298	1	0.126	41	315.8	343.3	164.4	.547	329	1	0.177	56	475.0	530.7	226.9	.297
299	1	0.086	41	319.4	343.3	164.4	.872	330	1	0.086	56	479.9	530.7	226.9	.849
300	1	0.204	41	327.7	343.3	164.4	.139	331	1	0.204	56	491.5	530.7	226.9	.141
301	1	0.155	41	334.1	343.3	164.4	.303	332	−1	0.312	56	473.8	530.7	226.9	.359
302	1	0.177	41	341.4	343.3	164.4	.208	333	1	0.301	56	490.9	530.7	226.9	.034
303	1	0.301	41	353.8	530.7	226.9	.006	334	−1	0.312	56	473.2	530.7	226.9	.360
304	1	0.204	56	365.3	530.7	226.9	.158	335	1	0.155	56	482.0	530.7	226.9	.392
305	−1	0.262	56	350.5	530.7	226.9	.436	336	1	0.072	56	486.0	530.7	226.9	.996
306	1	0.177	56	360.5	530.7	226.9	.279	337	1	0.086	56	490.9	530.7	226.9	.837
307	1	0.072	56	364.6	530.7	226.9	.913	338	1	0.155	56	499.7	530.7	226.9	.375

No.	±	value	X	n	A	B	val		No.	±	value	X	n	A	B	val
339	1	0.086	56	504.6	530.7	226.9	.861		370	1	0.204	79	675.5	801.7	317.2	.176
340	−1	0.196	56	493.5	530.7	226.9	.604		371	1	0.112	79	684.3	801.7	317.2	.606
341	1	0.072	56	497.6	530.7	226.9	.929		372	1	0.097	79	692.0	801.7	317.2	.788
342	1	0.126	56	504.7	530.7	226.9	.592		373	1	0.301	79	715.9	801.7	317.2	.022
343	1	0.097	56	510.2	530.7	226.9	.757		374	1	0.301	79	739.8	801.7	317.2	.051
344	1	0.126	56	517.4	530.7	226.9	.591		375	1	0.143	79	751.1	801.7	317.2	.470
345	1	0.301	56	534.4	801.7	317.2	.082		376	−1	0.156	79	738.7	801.7	317.2	.786
346	1	0.204	79	550.6	801.7	317.2	.102		377	−1	0.196	79	723.2	801.7	317.2	.634
347	1	0.112	79	559.5	801.7	317.2	.688		378	−1	0.350	79	695.4	801.7	317.2	.218
348	1	0.086	79	566.3	801.7	317.2	.848		379	1	0.072	79	701.1	801.7	317.2	.900
349	1	0.072	79	572.0	801.7	317.2	.954		380	1	0.143	79	712.5	801.7	317.2	.475
350	−1	0.156	79	559.7	801.7	317.2	.722		381	−1	0.196	79	696.9	801.7	817.2	.687
351	1	0.177	79	573.7	801.7	317.2	.212		382	1	0.097	79	704.6	801.7	317.2	.732
352	−1	0.156	79	561.3	801.7	317.2	.786		383	1	0.097	79	712.3	801.7	317.2	.792
353	−1	0.196	79	545.8	801.7	317.2	.609		384	1	0.126	79	722.3	801.7	317.2	.532
354	1	0.301	79	569.7	801.7	317.2	.031		385	1	0.204	79	738.5	801.7	317.2	.124
355	1	0.097	79	577.3	801.7	317.2	.713		386	1	0.155	79	750.8	801.7	317.2	.393
356	1	0.301	79	601.2	801.7	317.2	.041		387	1	0.177	79	764.8	801.7	317.2	.218
357	1	0.204	79	617.4	801.7	317.2	.198		388	1	0.143	79	776.2	801.7	317.2	.468
358	1	0.126	79	627.4	801.7	317.2	.572		389	−1	0.350	79	748.4	801.7	317.2	.293
359	−1	0.262	79	606.6	801.7	317.2	.400		390	1	0.177	79	762.5	801.7	317.2	.216
360	1	0.112	79	615.5	801.7	317.2	.650		391	1	0.086	79	769.3	801.7	317.2	.859
361	1	0.143	79	626.8	801.7	317.2	.484		392	−1	0.156	79	756.9	801.7	317.2	.709
362	1	0.177	79	640.9	801.7	317.2	.272		393	−1	0.156	79	744.5	801.7	317.2	.745
363	1	0.155	79	653.2	801.7	317.2	.343		394	1	0.155	79	756.8	801.7	317.2	.336
364	1	0.155	79	665.5	801.7	317.2	.382		395	1	0.072	79	762.5	801.7	317.2	.952
365	−1	0.124	79	655.6	801.7	317.2	.926		396	1	0.312	79	737.8	801.7	317.2	.380
366	1	0.072	79	661.3	801.7	317.2	.965		397	1	0.143	79	749.1	801.7	317.2	.439
367	1	0.097	79	669.0	801.7	317.2	.781		398	1	0.112	79	758.0	801.7	317.2	.623
368	−1	0.235	79	650.4	801.7	317.2	.545		399	1	0.112	79	766.9	801.7	317.2	.643
369	1	0.112	79	659.3	801.7	317.2	.648		400	−1	0.398	79	735.3	801.7	317.2	.104

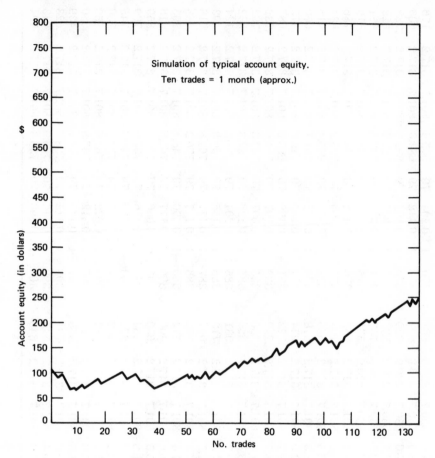

Figure 61. Graph of simulation No. 2.

the almost-random, helter-skelter nature of account growth on its way upward, the wait can be quite rewarding. By holding on, the investor would have a kitty of $776.20 by trade No. 388, more than a 600% increase in his account!!

LESSONS TO BE LEARNED

First, don't be so narrow-minded as to expect gains to compound monotonously upward. Any winning system with unknown sequences of gains and losses *will* have some periods of relatively large cumulative

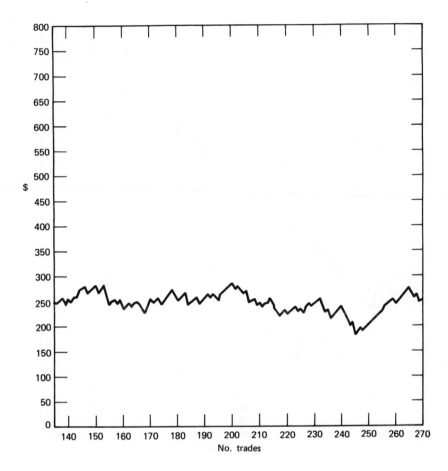

losses. And they can happen *any* time: sometime after you have started trading, or right at the beginning.

Like the coin-toss, we have little control over the sequences of tails (losses), only over (hopefully) the end result—long-run profits. As with the coin-toss, wherein the account value (cumulative net heads over tails) will frequently cross the starting line, the managed account should grow upward over a large number of trades, assuming past simulated market conditions match future ones in general. But it will not grow smoothly or straight up, just as the coin toss did not stay near the starting line.

Second, don't think because the account falls immediately that the

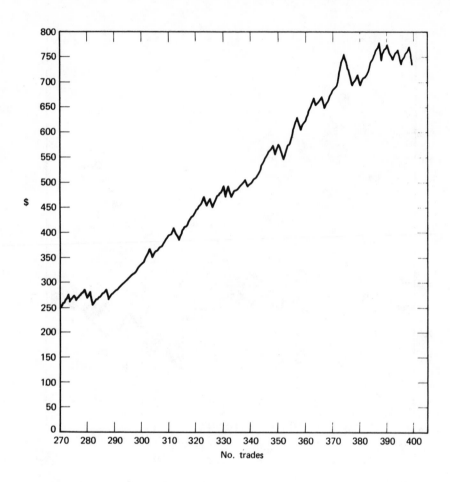

methods have failed, that you have somehow jinxed things, or that "this is a bad time to start." None of these are true. The rises and falls are neither predictable in size, length, or starting point. We can only tell on the average (or in terms of probability) how large a rise or fall might be when it comes, but most likely never be able to tell you when it will occur.

However, one general observation can be made from all these uncertainties: the account will grow strongly (though seemingly haphazardly) over time, especially compared to other types of investments (stocks, bonds, etc.). This assumes, of course, that future market conditions over a long period somewhat resemble today's conditions.

CHECKING WHETHER THE ACCOUNT
IS ON SCHEDULE

How can an investor monitor his managed account to assure himself that
it is producing results reasonably within expectations? A fair question.
An unequivocal set of numbers cannot be given, as trading conditions
may change from what is currently happening, producing a higher or
lower growth rate with attendant higher or lower volatility (cumulative
losses or gains) around the growth.

But if current market conditions persist (generally stable, lower
prices than the 1972–1974 inflationary price spiral), the investor should
expect from the above modeled account the following: a success rate
(no. of successful trades out of total attempts) of around 75%, average
gain of about 13% per gaining trade on committed funds, average loss
of about 25% per losing trade, an average drop from start or subsequent peaks in the account of 10–20%, and occasional (10–20% probability) drops from start of peaks in the account of 30% or so. From a statistical viewpoint the averages mentioned above can only be meaningfully
arrived at after a hundred trades or so. The investor may be a bit fidgety
to wait for a hundred trades, especially if he's losing 25% in the account—so he should check the account against the "occasional drop" figure to keep assuring himself that the account is still on target. Of course,
the account could suffer much larger loss and still come back in a blaze
of glory, but this drop is less probable (though still real).

CHECKING OTHER BROKER'S ACCOUNT
GROWTH CLAIMS

Even if a potential client of a broker never becomes one, or has an account with another broker/advisor now, he should pose the same account growth questions and use the same standards of judgment.

Ask him (her) to show you the average success rate, average gain
size; average loss size; average account drop size (from start or peaks in
the growth); probabilities of a drop of 10%, 20%, 40%, 60%, and 80% in
your account's value; how he expects to reinvest profits; and the effects
on account growth. These questions and full, precise answers, should enable you to compare with others results and generally determine if the
broker's account would grow faster, more evenly, or not at all.

If a broker's success rate is higher and average gain size larger, the
loss size is smaller than others' and he commits no more to each trade

than others do, then his account will grow faster and with less and smaller drops in value. Likewise, if these statistics are reversed, the others will do better. A mixed bag of comparisons is difficult to evaluate. Generally if the success rate is significantly lower (like ½ of this example) but the average gain is two, three, or four times larger and losses the same, then this broker's account will grow faster at some points and suffer larger drops than the others' at other points.

You should beware of false claims, too. If your broker (or broker-to-be) makes fantastic claims about success rates, average gain size, and so on, check his verifiable past results to see if he did his arithmetic properly. If he has a new system only on paper, get the set of statistics listed, and run a simulation based on that data. You can then check the average growths, drops, and so forth from the simulation discussed earlier against his actual results from then on.

23 Investment Discipline

The fifth, and in many ways most crucial, element in a successful trading system is the ability of the human trader to implement and follow the mechanics of the system—in short, to be able to follow a system.

It has been said (see trading method references) that discipline is 90% of trading success. Proper timing of trades and efficient diversification of assets may be great, but if the trader can't follow timing signals and actually commit capital to trades, he might as well throw out the whole trading system.

Actually, the human trader is part of the trading system. Like a cart without a cooperative donkey, the system won't go anywhere without a disciplined trader.

Personal discipline and fortitude have earmarked individuals in history to rise above others and become famous. The Napoleans, Washingtons, and Churchills have literally turned the course of events because of strong beliefs in their causes and the determination and organization to carry through to the end. When General Washington had 25% of his troops left and hardly surviving a rough winter at Valley Forge, the cause of the revolution seemed doomed by almost any rational person's conjecture. Yet he knew the time was ripe for severance from Britain, even though current conditions nearly counted him and the cause out.

Commodity traders don't go through quite as epic a struggle as Washington and others did, but sometimes they feel their wallets are pretty slim. Yet successful ones do have two things going for them— basic, good trading systems and realistic, disciplined selves to implement the rules. "Know thyself" says the ancient Greek oracle, and this certainly holds for commodity traders. Perceive your limitations, strengths, and follow good emotion-controlling rules of behavior.

This chapter addresses trader discipline habits to follow to better implement the trading system so the cart and donkey get somewhere. The following list and brief discussions outline what many consider to be primary attributes for being able to run a good commodity-trading plan.

1. First, and certainly foremost, a trader should have the ability to follow all timing signals vigorously and to commit the amount of capital called for under capital allocation. Often a trader will feel "Hogs are too high, don't buy" as prices approach old highs. Despite his personal, interpretative analysis, he must buy, sell, or reverse for *every* signal. Failure to follow could mean omission of big gains (for some reason they often happen on trades an individual thinks are repugnant).

2. Second, and a corollary of (1), he must continue to trade even when he encounters a losing streak. These losses are accounted for in the total for all trades (as he has simulated in the past or actually experienced), and are *bound* to occur, *over and over in time*. Every timing system has periods of whipsaw losses. Trended ones, like moving averages, get tangled up in tight trading markets, whereas contrary type methods experience strings of losses in long, trended markets, when many contratrend positions are continually tried.

3. The trader should not change his methods—timing, allocation parameters, or even the basic methods themselves—due to short-term results. He may feel that the markets are not trended right this month, or the meats have entered a dormant stage and he should switch to coffee because the effects from the recent freeze are still continuing. Yet all this is explainable by and accounted in long-term account results. He selected hogs because over the recent past they have proven to have better over all profit opportunities than coffee, which is strictly one-event oriented.

4. Our redoubtable investor must yet be flexible about broad changes in his system—for example, timing methods or allocations. For instance, the grains were strongly vacillating up and down and provided great profit opportunities with trend-following methods in 1972–1974, but thereafter have gone into tighter trading ranges. That

period could be seen from long-term analysis (last thirty years) to have been a warm spot in the ice age of relatively dormant prices. Hence he may conclude that contrary type techniques should be used until that warm spell appears again. Likewise, more money can now be committed for trades because general price volatility (and returns) and hence account volatility have diminished.

5. The trader must have the ability to shut off outside influences. Board-room tips, news events, other traders' plans, personal problems (fighting with in-laws, wife, or kids) must not be allowed to inter-fere with the execution of the trading system's plans, lest sporadic use of the system and hence lost profits or even losses, result.

6. He must have the ability to treat commodity trading as a game. Monetary gains and losses must be considered just numbers in a great Monopoly game—that, with the correct strategy (the trading system), will lead him to own Park Place and Boardwalk, enabling him to walk away at the end with all the money. As shown in simula-tion examples in Chapter 22, gains and losses occurred haphazardly, the account went up and down rather randomly, but the end result was long-term profits (the *drift*, in random parlance).

7. Our investor should have the ability to relieve the pressures and ten-sions by crying, jesting, and generally downplaying the importance of trading results. The rigors of trading, the leverage and subsequent profits and losses—all place intense pressure on an individual. This must be lessened lest mental breakdowns occur.

8. The trader must be open minded. He should refrain from wearing horse blinders, lest narrow, local analyses of losses and current con-ditions make him conclude that trading is not profitable, now or in the future. He must be sophisticated enough to realize and accept the concept of a string of losses as being nothing more than a result of certain markets—they are bound to occur and do not portend (from a short-term analysis) any long-range conditions.

9. He must develop and exude confidence. Like psychology in tennis, the more you believe that you will win, the more probable it is in fact. Often tennis matches are won on turn around in momentum, that time in the game when the fellow on top starts coasting and the other one starts building up points, games, and momentum, to even-tually overtake and beat the leader.

10. The trader should follow no more commodities than he can per-sonally handle. He may wish to follow all commodities to be ready and catch all profit opportunities around, but it may mean loss of accuracy in recording prices, making calculations, or lateness in plac-ing orders.

11. Our investor should always act promptly. If he obtains a signal at today's close to buy pork bellies, he should not procrastinate or delay at all; for one, two, or more days (even minutes, sometimes) can mean vastly different prices at the time of execution, or no execution at all if he tries to buy or sell at particular prices—the trend could have become full blown by the delay of a day or two.

12. Don't be greedy. If the timing plan calls for profits to be taken at a certain price or time, take them, even if prices are still heading strongly in your trend direction. Even limit moves in favor of the trader's position can often mean little carry-over the next day, and sometimes even a reversal to loss during the following day (and even today—the limits don't hold!).

13. The trader should depersonalize himself from the markets. The markets are not out to get him, so he shouldn't get into a vengeful or truculent mood.

14. He should demonstrate patience. He must accept individual and strings of losses (the market is not about to act exactly as he desired) and be able to hold on for long periods of time, for the long-term net profits in the account. Often club members sell out their part of the club at a bottom in the account's value, just before it started rising. This seems to be a phenomenon akin to lemmings rushing headlong into the sea, as the general public seems to have a propensity to buy a stock near the top and then sell in disgust at a bottom, just before the stock begins to rise anew.

15. The trader should have humility. Just because he is on the commodity scene, everyone is not going to rush to him and give him profits. He will have to fight, get scars, and earn his way to long-term profits. He must accept losses graciously, lest a bad temper flare-up influence his ability to handle the trading system's demands.

16. Excessive fear should be cast out. Great fear can inhibit a trader from ever taking a position, for his feelings give rise to counterposition limit moves and heavy losses. A small amount of fear is good, to enable him to get out of losing positions when his methods tell him to, lest he daydream, procrastinate, and hope for a price reversal to profitable territory after a stop has been hit.

17. The trader does not need, and in fact should avoid, the approval or admiration of others. If he waits for general boardroom approval, or even analysis of each of his trades, he is doomed to losses. Admiration and swooning over his results by others can have the adverse effect of making him vulnerable to taking his own personal advice, delaying execution of trades, holding onto gains or losses too long,

and rendering him unprepared and unable to handle losing periods later on.

18. He must exhibit personal fortitude. Every trade carries with it a great amount of risk because of the leverage and money committed. Some trades are unpopular. Like Washington crossing the Delaware at one of the lowest ebbs in the Americans' fortunes in the war, the trader must have the bravery to ford cold, icy streams of losing periods to see the lonely fight through to ultimate profits.

Investment Methods Bibliography

The following list of articles, books, and other publications is designed to encompass major theory, application, or critiques of investment trading methods, especially related to commodities. The list is broken down into a number of categories. The reader should be careful to cross reference several if he cannot find a topic or specific reference in any one category.

FORECASTING METHODS

1. Associate Staff Educational Program, *The Smoothing of Digital Data*, Applied Physics Laboratory, Johns Hopkins University, Silver Spring, Md., 1959.
2. Box, G. E. P., *Forecasting, Diagnostic Checking Models for Prediction and Control*, Vols. I–VIII., University of Wisconsin, Madison, Wisc., February 1967.
3. Box, G. E. P., *Discrete Models for Forecasting and Control*, University of Wisconsin, Madison, Wisc., June 1966.
4. Bossons, John, "The Effects of Parameter Misspecification and Non-Stationarity on the Applicability of Adaptive Forecasts," *Management Science*, 12 (9), 659–669 (1966).
5. Brenner, J. L., D'Esopo, D. A., and Fowler, A. G., "Difference Equations In Forecasting Formulas," *Management Science*, 15 (3), 141–159 (1968).

6. Brown, Robert G., *Smoothing Forecasting and Prediction*, Prentice-Hall, Englewood Cliffs, N.J., 1962.
7. Brown, Robert G., and Meyer, Richard F., "The Fundamental Theorem of Exponential Smoothing," *Operations Research*, Eighth Annual Meeting, New York, May 18, 1960.
8. Couts, D., Grether, D., and Nerlove, M., "Forecasting Non-Stationary Economic Time Series," *Management Science*, **13** (1), 1–21 (1966).
9. Dobbie, James M., "Forecasting Periodic Trends By Exponential Smoothing," *Management Science* (unknown issue).
10. Goodman, M. L., "A New Look at Higher Order Exponential Smoothing for Forecasting," *Operations Research*, **22** (4), (1974).
11. Harris, Lawrence, "A Decision-Theoretic Approach on Deciding When A Sophisticated Forecasting Technique Is Needed," *Management Science*, **13** (2), pp. B66–B69 (1966).
12. Hinich, Melvin, and Farley, John U., "Theory and Application of an Estimation Model for Time Series with Non-Stationary Means," *Management Science*, **12** (9), (1966).
13. Jiler, Harry, Ed., *Guide to Commodity Price Forecasting*, Commodity Research Bureau, Inc., New York, 1965.
14. Kirby, Robert M., "A Comparison of Short- and Medium-Range Statistical Forecasting Methods," *Management Science* (paper delivered at Institute of Management Sciences 1965 National Meeting).
15. McDonough, R. N., and Huggins, W. H., "Best Least Squares. Representation of Signals by Exponentials," *Institute of Electrical and Electronic Engineers Transactions on Automatic Control*, AC-**13** (4), 408–412 (1968).
16. Nerlove, M., and Wage, S., "On the Optimality of Adaptive Forecasting," *Management Science*, **10** (2), 207–224 (1964).
17. Stekler, H. O., "The Federal Budget as A Short-Term Forecasting Tool," *Journal of Business*, **40** (3), 280–285 (1967).
18. Theil, H., and Wage, S., "Some Observations on Adaptive Forecasting," *Management Science*, **10** (2), 198–206 (1964).
19. Thompson, Howard E., and Beranek, William, "The Efficient Use of an Imperfect Forecast," *Management Science*, **13** (3), 233–243 (1966).

GAME THEORY

1. Barish, Norman N., and Siff, Frederick H., "Operational Gaming Simulation with Application To a Stock Market," *Management Science*, **15** (10), B530–B541 (1968).
2. Bellman, Richard, *The Theory of Games*, RAND Corporation, Santa Monica, Calif., April 15, 1957.
3. Kahn, Herman, *Game Theory*, RAND Corporation, Santa Monica, Calif., July 30, 1957.
4. Nemhauser, G. L., and Ullman, Z., "Discrete Dynamic Programming and Capital Allocation," *Management Science*, **15** (9), 494–505 (1969).

GENERAL

1. Barnes, R. M., "Evaluating Trading Performance," *Journal of Commodity Trading*, 8 (4), (1973).
2. Barnes, R. M., *Dow Theory Can Make You Rich*, Arlington House, New Rochelle, N.Y., May, 1973.
3. Barnes, R. M., "Illusion or Reality," *Journal of Commodity Trading*, 4 (1, 2) (1969).
4. Barnes, R. M., "Looking Both Ways at Commodities," *Capital District Business Review*, Albany, N.Y. (January 1975).
5. Bauer, Douglas, "Prince of the Pit," *New York Times*, April 25, 1976 (magazine section).
6. Brigham, Eugene, and Pappas, James L., "Rates of Return on Common Stock," *Journal of Business*, 42 (3), 302–316 (1969).
7. Economic Research Service, USDA, *Margins, Speculation and Prices in Grains Futures Markets*, Washington, D.C., December 1967.
8. Fisher, Lawrence, and Lorie, James H., "Some Studies of Variability of Return on Investments in Common Stocks," *Journal of Business*, 43 (2), 99–134 (1970).
9. Gold, Gerald, *Modern Commodity Futures Trading*, Commodity Research Bureau, Inc., New York, N.Y., 1959.
10. Heiser, Ralph A., and Smith, William, "Decision-Making, Personality Traits and Commodity Trading," *Journal of Commodity Trading*, 3 (6), 6–9 (1968).
11. Hieronymus, Thomas A., *Economics of Futures Trading*, Commodity Research Bureau, Inc., New York, N.Y., 1973.
12. Keltner, Chester W., *How to Make Money in Commodities*, Keltner Statistical Service, Kansas City, Mo., 1960.
13. McCrachen, James, "The Lonesome Bull of LaSalle Street," *Commodities Magazine*, 3 (3), 9–14 (1974).
14. Smidt, Seymour, "Amateur Speculators: A Survey of Trading Styles, Information Sources, and Patterns of Entry and Exit from Commodity Futures Markets by Non-Professional Speculators," Graduate School of Business, Cornell University, Ithaca, New York, 1965.
15. Tewles, Richard J., Harlow, Charles V., and Stone, Herbert L., *The Commodity Futures Trading Guide*, McGraw-Hill, New York, 1969.

PORTFOLIO SELECTION AND PERFORMANCE

1. Agnew, N. H., Agnew, R. A., Rasmussen, J., and Smith, K. R., "An Application of Chance Constrained Programming to Portfolio Selection," *Management Science*, 15 (10), B512–B520 (1969).
2. Barnes, R. M., "Initial Capital Requirements," *Journal of Commodity Trading*, 8 (2) (1973).
3. Blume, Marshall E., "Portfolio Theory: A Step Toward Its Practical Application," *Journal of Business*, 43 (2), 152–173 (1970).
4. Breen, William, and Savage, James, "Portfolio Distributions and Tests of Security Selection Models," *Journal of Business*, 43 (5), 805–819 (1970).

5. Cohen, Kalman J., and Fitch, Bruce P., "The Average Investment Performance Index," *Management Science*, **12** (16), B195–B215, 1965.
6. Cohen, Kalman J., and Pogue, Jerry A., "Some Comments Concerning Mutual Fund Versus Random Portfolio Performance," *Journal of Business*, **41**, 180–190 (1968).
7. Cohen, Kalman J., and Pogue, Jerry A., "An Empirical Evaluation of Alternative Portfolio-Selection Models," *Journal of Business*, **40** (2), 166–193 (1967).
8. Cranshaw, T. E., "The Evaluation of Investment Performance, *Journal of Business*, **50** (4) (1977).
9. Elton, Edwin J., and Gruber, Martin J., "On the Optimality of Some Multiperiod Portfolio Selections," *Journal of Business*, **47** (2) (1974).
10. Elton, Edwin J., and Gruber, Martin J., "Risk Reduction and Portfolio Size: An Analytical Solution," *Journal of Business*, **50** (4) (1977).
11. Fisher, Lawrence, and Lorie, James H., "Some Studies of Variability of Returns on Investments in Common Stocks," *Journal of Business*, **43** (2), 99–135 (1970).
12. Friend, Irwin, and Vichers, Douglas, "Reevaluation of Alternative Portfolio Selection Models," *Journal of Business*, **41** (2), 174–178 (1968).
13. Hanssman, Fred, "Probability of Survival as an Investment Criterion," *Management Science*, **15** (1), 33–48 (1968).
14. Jensen, Michael C., "Risk, The Pricing of Capital Assets, and the Evaluation of Investment Portfolios," *Journal of Business*, 167–247 (unknown issue).
15. Latane, Henry A., Joy, D. Maurice, and Jones, Charles P., "Quarterly Data, Sort–Rank Routines, and Security Evaluation," *Journal of Business*, **43** (4), 427–439 (1970).
16. Manne, Alan S., "Optimal Dividend and Investment Policies for a Self-Financing Business Enterprise," *Management Science*, **15** (3), 119–129 (1968).
17. Mao, James C., and Särndal, Carl Erik, "A Decision Theory Approach to Portfolio Selection," *Management Science*, **12** (8), (1966).
18. Markowitz, H. M., *Portfolio Selections: Efficient Diversification of Investments*, Wiley, New York, 1959.
19. Mossin, Jan, "Optimal Multiperiod Portfolio Policies," *Journal of Business*, **41**, 215–229 (1968).
20. Porter, R. Burr, and Bey, Roger P., "An Evaluation of the Empirical Significance of Optimal Seeking Algorithms in Portfolio Selection," *Journal of Finance*, **29** (Dec. 1974).
21. Renwick, Fred B., "Asset Management and Investor Portfolio Behavior: Theory and Practice," *Journal of Finance*, **24** (2), 181–222 (1969).
22. Sandmo, Agnar, "Capital Risk, Consumption, and Portfolio Choice," *Econometrica*, **37** (4), 586–599 (1969).
23. Sharpe, William F., "A Linear Programming Algorithm for Mutual Fund Portfolio Selection," *Management Science*, **13** (7), 499–510 (1966).
24. Simon, Julian L., "Does 'Good Portfolio Management' Exist?," *Management Science*, **15** (6), B308–B321 (1969).
25. West, Richard R., "Mutual Fund Performance and the Theory of Capital Asset Pricing: Some Comments," *Journal of Business*, **41**, 230–234 (1968).

26. Winkler, Robert L., and Barry, Christopher, "A Bayesian Model for Portfolio Selection and Revision," *Journal of Finance,* **30** (1975).

PRICE MODELS

1. Alexander, Sidney S., "Price Movements in Speculative Markets: Trends or Random Walks, No. 2," *Industrial Management Review,* **5,** 25–46 (Spring 1964).
2. Barnes, R. M., "Fundamental Questions to Stock and Commodity Investors," *Journal of Commodity Trading,* **2** (7, 8) (1967).
3. Barnes, R. M., "Critical Reaction Calculations for Commodities," *Journal of Commodity Trading,* **3** (1), (1968).
4. Bolton, Hamilton, *The Elliot Wave Principle,* Bolton Tremblay Ltd., 1964.
5. Bracken, Jerome, and Soland, Richard M., "Statistical Decision Models for Brokering," *Management Science,* **15** (11), 619–625 (1968).
6. Brada, Josef, Ernst, Harry, and Van Tassel, John, "The Distribution of Stock Price Differences: Gaussian After All?," *Operations Research,* 334–340 (1966).
7. Cootner, Paul H., *The Random Character of Stock Market Prices,* MIT Press, Cambridge, Mass., 1964.
8. Dryden, Myles M., "Share Price Movements: A Markowian Approach," *Journal of Finance,* **24** (1), 49–60 (1969).
9. Ehrich, R. L., "Cash-Futures Relationships for Live Beef Cattle," *American Journal of Agricultural Economics,* **51** (1), 26 (1969).
10. Emerson, Peter M., and Tomek, William G., "Did Futures Trading Influence Potato Prices?," *American Journal of Agricultural Economics,* **51** (3), 666–672 (1969).
11. Fama, Eugene F., and Laffer, Arthur B., "Information and Capital Markets," *Journal of Business,* **44** (3), 289–298 (1971).
12. Flumiani, Carlo Maria, *The Cylinder Theory,* Institute For Economic and Financial Research, 1961.
13. Goss, B. A., *The Theory of Futures Trading,* Routledge and Kegan Paul, Boston, 1972.
14. Harlow, Charles V., Jr., and Teweles, Richard J., "An Inquiry into Non-Random Elements of the Commodity Futures Markets," *Journal of Commodity Trading,* **4** (4), 6–24 (1969).
15. Jacob, Nancy, "The Measurement of Market Similarity for Securities under Uncertainty," *Journal of Business,* **43** (3), 328–354 (1970).
16. Kassouf, Sheen T., "An Econometric Model for Option Price With Implications for Investors' Expectations and Audacity," *Econometrica,* **37** (4), (1969).
17. Mandelbrot, Benoit, "The Variation of Certain Speculative Prices," *Journal of Business,* **36,** 294–419 (1963).
18. Mandelbrot, Benoit, "On the Distribution of Stock Price Differences," *Management Sciences* (unknown issue).
19. Niederhofer, V., "Clustering of Stock Prices," *Operations Research,* **13** (2) (1965).
20. Niederhoffer, Victor, and Osborne, M. F. M., "Market Making and Reversal

on the Stock Exchange," *Journal of the American Statistical Association,* **61,** 897–916 (1966).
21. Osborne, M. F. M., "Some Quantitative Tests for Stock Price Generating Models and Trading Folklore," *Journal of the American Statistical Association,* **62,** 321–340 (1967).
22. Press, S. James, "A Compound Events Model for Security Prices," *Journal of Business,* **40** (3), 317–335 (1967).
23. Renwick, Fred B., "Theory of Investment Behavior and Empirical Analysis of Stock Market Price Relatives," *Management Science,* **15** (1), 57–71 (1968).
24. Simmons, Donald M., "Common Stock Transaction Sequences and the Random Walk Model," *Operations Research,* 845–861 (July–August 1971).
25. Stoll, Hans R., "The Relationship Between Put and Call Option Prices," *Journal of Finance,* **24** (5), 801–824 (1969).
26. Tiao, S., *Modeling the Consumption of a Frozen Concentrated Orange Juice: A Case Study of Time Series Analysis,* University of Wisconsin, Madison, Wisc., March 1970.
27. Venkatoramanan, L. S., *The Theory of Futures Trading,* Asia Publishing House, New York, 1965.
28. Wilson, Robert, "Investment Analysis Under Uncertainty," *Management Science,* **15** (12), B650–B664 (1969).
29. Ying, Charles C., "Stock Market Prices and Volume of Sales," *Econometrica,* **34** (3), 676–685 (1966).

RISK MODELS

1. Brealey, Richard A., *An Introduction to Risk and Return from Common Stocks,* MIT Press, Cambridge, Mass., 1969.
2. Briscoe, G., Samuels, J. M., and Smyth, D. J., "The Treatment of Risk in the Stock Market," *Journal of Finance,* **24** (4) 707–714 (1969).
3. Fama, Eugene, "Risk, Return and Equilibrium: Some Clarifying Remarks," *Journal of Finance,* **23** (1), 29–40 (1968).

TESTING METHODS

1. Barton, D. E., and David, F. N., "Multiple Runs," *Journal Royal Statistical Society B* (1957).
2. Cochran, W. G., *Sampling Techniques,* 2nd ed., Wiley, New York, 1963.
3. Dryden, Myles M., "A Source of Bias in Filter Tests of Share Prices," *Journal of Business,* **42** (July 1969).
4. Edgington, Eugene S., "Probability Table for Number of Runs of Signs of First Differences in Ordered Series," *Operations Research* (unknown issue).
5. Harter, H. Leon, "The Use of Order Statistics in Estimation," *Operations Research* (1968).
6. Krishnaiah, P. R., and Murthy, V. K., "Simultaneous Tests for Trend and

Serial Correlations for Gaussian Markov Residuals," *Econometrica*, **34** (2) (1966).
7. Owen, D. B., *Handbook of Statistical Tables*, Addison-Wesley, Reading, Mass., 1962.
8. Shelton, John P., "The Value Line Contest: A Test of the Predictability of Stock Price Changes," *Journal of Business*, **40** (3), 251–269 (1967).
9. Swed, Frieda S., and Eisenhart, C., "Tables for Testing Randomness of Grouping in a Sequence of Alternatives," *Management Science* (unknown issue).

TRADING METHODS

1. Arms, Richard W., Jr., "Equivolume—A New Method of Charting," *Commodities Magazine*, 18–24 (April 1973).
2. Barnes, R. M., "A Statistical Method for Setting Stops in Stock Trading," *Operations Research* (July–August 1970).
3. Barnes, R. M., "A Model of Commodity Trading," *Journal of Commodity Trading*, **2** (6) (1967).
4. Barnes, R. M., "A Systems Approach to Commodity Trading," *Journal of Commodity Trading*, **3** (2) (1968).
5. Barnes, R. M., "A Marriage of Trend and Contrary Methods," *Commodities Magazine* (July 1976).
6. Belveal, L. Dee, *Charting Commodity Market Price Behavior*, Commodities Press, Wilmette, Ill., 1969.
7. Dunn, Dennis, and Hargitt, Edwin, "Martingale for the Very Rich," *Journal of Commodity Trading*, **4** (5), 14–15 (1969).
8. Edmunds, Philip W., "A Guide to Maximizing Profits Using A Technical Trading Method," *Journal of Commodity Trading*, **3** (5), 6–12, 28 (1968).
9. Edwards, Robert D., and Magee, John, *Technical Analysis of Stock Trends*, J. Magee, Springfield, Mass., 1951.
10. Ferguson, Robert L., and Jones, Curtis H., "A Computer Aided Decision System," *Management Science*, **15** (10), B550–561 (1969).
11. Heiser, R., and Keltler, Paul C., "Standard, Linearly-Weighted and Exponentially-Weighted Moving Averages," *Journal of Commodity Trading*, **2** (1), 5–8 (1967).
12. Hite, Lawrence D., and Feldman, Steven, "Game Theory Applications," *Journal of Commodity Trading*, **7** (2), 10–14 (1972).
13. Hull, M. Blair, Jr., and Loops, Lester W., "Hypothesis Testing and Trading Methods," *Journal of Commodity Trading*, **5** (2), 14–19 (1970).
14. Investors Intelligence, Inc., *Encyclopedia of Stock Market Techniques*, Larchmont, N.Y., 1965.
15. Kaufman, Perry, *Commodity Trading Systems and Methods*, Wiley, New York, 1978.
16. Langford, Gordon L., "A Decision Theory Model," *Journal of Commodity Trading*, **8** (3), 30–36 (1971).
17. Levy, Robert A., "Relative Strength as a Criterion for Investment Selection," *Journal of Finance*, **22** (4), 595–610 (1967).

18. Levy, Robert A., "The Predictive Significance of Five Point Chart Patterns," *Journal of Business,* **44** (3), 316–323 (1971).
19. Livermore, Jesse L., *How to Trade in Stocks,* Investor's Press, Inc., Palisades Park, N.J., 1966.
20. Norfi, Eugene, "The Phase Congestion System," *Commodities Magazine,* 24–33 (September 1975).
21. Pelletier, Robert C., "Money Management for Martingale Commodity Trader," *Journal of Commodity Trading,* **4** (3), 17–20 (1969).
22. Sibbet, James H., "Contrary Opinion Theory and Commodity Trading," *Journal of Commodity Trading,* **3** (5), 23–28 (1968).
23. Steinberg, Jeanette Norfi, "Timing Market Entry and Exit (The Congestion Phase System)," *Commodities Magazine,* 24–33 (September 1975).
24. Taylor, Howard M., "Evaluating a Call Option and Optimal Timing in the Stock Market," *Management Science,* **14** (1) (1967).
25. Taylor, Robert Joel, "The Major Price Trend Directional Indicator," *Commodities Magazine,* 17–22 (April 1972).
26. Taylor, Robert Joel, "Technical Personalities," *Commodities Magazine* (unknown issue).
27. Viskochil, M. H., "The 'Big Five' Moving Average System," *Journal of Commodity Trading,* **4** (1), 16–17 (1969).

Index